A GOD'S SILENCE

A Fantasy Noir Tragedy

JESSE WOODWARD

ISBN 978-1-967362-29-5 (paperback)
ISBN 978-1-967362-30-1 (hardcover)
ISBN 978-1-967362-31-8 (digital)

Printed in the United States of America

Whirling round the widening spire
I lose sense of who I am.
When above leaves them behind
Who is left to govern man?

CITY OF OPHIDIA

EST. POPULATION 800,000

A. UPPER WEST GROVE
B. FORT SCHID
1. DOWNTOWN SNAP
4. PRAEPERVUNT'S DOCKS
5. FOUNDER'S SQUARE
6. LASIRGWOP ROW
6. GUSILP CROSS
8. DIXUN'S CULVERT
9. CHIMEG ACRE
10. PLIMREG YARD
10. XAGGIN WEST
12. STONURWASP CENTER

JB
'21

CHAPTER 1

I 've done it again. I promised I wouldn't drink last night, but the boys in Karnagen Hall convinced me otherwise. I indulged in another evening of carousing and petty rebellion. Our frequent defiance of expectation, of how young scholarly gentlemen like us are supposed to behave. But because I drank far more than I should have, the night had flown past in a blur, rabble rousing scarcely remembered, and I woke up dazed and confused on some freight ship. I had to run my way to the nearest tram station, doubtlessly late for morning courses yet again. Not that any trouble will come from all this. Another scolding from creaky old Dean Clemens, most likely, and then I'm on my way for the day. My entire future rides on graduating from this chore of a college; he's not enough of a sadist to hit me with any harsher punishment.

Thus, here I sit, hungover and with eyes half-shut. Eyes that look up past the modest skyline of the Docks to Hodren's Wall, that bulwark that pens in our vast city. As tall as sixty men, made of stones taken from the World Spine Mountains, and laid immaculately by a dwarven clan that's been long extinct, it runs all along Ophidia's perimeter. Right up to the Great Blue Expanse.

Sometimes I wonder what life is like past it, out on the frontiers in the realm of change and chaos. The plants out there are constantly changing, they say, never retaining a single form for long. If one ventures out far enough, they can see a mighty tree shift and regress into a single flower.

All traces of native flora were cleansed from Ophidia some years ago, before my family got here, deadened and controlled by a nullification powder laid weekly along the streets. Hundreds of thousands of sentient-folk go their whole lives living in this city, never venturing further into New Colonia. Sentient-folk just like me.

The tram leans to and fro on the twists of the track, dropping slightly and getting picked back up in rapid sequence. As this happens, the wide harbors and short buildings of Praepurvant Docks give way to the mighty Grengara River; murky waves lapping against the beams of the tramway bridge. A sharp and dismal fall that would be. Save me the trouble of the day, though. This is the Counter-Circuit of the tramway line, then. Instead of going straight to Gusilp Cross, it'll be hitting every other district first, making me even more late.

Just then, a rotting assault on my olfactory brings about a familiar response of nausea. It has been some time, Plimred Yard. The tram is high up above the rooftops that are filled with laundry lines flying tattered blankets and hole-ridden trousers. Homemade scaffolding forever encases the buildings of the Yard, those poor crumbling brick structures that will never see renovation. Below all that on street level, various humans and orcs mill around in their mundane fight for survival. I can even make out the odd dwarf and elfblood. Piles of detritus layer the sidewalk corners, and there's more ruined machinery, burned-out cars, and abandoned carriages than one can take count of. Some folks are pushing along wooden carts and picking through the garbage, hoping to find something worthwhile enough to pay for food and rent. What a curse it must be to be poor.

The Yard slips past quickly, as this tram line doesn't make any stops in the low districts. The overcast sky retreats behind a wooden facsimile of a jovial woman's face, sipping on a glass of brandy. Tenmen's Own, to be precise. The banner flies past the window, and a sweeping view of Parkland Avenue presents itself.

Chimeg Acre, the beloved realm of consumerism. Even at this early hour, the widened street is packed with cars, carriages, and trucks of every make and model. Steel-framed high rises sit along-side the avenue and are covered in banners and signs beckoning the viewer to wondrous delights, all of which are just a small purchase away. A dwarf in a suit smiles and presents his perfect life, all thanks to the Firebeard Clansmen Lumber-Efficient Fireplace. A whole-some human family is enjoying a cityside drive in the new Wayward Industries Family Vehicle Model 11. A wooden amalgamation of an elfblood gyrates and waves the viewer's attention to the Yew Electric Radio, home to the Last Paladin radio drama. All these banners and advertisements are placed as close together as possible, sometimes covering one another. Lines of lights also run along the edges of some of the more complex banners, but they're only active at night. The visual overload is both nerve-wracking and breathtaking.

As much as I want to complain, all in all, it is a little nice, this sort of tedium. To have such trite things be the depth of my woes. Was this the future you had in mind, Caddock? The fate you wanted for your special young man?

The tramcar strikes a bump in the rails and jostles me from my internal reverie, as well as reawakening my headache.

It is far too early in the morning to be thinking this much.

"Excuse me, sir," I say to the man beside me. "Could you wake me when we get to the Cross, at the Waterford Pass Station?"

"Of course, I'm stopping there myself."

I nod my appreciation to him and close my eyes, hoping to get a few minutes of shuteye. But all I get is the rocking sounds of metal and murmurs of quiet chats.

...

"We've arrived."

A brief period of sleep managed to slip in, but all the same, I returned.

"Thank you," I say.

3

We all rise once the tram bustles to a stop and go through the lengthy social process of filing out and apologizing when we get in the way of one another. Eventually, it's all sorted, and I set foot out onto the station. Men and women in suits with briefcases mill about and wait for their trams to arrive.

I step out of the station and out onto Waterford Pass. Bookstores and Keeper's Studies, those holy places of worship, dot along the street. People are filing out of the latter with stacks of paper for their prayer-keeping; morning worship must have just finished. Many of said prayers will likely be nailed outside of tenements and apartments to get the Keeper's attention. 'Mind the suffering here.' 'We wish for your gaze,' they will likely say. I've seen such things a thousand times. A queer thing, that whole ritual.

I pull my pocket watch from my coat to get a sense of the time, only to find its glass cracked and machinations ajar, gears pushing up the watch face on the edges. The sight of it strikes me more deeply than I would have anticipated. What crimes did I commit last night? Your timepiece, the so-called Neverending Watch, reduced to this. That seems about right. The clocktower a few blocks away tells me that the morning bell only rang a short time ago. I still have a chance to make it in time. My feet stamp at a quicker yet still socially appropriate rate. I weave between passing businessmen and bookkeepers.

A street interrupts the faded brickwork of the surrounding establishments, revealing a stone archway. OXLEN UNIVERSITY, a large sign affixed to it reads. My home and calling. The campus is grandiose, with its acreage sprawling over five city blocks. I cross the street and pass under the archway.

The pathways between the lecture halls and dormitories are surrounded by mineral statues of plants and one strain of tree, the only one that can survive the nullification powder that blankets the streets. The powder's the one thing saving us all from the beastkin savages that will bring madness to our front doors with their strange shamanic magic. Or at least that's what the papers tell us.

The campus paths are empty when I arrive. It took longer to get here than initially thought. I was never good at arithmetic. Numbers are for the birds. The doors of Gregory Guillihon's Hall of Rhetoric moan and echo down the halls, declaring my tardiness. I rush up the nearby flight of stairs, straighten my tie, and skulk into the classroom. Despite my best efforts at stealth, Dr. Yuikan's gaze turns to me. A slight shake of my head, and he sighs and concurs that the verbal flogging isn't worth his time. I quickly and quietly find my way to a seat as he returns to his lesson.

"...So with the damning argument made by Sigesar's advisor, Fucius," he shouts to the class, "the Highrock Dwarven clans that came to inhabit the Death-Pass Mountains were convinced to help provide schematics and resources in the war against the elven and beastkin tribes. Fucius's address is an excellent balance of the appeal to emotion and use of rational arguments to convince a neutral-but-stubborn party that is typically associated with our"—he turns to see a few young dwarves seated in the front row— "more headstrong kinsmen."

A girl to my left taps my shoulder and points to the door. A disapproving prefect instructs me to join him with a wagging finger. My executioner beckons. It's for the best, though. I could do without yet another lecture on the foundations of the Civilized Empire. Even though this is the second Historical Analysis course, Dr. Yuikan loves to fixate on the beginning, the first few centuries post-Exodus. Way back when our ancestors were little more than refugees. After losing a war for survival against the Great Undeath in the World Before, sentientkind somehow found themselves here, stripped of all ties to home, hearth, and heritage.

Whispers spread through the class as other groups of students begin to make the connection between the prefect and me. Gossip and theories are already propagating at breakneck speed. Who knows what nonsense tales there will be by the end of the day?

I rise and take my time back down the steps of the lecture hall to meet the prefect. May as well indulge the rumors a little.

"Morning," I whisper once I reach him. "Clemens sent you?"

The prefect nods and opens the door, motioning for me to leave. I look back into the classroom one more time and then set out into the hallway.

The march to the Dean's office is choked with silence. The prefect has a pensive scowl on his face. Like I am nothing more than another bit of refuse to be handled throughout the day.

"Any chance you could tell me how the good dean is doing?"

He looks at me for a moment before returning his gaze straight ahead.

"Fair enough."

Soon the bulky wooden door of Head Dean Phillip Clemens appears. The prefect stops beside it in a dutiful manner that is oh so impressive.

"You are to enter his office," he commands.

Part of me wants to say something. Something concise and cutting, fitting for this farce of an authority figure.

Instead, I smile and enter the office. A submissive wooden chair sits before a mighty desk and four sets of filled bookshelves. The respectfully corpulent shape of the dean is bent over an assortment of papers, his pen moving in a slow and measured rhythm, glasses resting just above the tip of his nose. His grip on his favorite fountainhead pen is that of a corpse in the throes of rigor mortis. He's stressed, more stressed than I've ever seen him.

Seeing him in such a state creates two senses within me: satisfaction and guilt. In the beginning, he was little more than a pawn for you, wasn't he, Caddock? Another stepping stone on the destined path you've made for me. Get chummy with the dean of Oxlen, donate to help build a new hall, and my academic success would be all but guaranteed. A blind eye at the very top. But then the worst happened, a tragedy I naively assumed I would never experience, and this overly wrinkled man just *had* to step in as my guardian. He took me into his home, and I endured one year of torture before I was freed to a dorm room. One year of pitiful glances, half-hearted hugs, and anemic life advice. He's living proof that age doesn't correlate to wisdom.

But he was also very forgiving in my more impatient and child-ish moments, and he deserves credit for that. These days, it's best for both of us to be cordial from a distance.

He looks up from his studious trance, and his brow and mouth sink a few degrees.

"There you are," he says, with a stern monotone voice. "Please, have a seat."

The aged wood of the seat detests my weight.

"We both know why you're here, Mr. Fey," he sighs, looking out the window to his left. This building is the highest on campus. The sight is similar to looking over the top of a maze. A maze topped with tiled roofs and chimneys.

"Mr. Fey, this morning, am I?" I follow his gaze out the window. "How are you?"

He returns to the moment and looks at me.

"I'm fine, thank you for asking."

"Happy to hear it. I'm always glad to be called in like this. So, what sentence awaits me for my third offense?"

"Fifth! This is the *fifth* act of delinquency, Arthur, just for this quarter! So, let us drop the feigned niceties, shall we?"

The immediate hostility forms into a lump in my throat. The old man never starts out this aggressively.

"Yes, sir. I apologize."

"I've already received reports of what you and your comrades got up to last night, so let's see here."

He turns back to his desk and files through a pile of folders to his right.

"Your House Monitor hasn't been notified of your where-abouts in two days. A fight broke out in The Sleeping Maiden on 68th Avenue in Praepurvant Docks, and you and three others were witnessed as the instigators. Shortly after that, a statue about three blocks away was defaced. And that doesn't even cover what occurred after the midnight bell!"

The zeal of the moment leaves him when he sees that I'm not putting up any defense to my actions.

"Forgive me, let me calm back down for a moment," he says, taking off his glasses. "I never liked screaming at you like this, Arthur. You know that. When your dear father and mother... Passed... and you were left in my care, I swore to myself to be as patient and atten-tive as I can be with you. To give you whatever you need to succeed and get ahead in life."

"You have, Clemens, and I thank you for that."

He stops for a moment before continuing, straightening out some papers. Hearing validation like that makes him relax his shoul-ders a little, easing up on some of the tension.

"But," he says, "Everything has its limits, Arthur, and I have other duties in my life. Imagine being in my position. Oxlen University is renowned for its prestigious tutorship and dignified students. But every once in a while, you get a young man who insists on sowing bedlam wherever he goes and wasting away his parent's wishes, even though he's a bright lad and holds a wealth of promise. I just don't understand, Arthur. You are the last of your line. Doesn't that fill you with a sense of..." He waves his upturned hand in a circular motion as he searches for the word. "Duty? What would your mother say? Or your father?"

A quick bolt of anger shoots through me. He always does this, using your passing to guilt me into capitulation. It's always an unfair tactic, isn't it?

"There's no need to bring them into this, Dr. Clemens," I say.

"Forgive me, lad," he says. "I only want to get through to you. But at this point, I've tried everything."

Dr. Clemens leans back into his chair and moves his glasses so that he can rub the bridge of his nose. As shameful as it is to admit this, I'm glad he's finally been tired out and is coming to his senses. There's really no sense for this exhausting dance of ours. He may finally now give me the freedom I've so dearly needed.

"I'm glad you've come to this conclusion," I say. "Perhaps a laxer approach at your end is needed. I'll straighten out, I promise, I just need time."

"That... That isn't what I mean, son."

"Then what do you mean? Even more afternoons scrubbing the floors?"

"Just give me a moment. I need to prepare myself. You've no clue how much it wounds me to say this." He swivels his chair to face the window, too exasperated for eye contact. "I think," he says, "your time at Oxlen is at an end, for now."

Wait, what?

"What do you mean?" I ask, voice cracking and revealing my anxiety.

"You don't seem to care much for your education, and as much as I owe to your father, Keeper saves his legacy, I can only bend the law so much. Your obsession with being a miscreant has no place here, son. I'm sorry, but this is for the best. Perhaps some time in the real world will do you good."

I rise from the chair and drop to one knee, losing all sense of composure.

"You can't do this, Dr. Clemens. Please! You know I have nowhere else to go. Oxlen is my home, my future. To get expelled from here is to live out my days as a convict. Nowhere of prestige will hire me. Where do you expect me to go?"

"Please don't make this any harder, son. You have no idea how much slack I've granted you, for both you and your father's sake."

"Don't you *dare* bring him into this again. His ashes have barely cooled, and here you are, throwing me out of your meager little school. And while he breathed, you took his silvum all too eagerly, didn't you?"

He turns and looks at me with eyes of such widened scorn, I know I've struck a nerve.

"Mr. Fey, that is enough!" he shouts. "Barely cooled? For the Keeper's sake, it's been two years, boy! How much longer will you refuse to move on from this?"

"Oh yes, I should simply move on, is that right? Move on into what? Nothing! Nowhere!"

I rise to my feet, and for a fleeting moment, I want to pick up this decrepit fool's ledger and strike him with it. To beat him senseless and make him feel how much he's ruined my future. But there's no point to it. A few years in a penitentiary is all that would give me.

I simply groan and fall back into the chair.

"So, this is it then," I say. "This is all my time here has given me."

"I'm afraid so, son," Clemens says. "I can see you falling into despair, but there's no need for it. You can re-apply in four years' time when your academic suspension expires."

"Four years? But that's a lifetime from now! And you know as well as I do that traditional applications never get considered for this school." It takes all of my energy not to break down into tears at this very moment.

"Oh, don't be so melodramatic," he says. "Almost a tenth of all applicants enter that way every year. Besides, you should have thought of all that before committing to this destructive cycle you're on. Now, I'm going to lift the restriction of access to your family's trust fund. And you'll just have to decide what to do with your life yourself. We have a reputation to maintain here. I'll even let you go stay in your old room, in my home. Just until you get on your feet."

He attempts it again. To take over your place as guardian and mentor. It's just sickening, isn't it?

"What of the rest of my tuition, for the years I haven't completed?" I ask. "Is that to be refunded alongside my trust fund?"

He turns away from me once more, squirming with discomfort.

"I'm… afraid not," he says. "That's nonrefundable and isn't up for negotiation."

After a moment, I scoff in astonishment.

"You're serious? Enough silvum for a down payment on a house in the Row, more than enough to sit well alongside whatever meager fortune my family left me, and you're keeping it?"

"Yes, yes, so don't linger upon the point!"

First, I sit there dumbstruck, then I can't help but laugh. It's all so absurd. Absurd and maddening.

I get up once more and take a few steps over to his little desk and pound both of my hands onto it. Clemens flinches and retreats into his large resting chair.

What was that thing you always said? One of your many pithy phrases? Oh right. *"If you're going to be defeated, at least do so with gusto."*

"To the *void* with you, old man, and your 'hospitality.'" I point my finger condemnably at his wrinkled face. "All the books in the world sit in this rotten institution, from a dead time, written by dead men, and you'll soon join them. I'd rather be flayed alive than stay another day in your care. It's always been so *suffocating*."

"Please, son, there's no need to be so undignified."

"Oh, I'll show you undignified."

I go past his desk to one of the bookshelves. I wedge my hand into one of the lines of books.

"Don't you dare," he warns.

With a swift motion, I swipe several first editions onto the ground.

"Arthur!"

"There. That'll do for a tantrum, don't you think?"

"Joseph!" he yells at the door.

His wetnurse appears in an instant.

"Yes, sir?"

"Escort this boy to his room to fetch his affections, then remove him from the premises, will you?"

"Right away, sir."

The prefect rushes over and grabs my shoulders. He's a head taller than me, but in my rage, I shake him free.

"Leave it, will you?" I shout. "I'll play along. Save your fetish for authority for your policing career."

He steps back and channels his intimidation into his gaze, brows as furrowed as the anatomy allows. I turn back to Clemens.

"I'm not the first, and I won't be the last. Oxlen's days are numbered."

Clemens lowers the corners of his eyebrows as he struggles to understand what I mean. To be honest, I'm not even sure myself. The last of my cocktail of anger and sadness spilled out, and that was the result.

I walk out of the office, and the prefect is one step behind me at all times. We begin the march of shame towards my dormitory.

I stop for a moment and rub my temples. Regret starts to seep in. Such a simple last wish from Rose and you, to simply finish this education, and I couldn't even do that right.

"It's too late to second-guess, you know…" the prefect mutters.

"I'm aware of that," I spit back at him. His eyebrows are much too thick. I'd peel them off if I had the chance.

What am I getting so upset over? This place was a waste of time, anyway. What could be done with a rotten Distinction in Rhetoric? What would I become? A politician? A socialite that goes to parties and prays that those with actual acclaim will notice me? Please. The life of aristocrats is a stuffy and hollow one. I wanted no part of it, anyway. Never did. Come to think of it, this expulsion may be a good thing, actually.

We entered the lounge of my dormitory. The usual suspects are missing from the quiet hall. The only present that I was with last night was Todrey. I stop beside him while on my way up the stairs. He's comfortably seated in a reading alcove, tucked in behind a pillar. His gaze sits behind a pair of thick spectacles, looking intently into some history book.

"So..." I awkwardly chuckle. "I suppose this is it, friend. Clemens gave me the boot, finally. Didn't think that old bat had it in him."

His attention on the yellowed pages intensifies. I swear I can see him lean in just a touch further to avoid having to look my way.

"Where's the rest of the crew? The ones that we were a part of last night? I owe them one last goodbye at least, surely."

Nothing. No response, no laughter, no promises of meeting up sometime in the future. Not even a glance of pity.

As much as it rips my heart open, I can't say I blame him. We've all seen this happen before. Once someone gets expelled, they may as well cease to be. Nothing's worse in these circles than being associated with someone disgraced from a place like Oxlen. I'd prefer to be looked upon as one does a leper at this point. At least then, I'm acknowledged.

As much as the students here play at rebellion, skirting curfew and drinking with the commoners, they're trapped in this life all the same. The thought of leaving it behind is terrifying.

So, here I am, alone and exiled. It's finally setting in. Keeper above, I really do have nothing left, don't I?

Pressure builds in my throat, choking and burning. With it comes the rapid onset of faintness and nausea. I picked the worst day to be hungover. I have to sprint to the nearest waste bin to ensure I vomit into something instead of onto something, crashing down on my knees as I let loose.

It's nothing of substance, just acidic liquid.

No sounds of surprise or disgust come from the prefect. Todrey's equally quiet.

"My apologies to whoever has to clean that," I say.

"Shall we get to your room?" the prefect asks.

"Right," I say, wiping my lips. "Sorry, let's get on with it."

I can feel Todrey looking at me as I leave, but I don't stop again, keeping my pace past him and up the stairs. Let him live with regret, as well.

My door slowly yawns open, and I look about my room. It's a modest affair. Only a cupboard, trunk, bed, and desk furnish it. Keepsakes and mementos from last year fill the desk beside my bed. A family photo in front of our manor back in Veneria lays on it beside an open book. I take it and stuff it inside my breast pocket before turning to leave.

"Um, shouldn't you begin packing?" the prefect asks.

"Not necessary," I say. "No need for any of it. I don't recall asking for your opinion, either."

"A day's clothes at least, surely." His furrowed brow smoothed into one of concern.

Some sense seeps into my mind. He's right; I'm just in a frenzy to leave as soon as possible. The hairs on the back of my neck haven't gone down since leaving Clemens's office. It stings to still be on this campus.

"Yes," I say. "Yes, you're right. My apologies for taking all this out on you."

Childish, Fey, so childish. I pull a steam trunk from beneath my bed. A few days' worth of suits, sleeping clothes and such will be enough. I refuse to plan past that point.

The final stroll through campus is a bitter one, with no sweet to accompany it. The beauty of the cobblestones and statues is just drenched in grey. Dull, dull gray.

We shall see how dour my circumstances shall really be. At least I can finally see what sort of fortune you've left me. Let that dictate my future.

Once I pass the college gates, I turn to the right and head down the street toward the telegraph office.

CHAPTER 2

For the lowly sum of 500 silvum, this state-of-the-art shifting lamp can be yours!

These catalogues call every appliance state-of-the-art. A bright half-page illustration shows a housewife agasp, both hands on her face, as a lamp with a rotating set of shades changes the color of her dining room. A small list of phone numbers and order instructions sit below it.

Looking at this tiny woman and her big smile provides barely any distraction. The wait to see how rich or poor I truly am is killing me.

"Mr. Fey," a tinny voice says from the waiting room speakers. "Would you approach desk number fourteen, please?"

I rise from my seat and set down the paperbound collage of consumerism, making my way along the row of inset booths on the left wall. Women send off notes to their enlisted beloveds. Middle-aged men wring hats in their hands as they receive bad news from military outposts and company towns on the frontier. A few booths also have men doing what I'm attempting to do: get their balance from their banks and investment portfolios.

The awareness of how much sweat is forming in my armpits is just now coming into focus. Dean Clemens never allowed me to take from my estate's treasury since my parents' passing. He would always say that I'd burn through it without even noticing. Now that it's all I have, I'm starting to read between the lines of what he meant. I doubt he characterized me as that excessive of a spender. Perhaps he meant it as there wasn't much silvum in my inheritance, to begin with. Just how much did you gamble away, I wonder?

It couldn't have been that much. We were millionaires when we immigrated here. And the government was eager for the coming of old blood and gave us even more in subsidies.

What meager comfort that notion brings.

I approach a middle-aged woman who sits behind a pane of glass with an array of holes punched through the middle of it.

"Your telegram from Venerian Ancestral Bank has returned, sir," she says.

"And?"

"It states that the current balance of your account is 2,600 silvum."

"*What?*"

"It states that the current balance of your acc—"

"No, no, sorry I heard you the first time. It's just. That can't be right. Can you telegram again?"

"I could, but it would be the same amount. Venerian Ancestry is never wrong in its counting, Mr. Fey."

"There's just no way. That's almost nothing."

"I'm sorry if this alarms you in some way, but this is the current amount in the account you gave me."

I tap my fingers on the wooden counter, scattering for some sort of answer. All that's left of my family's treasury. The cost of one month's rent in some two-bedroom apartment in the Acre.

I sigh and resign to reality.

"Can you notarize that for me, please?" I ask.

"Of course, sir."

She brings down a large stamping device onto the telegram, with an audible thunk, before signing the telegram office's location atop it and handing it to me.

Good Keeper above! I can't help but feel cornered by financial dread. That small amount would barely last long enough to find a job. I'd be forced into a small hotel room somewhere in Lagiagwop Row, cramped between struggling and underfed families. Each day would be spent filling out applications and shaking hands, hoping and writing prayers that some manufacturing company or, Keeper forbid, steel mill hires me on and slaps me on the back. In the absolute worst case, I'd fall into some sort of debt servitude and have to serve a term at the brutal Wayward Industries company towns to the north, where 1 in 20 don't even make it back. Adulthood and its full horror are starting to creep in. It should never have been this sudden. How much worse can this day get?

When I return outside, I can't help but stand still among the wave of busybodies. I read the words of the telegram over and over again.

The current balance of the Fey treasury as of its latest counting is 2,600 silvum.

This is it, the last of my family's estate—such a small sum for centuries of history. From the harrowing escape of our collective forefathers during the Exodus, chased out by the Great Undeath, to the conquest of this land by Sigesar the Revered and my ancestors in his War Council. Kingdoms rose and fell, the aristocracy in its feudal incarnation receded from political relevance, and a few generations later, I became alive before you and mother. You lose your position as governor of a county in Veneria, we come here, and now here I am. And this is all that's left.

All that's left. They never get less painful, the memories and their yearning aches. The slow limp of mother's passing through the hallways, the low echo of your chuckling from the parlor. Childhood and its vile nostalgia bring pangs of loss.

Stop it, move on.

To the void with it, if I'm going to fall victim to some depressing circumstance, that's in the future. I'm going to flip this whole situation on its head. Time for one last hurrah.

I climb into a telephone booth and pick up the receiver. There's one last man I know that can help me here. A certain party animal and social leech known as Wolfrind. He scurries off like a rodent when the sun shines but is the one to go to for a riotous time.

After putting in a few coins and listening to the buzz of the line, the operator answers.

"Operator speaking, what number will I be connecting you to?"

"Hello, yes, I'd like to call Ophidia, 17-990-46."

The receiver buzzes for a short time before being interrupted by a scratching noise of something being dragged along fabric.

"Hello?" whispers his hoarse voice.

"Good morning, Wolfrind," I say.

"Who is this?"

"It's Arthur."

"What are you doing calling me this early, Fey? Has the dawn bell even rung yet?"

"Yes, it has, a few hours ago. Listen, I need your help putting together one last big bash on my behalf."

"One last bash?"

Some more shifting of fabric comes through the line. He must be sitting up.

"Are you leaving somewhere?" he asks.

"In some respect. Call it the death of an aristocrat, if you will."

He stops talking, and I can hear more fabric moving about. He's rising to his elbows.

"Fey."

"Yes?"

"You're not going to end it, are you?"

"Of course not! Not a literal death, I'm just going to be bankrupt soon and want to throw together a big party before then."

"Oh," he slowly lets out before chuckling. "You could've just said that and saved the melodrama, yes?"

"I'm sorry, darling, I'll be sure to keep your tender heart in mind next time."

"Oh, shut it. How about," he grunts with the effort of standing up, "You meet me at the café off of Duavare Street? How's that sound?

"It's a date. See you there."

The phone clicks as I hang it up and shift back out into the wide world. It's not even midday yet, and my world has been turned on its head. A semblance of shock wishes to creep in, but I fight it. Nothing's really been lost—just a worrisome education. Millions of folk seem to get on fine without one. Wolfrind is onto something; a cup of blackbrew and sandwich should remedy things. Hopefully.

One awkward wave at an oncoming car and I'm across the street. Duavare Street is only a few blocks away, and Wolfrind doesn't live too far off. The traffic lights maintain their monotonous ticks and beckon the beeping trucks and jalopies. The day is humid, causing many loft windows to yawn open for some blessed breeze. A bead of sweat trickles down my temple, and I loosen my tie and undo a button on my shirt. I've never been fond of the smell that emanates from people when the day is too warm.

The bell above the café door tinkles in response to the opening door. I find my way to a cushioned chair at a table near the entrance. A few patrons mill around the premises. Some are peering into the glass display of baked goods, while another is at the till, patting his pockets for his wallet. A scene so frequently played out, it probably happens a hundred times a day. A server spots the new arrival and comes to my table.

"Good morning, sir. What can we get for you?"

"I'll have a blackbrew. No sweets or cream added, and an axe-boar sandwich, please."

"Very good, sir. Would you like today's paper while you wait?"

"Yes, please."

Her footsteps recede, and I gaze back out the store window into the street. The custodians are out in force, spreading nullification powder on every crack and crevice in the cobblestone and sidewalk.

It's likely a day or so too early for them to be out in so many numbers. Something quite wicked must have happened recently to get the Ophidian Security Council to add this expenditure to their budget.

A wrinkled newspaper is set on my table. I turn to the grinning server that set it down and return the expression. Time to get in touch with the world around me.

TRADE TALKS BECOME A BUDDING TOPIC OF CONTROVERSY

Negotiations between New Colonian and Gaal Fateux dignitaries have entered their seventh consecutive day today. It's only been a few decades since the two countries were at war over ancestral land disputes, and many are still vocal in their resistance to the idea of cooperation, including Statehouse Representatives from Ophidia and Northsend. This resistance is made manifest in the outcry against the New Colonian Parliament's proposed legislation dubbed the 'Business-Trade Market Proposal,' wherein foreign businesses will have the opportunity to invest in domestic businesses, as well as any New Colonian citizen with the silvum to afford it. Wayward Industries Executive Howard Wayward, however, had this to say:

"The time of unceasing bounty from within New Colonia's borders is, unfortunately, waning. Our many properties across the north have been reporting declining output in both raw and refined products year-over-year. Not all hope is lost, however. Our industrial processes are in need of a proper revitalization, and right now it seems foreign investment is the surefire way to achieve that. I'm afraid if this Proposal doesn't come to pass, we're all going to need to tighten our belts for some time."

"Did you get to the story about the woman and her disappearing baby yet?"

I look up to see Wolfrind and his unshaven face, unbuttoning his shirt and taking a seat across from me, sweat dripping from his brow.

"You really need a shave," I say. "No, I haven't."

"It's a strange one. They say it's probably due to the poorer districts being unable to receive as much powder as the rest of us. The police took the kid away for 'state investigation.' Whatever that means."

"Our benevolent country always looks out for us."

"Spoken like a true politician."

Once he's situated, the server returns, and he orders his breakfast while she sets down two cups of blackbrew for the both of us.

"So, let me get this straight," he says. "Instead of being frugal with the little money your mom and dad left you, you're going to blow through it in one fell swoop?"

"Not all of it, but that's more or less correct."

He narrows his eyes, sly grin on his face.

"That's why I like you, you know that?"

"I've had my suspicions."

The server comes with our plates of food, and we make short work of it all.

"Tell me what we got for the playing-around fund," Wolfrind mumbles through a full mouth.

"Well, I'd like to not be homeless after tonight's affairs, so let's say 1,000 silvum."

"I see. We're not having a night at the castle, but that's not too bad. We can still have a great time."

"What are you thinking about venues?"

He takes a moment to get another sip from his cup.

"If we're thinking of inviting those we usually go about with, and a place that will set up on such short notice, I would say either The Superb off of Mainford Avenue or Monarch in the Snap."

"That is a tough choice. The Superb is on the riverside, but they have that pesky drink limit."

"You're looking to get bashed," he smiles.

"I'm always looking to get bashed," I smile back.

"That's my boy. Are we going to let in newcomers if they notice our good time?"

"As long as they don't start trouble, I don't mind."

"Very well, Monarch it is. I'll get to work on setting things up. Do you have the notarized slip?"

I take the telegram from my pocket and slide it across the table.

"Thank you, good sir," he says.

I feel a tinge of shame handing off my estate to the likes of Wolfrind.

"Well, Mr. Aristocrat," he says, "let's make sure you get the proper send-off, shall we?"

CHAPTER 3

The woman on stage whips her body in a mesmerizing fashion. Legs, hips, and arms move in tandem with one another, harmonious with the spastic rhythm of the tuxedoed band behind her. Strands of fabric on her short dress whirl around her waist. Her grace and motion are beautiful, although, in scant moments, the facade breaks, and I can see her boredom. Her face will catch the full light from one of the stage lamps, and her expression is always flat. The result of doing this routine hundreds of times. Still, her body shows something completely different. There's a certain beauty to maintaining a mask so well.

From the private section of the cabaret, I'm able to look down on the entirety of the scene. Purple drapes all along the stage match the deep lavender color of the plain wallpaper. The electric sconces that line the walls are half-lit with an array of orange hues, affording a sort of warm ambiance. Clouds of smoke drift through the air from the regiment of lit tobac pipes that fill the space. The acrid smoke and flowery perfume combine into an odd bouquet of scents.

The dance floor in front of the stage has a fair number of participants, mostly humans. Men and women pair off and hold each other close, moving their legs back and forth to the rapid pace of the music. But the majority of patrons are more self-conscious and stay at their tables to enjoy their colorful drinks.

My attire for this occasion is more casual than I'd like, but the haste to evacuate Oxlen didn't leave me with much choice. I put my suitcase away in a small room at a nearby hotel. All that is in it is a few more pairs of day suits and a sleeping gown because I'll be hexed if I have to sleep in a blazer and slacks.

"Here's your Bullwolf Cocktail, sir."

I turn to the waitress, setting down a drink on my standing table.

"Thank you, miss."

A small paper parasol sits inside the thick liqueur. It's almost a sort of syrup but goes down easily. The drink is sourer than I usually like, but at least it's disguising the burn of the spirits well.

Down to my right is the stairway up to our section, with a strapping middle-aged man guarding the entrance. In his hand is a written list of those who we, or Wolfrind, invited to attend. We'll keep up the air of exclusivity until near the midnight bell, then I've decided that anyone who wants to feel important can come up. Why not? It's not like I'll return here again anytime soon.

Keeper above, what a dark place that will be. An excessive amount of problems for future me. And the darkest of all would be admitting defeat and going back to live with Clemens, like a child. Horrid, absolutely horrid.

But that's another time. The music and drink are a welcome distraction.

It's still early in the evening, so the party won't reach critical mass for a while. Even on a workday, this place starts to swell, thanks to being located in the Snap. Little tribes have formed in the lower ranks of the club, as smiling faces look at one another and shake hands before waving toward the others and introducing themselves. Men attempt to be suave and reserved, while women have no such compunctions and explode with excitement, rising in pitch when they see both friends and strangers. A phrase appears again and again through the dull chatter and swell of instruments, in a hundred different voices: "Have we met before?"

"Hey, Fey," Wolfrind calls from the raised booth in the corner behind me. "Don't be an outsider. Join the rest of us, will you?"

I turn to see the booth filled with about two people I know and eight more that Wolfrind knows. He wasted no time using this as another opportunity to gather his pals and drink to oblivion.

What knee-jerk cynicism, myself. That's why I put this together.

Drink in hand, I walk over and squeeze my way onto the edge of the booth while everyone else wiggles around to make room for my wiry frame. The faces I recognize are Wolfrind, and my large half-orc friend Gren, at the other end of the booth. As soon as I see Gren, a wave of nostalgia washes over me. A great friend from another time. How Wolfrind managed to find and invite him is a mystery. His skin is a light red-brown, with eyes to match. His thick brow and bald head are covered in small scars and nicks, the result of a life of violence in Plimred Yard, and not really caring about how sharp his razor is. I've known him the longest out of anyone here but stopped seeing him once I started living at Oxlen. Looking back, I discarded him quite casually, choosing to be around the stiffs at college instead. What a rotten friend I've been.

He's the only non-human here and didn't bother to dress up, wearing a simple long-button shirt and trousers. He's also a head taller than anyone else at the table, and I think most of them find it off-putting.

It's too soon for anyone to have gathered enough drunken audacity to say anything, thankfully. Things are still very polite.

"You know, Margaret," a ginger woman in a yellow evening gown says, "I absolutely adore that dress you're wearing. Is that Bul'thana?"

"Oh, how did you know?" a blonde woman across from her says. "It's part of her new collection. Some are already calling it her magnum opus, but if you ask me, that's too soon to tell."

I don't care. It's my party, and I don't care.

"Incredible," I interrupt. "Say, Gren, what have you been up to? It's been a good while since we've seen each other."

"Since you left for Oxlen, just about."

Whether he meant it or not, guilt dripped from that statement.

"Has it been that long? I'm sorry about abandoning you like that, pal. What have you been up to in the meantime?"

"Oh, you know," he shrugs. "Same ol', same ol'."

"No, I don't. Fill me in."

He takes a look around the room.

"Well," he begins, "how does everyone here feel about, uhhh… What's the legal term? Assault and battery?"

"Oh, I'd rather not hear of all that, if you don't mind," the blonde woman says.

"That's about what I thought," he replies. "I'll go get us shooters."

Gren rises and sets off down the stairs.

"My word," pipes up another gentleman in the middle of the booth. "Are all of his kind like that?"

"Most of the ones I've met are like it," the man to his left smugly retorts. "You'd think having human ancestry would put some civility in their veins."

"Wolfrind," I whisper. "How did you find Gren, let alone invite him?"

"Bumped into him while I was out in the Acre," he whispers. "We frequent a lot of the same spots. Mentioned your name, and he blew up with excitement and almost begged to be invited."

"Sounds like he hasn't changed too much then," I say.

The girl directly across from me breaks up the exchange with a shriek of excitement, eyes pointed toward the stairs. I turn to see three more joining the party, the woman at the front crouched down in that excited way people tend to do when entering a social gathering. The booth starts to rise and leave the table to gather around the new incumbents. They must be pretty important. At least the party will start to expand out across the balcony. Wolfrind taps my upper arm to grab my attention.

"You picked the best time to return to the table. Everyone's so frigid today for some reason."

"Must be the weather. Tell me, have I been around any of these people before?"

"Not really. The majority of the usual crowd is either away on vacation or otherwise busy. I just asked the few I haven't seen in a while to bring whomever they like."

"Are any of them worth knowing?"

"If you ask me, anybody's worth knowing, as long as they aren't a spoilsport."

"You know what I mean."

"Well, there's maybe a few that even a misanthrope like you may enjoy. Let's try those three over there."

The waitress arrives in the nick of time with my refill, which I didn't even know I needed, and we set forth. The man in an auburn suit wastes no time introducing us to each other. His name is Wilhelm, and the other two, a brunette in a bright summer dress and a ginger in one of those shorter dresses that are coming into fashion, are Gedrie and Nelna.

"So, tell me, Arthur," the brunette, Gedrie, says. "If I may call you that…"

I rush to finish the sip of my cocktail.

"Fey's fine. Everyone calls me Fey."

"Alright then. Why did you decide to put this together, Fey?"

To be blunt or polite. The gentleman's dilemma.

"I recently came into a spot of silvum, so I decided to have a modest celebration," I say.

"That's rather fortunate. Where did it come from, if you don't mind me asking?"

"Death in the family, you know how it goes."

"Oh. I'm so sorry for your loss."

"Something like that happened to my cousin last month," Nelna interrupts. "Our uncle was ambushed on his way between cities by those wretched beastmen and didn't survive it. Although if you ask me"—she leans in, and we are compelled to do the same—"it happened right before he was going to sell his company, so I think it was planned."

"Men do enjoy playing those little games with one another," Nelna quips.

"Ambition is a man's game, is it not?" Wilhelm asks.

"It seems that way," Gedrie replies. "But I'd be miffed if we never got a turn."

The two women break into a giggling fit.

I finish my drink and start to feel the spell of the potion. A pleasant buzz settles behind my temples, and I feel the need to be more talkative.

"I spent all day today in my atelier, drenched in sweat," Nelna complains. "You'd think being by the ocean would bring some sort of cool breeze, but I suppose whoever's above has other plans."

"Where's what I've always wondered," I say. "The state has all sorts of sorcerers and such under lock and key, correct? Why can't we gather them up and have them whip up cool winds to bring up and down the city streets?"

Gedrie shuffles uncomfortably at the mention of magic, but Wilhelm and Nelna nod.

"Surely that would be a decent use of taxpayer funds," Wilhelm agrees.

"Surely," I say. "Who do we get on the telephone over this? Who has connections?"

Gentle chuckles pass between the four of them.

"I must say, Wolfrind, your friend is a right laugh to be around."

"He has his moments, that's for sure."

I spot Gren returning in the corner of my eye with a tray of short drinks. I excuse myself from the group and rush over to meet him.

"Gren, my boy," I boom, arms raised.

"Oh no, Fey's startin' to get a buzz," he smiles before hugging me with his free arm.

"Oh, you know it, my friend. You know it. I've been talking to a few of these people, and they seem alright."

"That's just the spirits talking. Here, do some shooters with me. I'm too sober for this."

He lines up two drinks for each of us, and we drink them heartily. The hunt for excitement is in full swing now.

"So, where have you been? It's been a few years since I saw you last," I ask Gren.

"Oh, you know, the same ol' gambit."

He sets the second shooter glass down.

"Although," he continues, "I'm not running in a crew anymore. Tryin' the solo thing for a while."

"How'd you get out of that? I thought it was a lifetime commitment."

"Orcs have certain rituals with that sort of thing, even for a rotten half-breed like me," he smiles.

"I think I've heard of that. It involves a fight-to-the-death sort of thing, right?"

"No, nothin' like that. Usually, it's an 'I yield' type of deal."

"Well, I'm glad to see you're moving up in the world. To freedom," I raise another short, and he responds in kind.

The two of us sit in the booth for a spell and look around. The party size has doubled since I last looked. So many faces. Drinking is a wondrous invention. With just a few sips, I turn into a social butterfly. A plan is quickly devised in how I can weed out the people worth knowing from the bores.

"You know something," I ask Gren, "I think 'to the void with these stuffs,' let's fill them in on the Gren lifestyle, eh?"

"I knew you'd have my back."

We spring from group to group, introducing ourselves and telling Gren's stories a few times. People were starting to loosen up, and some were actually receptive to our abrasive nature. I love being abrasive when I'm like this.

The room is starting to spin now. I go from talking to Wolfrind one moment to dancing with Gedrie the next.

"So, tell me, Wilhelm," I say, "how do you feel about the news story today about the… disappearing baby?"

"I didn't read that one, my friend," he slurs back at me.

"It was a strange one. Apparently, it was in the poorer districts, where the powder isn't spread around as much."

"Fey, you don't need to tell me that story. I'm the one who told you, for Keeper's sakes," Wolfrind jests aloud.

I dance on the table to a raucous crowd, basking in the glory of social validation. A blur of smiling faces and raucous laughter pass by faster than I can keep track of.

"Sir, we're closing soon. It's time for you and your friend to go home."

A man in a tuxedo wakes me from my slumber. I turn to Gren and shake him awake, and guide the two of us to my hotel room.

It was such a good time, and I had to go and fall asleep again. I never can find my limits, can I?

CHAPTER 4

"Good morning, my sleepy child."

I open my eyes to see Gren's stupefied grin before quickly shoving him away.

"Begone, you oaf."

He lets out a deep, hearty laugh. I rise and am further assaulted by a thumping headache. The blinds are still drawn in the dim hotel room. Thin shafts of morning light catch flecks of dust that flutter over the grubby table beside the door. A small radio sits atop that, still turned low on some acoustic music station from the night before.

"Get up," he says, going over to his boots. "It's time to get somethin' to eat."

"I'll be up, just give me a moment."

I rub my temples, and the consequences of my actions slowly seep into my mind. I burned through most of my family's last funds on a stupid party that I now barely remember. Keeper above, I am such a fool. I see your vicious, angry face screaming in mine over and over again, Caddock, and I can't shake it. Another of your lessons wasted on me.

A simmering melancholy settles over my being. I put on the previous day's suit out of sheer malaise and searched the pockets for my pack of pipes. Once found, a pipe is pulled and lit. The burn of the inhale is always strangely gratifying.

Once I leave the hotel room, I turn to see Gren leaning over the handrail beside the stairs, pipe hanging from his lips. I pull out my pocket watch on instinct to check it again, only to be reminded of its decrepit state.

"Oh yeah," I mutter. "Right."

"Is that your dad's watch?" Gren asks. "He gave you that after the crash?"

"It sure is, and he sure did. And it's busted. Because, of course, it is."

"I thought those types could never break."

"I assumed the same, but here we are."

"Great way to start the day," Gren chuckles. "You know, Wolfrind never told me why you did that little shindig last night."

"Oh. Uhh. Well... I..."

One look at Gren's rugged face and I lose all composure. As much as I want to remain dignified in front of him, we share a childhood of memories, of vulnerability and nonsense. He's just seen too much of me for lies to work.

"Escapism is what it boiled down to. A fool's gambit."

"Escape? From what?"

"I was expelled from Oxlen."

His brows and eyelids rise exponentially.

"Unholy void. How did you manage that?"

"Too much fun on the weekends, I suppose. They are an obstinate collective of finks, anyway. Not worth my time."

"What does that mean? They got a stick up their—"

"Yes, Gren, so let's not dwell on it, please."

"Alright, alright, your highness. So, what are you going to do now?"

"I have no idea. Try the Labor Office, I suppose, and get used to the horrid taste of discount liquor."

"They got nothin' for old blood like you in case stuff like this happens?"

"They did, and we used it all already. Caddock must've even burned through the Old Blood Subsidies that New Colonia gave out to migrate us out here. Those few years after the crash were rough."

"I never liked how you royal types call your parents by their first name. Too cordial."

"Yes," I smile. "I can see that. It's all about appearances in the upper echelons, I suppose."

"What about the other families? Could any of them help you out?"

I couldn't help but chuckle. "Aristocrats helping each other. That'd be new. No, no, none of them liked my family. Immigrants are still seen as immigrants, rich or poor."

"What about back home? In Veneria?"

"Not possible. Not enough money for the trip and the manor was sold long ago."

"Hex."

"I know."

A brief quiet settles over us as we smoke our pipes and get used to being awake. Men with worn suitcases set off for the day. Heat is already starting to come back. This hot flash of weather is staying longer than usual. Strange.

I look over and see Gren's affable face. I need to say sorry; I can't get past it.

"Say, Gren," I begin. "I'm. Uh. I'm sorry about just abandoning you like that once I got into Oxlen."

"What do you mean?" he asks.

"Once I began my courses, I just stopped going out or even being around you. And that's a terrible thing for a friend to do."

"Oh," he says. "Fey. You don't have to say a thing. The two of us were just apart for a bit, and that's life. No sense bein' sad over it. Besides, it looks like things are back to normal, right?"

He reaches over and slaps me on the shoulder with his big slab of a hand.

"Yes," I say, "I hope so."

"Good. Anyway, how's some mornmeal sound? My treat."

"I think that would be quite alright."

The two of us pass down the small set of outside stairs onto the sidewalk and stroll down the streets of the Snap. Closed signs on storefronts and restaurants are being flipped to welcome customers. Workers sweep the trash in front of their buildings into the gutter and hope that nature will take care of the rest. Cars let loose their shrill beeps in an effort to make my headache worse. As the sun rises, moisture begins to accompany the heat, becoming even more hot and humid than yesterday. My shirt is already clinging to my frame, damp with sweat. All efforts to shake off the mood of the day are abandoned.

Just as I was told again and again, I'm a failure with an acute ability to ruin any opportunity I come across. Your harshness was wasted, didn't even turn me into the prodigal son that everyone expected me to become. The reality is so depressing, it's hard for me to accept it.

Perhaps tensions with some foreign country will boil over, and I could get drafted. That would square things away for a while. What do you think about that, oh Holy Keeper? Feel like adding some spice into this horrid reality you pushed us into? I hope you're gone, as the New World pessimists say. Good riddance.

"And we've arrived," Gren chirps, holding the café door open for me.

We sit near the back of the restaurant, and the waitress sees us in short order, writing down our meal and setting back off to the kitchen.

"You're only having some biscuits? You're a growing boy, Fey. You need more than that."

"I know. That's what the blackbrew is for."

A wide grin smears across his face. "Come on, now. Cheer up, buttercup. At least you're not dead."

"No, but I may as well be."

"Oh, listen to you. All of a sudden, you've become, what's the word? Disenfaran—"

"Disenfranchised."

"That's the one."

Our cups of blackbrew arrive, and the bitterness helps wake me up. I swear this stuff helps with headaches, too. Truly a miracle concoction.

"Say," Gren starts, "you remember when we were kids, breaking into those big houses of the fairies who'd bully you in junior academy?"

"How could I forget? Especially that one we pulled toward the end when we convinced the butler to open the window for us, and it turned out he hated them as much as we did."

"You convinced him. You were always a real persuader."

"I can just read people, that's all."

"Do you ever miss it? The excitement?"

"Yeah," I lean back in my chair. "Sometimes. It did have a unique thrill, evading the law."

"Well…"

He turns and looks at me with a wide grin on his face.

"How would you like to do it again?"

What?

"What?" I say aloud.

"You heard me," he leans in closer, whispering so the busy room wouldn't hear him. "I've been keeping my eye on a score—a solo job. And you could be brought in on it. A real simple one. Slip in and out."

"Gren, we're not naive children anymore. Back then, if we got in trouble, it was just a slap on the wrist and a beating waiting for us at home. Now, we'd get locked up in a *penitentiary*, or worse, sent up north."

"Keep your voice down. Listen, that's only if we fail, and you know how long I've been doing this? Since before I met you. Long enough to not get caught."

"I'm not having this conversation in a café," I say, crossing my arms.

Right on cue, our food arrives. We eat in awkward silence, with Gren occasionally looking in my direction. My eyes stay locked on the window facing outside. He keeps clearing his throat, hoping that it's alright to speak again. I'm not humoring him. Who knows who's listening in a place like this. I'm honestly surprised his impulsivity hasn't gotten him killed at this point. We pay our tab and leave curtly. The city noise has since amplified twofold.

"If you're so paranoid about eavesdroppers, there's a nearby construction site we can go to."

I rub my eyes and wonder if I should even entertain this insane proposition. Amidst all the sense and rationality, there's an impulse, deep inside my mental recesses, to hear him out. What's the worst that could happen? I say no and walk away. And what choices do I have? I burned as many bridges as I had left in these last few days, so maybe it's not such a bad idea.

I despise being this at odds with myself at all times.

The sidewalk gives way to crunching gravel when we enter the empty lot. Grand machines lie dormant, waiting for their masters to grind them awake once more. I can't help but think that I would be like these machines if I were to get a job in civilized life. I would punch in, do as I'm told, and only leave when I'm given permission to. That continual, monotonous rigamarole is what made my uncle take himself out ten years ago. Sounds more tragic than being homeless.

I turn around to Gren's open eyes, corners of his mouth pouting downward.

"Stop looking like a sad house pet and get on with it," I snapped at him.

"I knew you'd listen to reason. So here's the deal. Some territory in the docks has recently come under some new ownership if you know what I mean."

"No, I don't."

"One of the major players in a family has died, and his heir took over. Think the gangs of the Yard, but more civilized, payin' off cops and things like that. So anyways, accordin' to a trusted source, some old-blood relic is bein' transported through the docks, and since no family is really running that portion of the docks, it's ripe for the picking for... independent contractors such as you and I."

"Okay," I put one hand out to stop his sales pitch for a moment while rubbing my eyes with the other. "This is nonsense, but I'll entertain it. Say we do this, and then what? You expect me to help you beat people senselessly and then rob them blind?"

"No, Fey, the opposite! You do some of that sweet-talkin' of yours, and no one needs to get hurt. The docks are barely guarded. It'd be a cinch. Besides, what other choice do you have?"

"I already asked myself that."

"And?"

"Not sure really," I eventually say. "But I don't know if a lack of prospects is a good enough reason to become a criminal."

"It's the perfect reason! Besides, you wouldn't just be a 'criminal.' Think about it." He wraps his arm around my shoulders. "The two of us, doing an odd job here and there, and in between, we'd be living the high life. Parties like last night would be a polite luncheon compared to what we'd get up to."

How is this impulsive half-orc persuading me?

"So, we wouldn't be joining a gang?" I ask.

"No. Never. I tried it once, and it's not worth the trouble."

"And I can stop whenever I want to."

"Of course. What am I, your owner?"

Well, to the void with it. My defenses have eroded. May as well enjoy life. High risk, high reward, as they say.

"Alright," I sigh. "I'm in."

Gren yelps and jumps up in the air. "I knew you'd listen to reason! Alright, let's go back to my place and go over the details. You don't need to do much, but I do have one question. Did your dad ever leave behind a gun?"

CHAPTER 5

So here it is, the crux of Gren's brilliant plan. I'm to enter the second-hand shop before me, Knife-Ear's Curios, and acquire an old firearm. And the reason the proprietor will bypass all legal mandates and regulations and simply hand me a weapon? Because he has a penchant for any manner of arcane items, and my neverending pocket watch, even though it's now broken, will be enough to convince him.

Oh, and "just use that trademark charisma, Fey, and it'll all work out." How a man with such a penchant for criminality is so sanguine is beyond my comprehension.

I'm through my second pipe in front of the store, working up the courage to go inside. The sweat that drips from my palms is enough to keep a man from dying of thirst. My heart can't decide if it wants me to break into a dead sprint or go into cardiac arrest. Today's humidity is choking, but at least that's a good excuse to be covered in sweat.

The store's on a quieter street in Chimeg Acre, so there aren't as many advertisements and banners hanging from buildings. Traffic on the street isn't at a total standstill, with movement being somewhat regular. The icon of the shop, an eye leering over a twinkling star, is etched into the brickwork of the building. These sorts of stores tend to be hole-in-the-wall types. Consumers in the magical-bauble market enjoy the sensation of discovering a shop within the cluttered maze that is this district.

The owner is apparently an elfblood. There's a rumor that their hearing is akin to that of a dwarf. One of the perks of having an elf in one's ancestry. Although I'm sure one wouldn't need that to hear the percussive instrument that's moved in between my lungs.

What am I even going to say to this man? "Hello, good friend. I'm a nameless vagabond who would like something to kill with, please. And do keep this anonymous. I'm just a law-abiding citizen looking for self-defense." There's no way he's going to refrain from asking questions. I can feel my mind twisting and turning in circles, desperate for an answer to put it to rest. This is going nowhere.

I look down to the tobac pipe, and the slow dimming of burning paper starts to soothe my mind, giving it something else to focus on. Another of your lessons for keeping composure start to brim forth. I can even hear your voice. *Whenever you feel like this, Arthur, turn your focus to your breath, and it'll ride itself out.* That sense of calm was something I never could get the hang of. Men aren't supposed to be so indignant during times like this, right?

"Ach." I drop the smoldering remnant of the tobac pipe. Small ashy burn marks stay on my fingertips.

To the void with this. Being terrified is starting to get old. I resign to my fate. Time to commit to these choices. I need to just pretend like I'm not in a state of panic, and all will be well. If it can work for that affable half-orc of mine, it can work for me. Hopefully.

I climb the few steps leading up to the door and slowly creak it open. A tin bell above it chimes. Once it closes, I immediately feel like a mouse packed into a cage. A brick cage lined with tradable castoffs.

The store is about thirty or so paces wide. Rows of shelves and clothes racks are filled with old clothing, religious objects, books, and other such trinkets. Portable shrines dedicated to the Keeper lie half-open. The small foldable triptychs depict the supposed god creating the book of reality, surviving the War of the Afterlife, and creating sentientkind. One shrine is so used, the prayer-sheets of the previous owner are still attached to them. They were very worried about some sort of disease in their household. A section off to the left is filled with all sorts of weapons from antiquity. Swords and axes and cross-bows, most missing the drawstring. It's strange to find something that killed so many feral elves and beastkin being resigned to such a fate—gathering dust and being forgotten.

About ten or so paces away is the counter, and behind that, a doorway with a patched, luminescent curtain hanging from it. It's an amalgamation of a few different animal hides, and they mesh surprisingly well.

"Hello," the doorway calls.

"Good day, friend," I say. "I'm here to shop for something."

I carefully weave between a row of thick frontier coats to get to the counter, stumbling on the odd bit of fabric on the way over.

A lanky, middle-aged man swishes aside the curtain. He has long, silky hair loosely pulled into a ponytail, and his glasses do their best to mask the bags under his eyes. "I would imagine. Onsario, at your service." He shakes my hand.

"Good day, Onsario. So, I hear you enjoy buying magical baubles."

"I do, but I thought you said you were shopping for something."

"Ah, well, you see, I do need to buy something, but I—"

"Why is your heart beating so much?"

What? Is the stereotype true? Oh, Keeper above.

"Oh, uh," I stammer, "that's because, you see, I'm a first-time buyer, for this sort of thing, and—"

"Empty your pockets."

"Excuse me?"

"I won't repeat it again."

In the span of a few sentences, I've been defeated. The first time I try something of this sort and I'm about to be arrested, or worse. My body wants nothing more than to crumple into a ball of nothingness and roll back into the street. I set my pocket watch, pack of pipes, and my wallet onto the counter. He picks up my wallet and inspects it before opening and leering into the front of my blazer.

"I didn't think so," he says.

"What's that?" I ask.

"You're not a detective. Too nervous. I can imagine what you're here for."

I look into his eyes with genuine confusion. He straightens out his forefinger and thumb and points it at my forehead, and bends his thumb.

"Am I correct?" he asks.

I meekly nod.

"And this is what you're going to trade with?" he asks, picking up the pocket watch. "How funny, a neverending pocket watch that's stopped. No matter, clansmen in Xaggik will be able to fix it. And what's this?"

He turns over the watch and notices the etched emblem on the back of it.

"The mark of the lineage of Vizegard the Wise," his hooded eyes open a little in astonishment. "Did you steal this?"

"No."

"Don't lie to me."

"I'm not, I'm of the F—"

"Shh, shh, shh," he puts his raised forefinger in front of my face. "I don't want to know. You truly must be in dire straits, then. No matter."

He sets down the watch and goes back behind the curtain.

"Well," he says, "it's my duty as a law-abiding citizen to try to lead you away from this dark path. No, don't do it. Buy a bauble of mine instead. All are Minor-Arcana classified, and thus perfectly legal."

He returns with a steel tray, atop which lie a few items. A dagger with a blade that pulses in and out of vision. A ring that has a small specter dancing around the gem. A pocket square covered in words, shifting over the fabric in Common and Dwarven runes. Finally, in the center of the tray, a small glass sphere is cut in half. Inside is a scene of a wooded glade. Two trees, a pond, and a lizard-like creature scuttling around. Nothing I haven't seen a hundred times in a noble's manor.

"These are quite tempting," I say to break the silence. "But I'm committed to this 'dark path.'"

"I thought so. Well, your item, while damaged, is still worth a decent sum. I know what would be an equivalent trade."

He turns around and opens a deep drawer in an armoire, and pops open a secret compartment, and reveals some sort of handgun. The metal is aged and scratched from hundreds of cleanings, and the words on the side of the barrel have been rubbed off, leaving only a few vague shapes instead. The cylinder above the handle has a few deep gashes, and I shudder to think where those came from.

"This should be perfect for your use. A Lucentfly 6.54 Caliber Repeating Revolver. An ancient model by today's standards, only houses five rounds, but it's more than enough to put someone down. I'll even throw in enough cartridges to load it fully."

He lightly tosses the gun upward, catching it again at the barrel, and holds it forward for me to take. There are no hard edges or gem-work to speak of, so it's definitely human-made. I've never heard of the company Lucentfly, so they must have gone bankrupt years ago. It's heavier than it looks, but as soon as I grip the handle, I immediately feel a sense of power. Like I'm able to shout down or stand off with anyone. Or mostly anyone. It's understandable why so many people can rob with simply a knife, let alone something like this.

"Yes, this will do," I mutter, setting the gun down.

"Excellent. Here are the rounds for it." A beat-up, hand-sized wooden crate appears next to it. "I won't be giving you a receipt. And of course, if anyone asks where you got it, you say it from a friend of a friend."

"As you say. Good day, friend."

"Good day."

I stash the gun and bullets into my coat pocket and quickly saunter out of the shop. As I creak the door back open, guilt reappears once more. One of the last few things I've kept of you, and I handed it off. So casually, as soon as it stopped being of use to me. I'm sorry, Caddock. I hope you can forgive me. Although, in a way, you're always still with me, right? In ways that I'll never want to let go of.

What am I doing? Speaking to my dead father like this, I'm truly going mad. Enough. Time to return to Gren and get to work.

As night settles over the docks, Gren and I march onward. Mist from the sea drifts up the street, carrying with it a scent of fish and decaying seaweed. A faint blue settles over everything. The dim chatter of a dozen conversations leaks from open windows; the street is filled with the crackling of tires and clopping of hooves on cobblestone. We hurry by a tenement with a disc player, crackling and reciting the muffled horns and violins from some unknown orchestra.

Even when I'm rushing toward my probable death, I can't stop taking all this detail in. Keeper above, if you're here, watch over us tonight.

The loaded handgun weighs down the left side of my jacket, and I'm tightly clutching a hempen face mask, or rather, a bag with eye holes cut out of it. Drops of cold sweat run down my armpits. My pulse hammers behind my ears. Gren doesn't look nearly as afraid. A smirk is carved into his features and refuses to leave.

"I never get sick of this," he exclaimed.

"That makes one of us."

"Don't be so coy. You used to love bein' a miscreant. Somethin' like that never changes."

We stop at an intersection. Across the street is a locked gate. Barbed wire lines the top. Gren pulls a set of steel biters from his pants and crosses, and I follow close behind. As he grunts with the effort of breaking the chain, I glance behind us to see if we've been found out. I can't help but feel like we're being watched. Someone must be right behind that post or that set of garbage bins and will hop out at any moment. I grip the handle of the pistol for courage, keeping it in my jacket.

A loud metal snap of the snipped chain echoes down the road, and we step a few paces away to pretend like we had nothing to do with it. Once it seems the coast is clear, we sneak through the gate and don our masks. A thick blackness surrounds most of my vision. I didn't cut my eyeholes wide enough. Criminal mastermind Arthur Fey, that's right.

We duck and weave between tall stacks of wooden crates of every shape and size. They're stacked about four or five times my height, and the resulting darkness makes it hard to see anything. Both Gren and I are wearing dark suits as well, leaving me to guess where he is half of the time. Each time I lose him, his massive frame is outlined by a dim electric lamp, and I have to rush over to catch up with him. Only for him to flatten against a stack of crates, lean out as gingerly as he can, and then rush off to the next junction, resetting the cycle once more.

Eventually, the stacks lessen in frequency, and a light appears ahead of us. We duck behind a crate, and a figure holding an electric torch slowly walks past us, about five paces away. Further beyond him is a closed gate with two more figures in front of it. Seabirds caw, and the ocean's tide rolls in the distance.

"Just as I thought," Gren whispers. "They only got clubs on 'em. This'll be cake."

"And the plan is?"

"Simple. I'm gonna charge 'em. They're barely awake, so it'll be real quick, and they won't even hear me comin'. Don't even have any broken glass to worry about here."

He stoops down and starts to peel his shoes off.

"Why are you taking your shoes off?" I ask, mystified.

"You'll see," he grins.

I sigh and rub my eyes in bewilderment and hear a rush of wind. When I reopen them, he's descending upon the first man. His body twists backward, shoulder muscles tensing, and arm drawing back. As soon as he's within a step of the guard, a punch springs from his frame into the man's unsuspecting jaw. I can hear the crack. The second guard is another ten steps away, yelps, and draws a pistol. Gren's stride grinds to a halt.

"Stop right where you are," he shakily commands.

You idiot! Gren, you utter, complete idiot!

As Gren raises his hands, I creep out of the darkness and draw my firearm, aiming it at the man. He was only *supposed* to have a club! That familiar drop of fear hits the bottom of my stomach. Once he sees me, he yelps again, switching his aim between the two of us. Every time his twitching barrel sweeps over me, something irrational threatens to overcome me, threatening to drop the revolver from my hands and fall down in complete surrender. Both my and his hands are shaking. I try to tense my arms as hard as possible to reduce the trembling. What a sorry scene this must be.

"Now, now, friend," I slowly begin, fighting for a sense of authority, "I would like you to take a moment to consider the situation. There's one of you and two of us. There's no way that little shooter of yours can kill the both of us fast enough. Especially not with the way your hands are shaking. If you shoot me, my friend here will charge you and make sure you're dead and hit you even harder than he did your comrade."

"Oh yeah, buddy?" he asks, voice cracking. "So, how about I shoot you first?"

His aim changes and stays on Gren. The change in dynamic mysteriously infuriates me, and the fear fades away—the nerve of this dockyard patrolman, threatening us like this.

"Then I shoot you in the stomach," I say through my teeth. "And your entrails fall out. This gun packs a big round, you know."

"I have backup nearby. All I gotta do is shout for him," the guard reaffirms.

"I can assure you," I whisper, "that you will be dead as soon as I see his torch."

An eternal moment passes. Gren's shoulders are tensed, with both hands clenched into fists. He's waiting for any excuse to tear this poor man apart. Physical threats were always a way to get him to change into something else. Something more sinister.

Eventually, tears start to flow from the guard's face.

"Fine, but please don't hit me as hard as you did Leeroy," the guard whimpered, setting his pistol down.

"You have my word," Gren replies. He walks over and jabs the guard, crumpling him immediately. I look over to Leeroy and see a dark liquid pooling from his mouth. I turn away before the thoughts of our actions can register.

Gren shoves the gate open, and I grab a torch.

"I can't believe he went for it," he laughs. "Who just gives up like that?"

"Save it. What are we looking for?"

"A small box with the emblem of a knight's helmet on it."

We rush through and knock over a few boxes before I stumble upon it.

"Perfect," Gren exclaims, picking it up.

"You two alright?" the voice of the third guard calls out. "I thought I heard something."

We turn toward the new voice and run out of the gated area, sprinting back the way we came. Gren stops and lets out a quick grunt before rushing back to grab his boots.

In a few moments, we're back to the main gate and peel off our masks. We pant as we make our way back to Gren's apartment. He puts his arm around my shoulders and shakes me.

"We did it," he shouts. "My ingenious plan worked."

"It could have used some more foresight, that's for sure."

"Oh, off with it. It all worked out great."

"I suppose. That shoeless stunt was something else."

"Knew it would. I've done it enough times. Without the thud of shoes, people don't hear you comin' until it's too late."

I can't help but feel confused. Our young lives were filled with thrills like this, and I felt it still all the same, but I've never felt so bad about it afterward. The scene of Gren's fist crunching into that man's face keeps replaying. I've never seen him do that to somebody.

"Gren..." I pull away. "I saw that man you hit the first time. He... He might be dead."

"Nah, I just broke his jaw. He'll be fine."

"Just broke his jaw?" I repeat, backing away further. "But you said we wouldn't have to do anything that violent."

"Plans change, Fey. He'll live and get to stay home for a while on medical leave. If anything, we did him a favor. Don't worry so much."

"So, when plans change, we just get to cripple a man? And that's all well and good? This is considered normal in your life?"

"Fey." Gren marches over to me and clenches both of my shoulders with his hands. "Stop. When folk start thinkin' like this, they fall apart. Sometimes people get hurt in life. It's just the way it is. Only rich people don't get hurt or have to worry about stuff like this, but you ain't rich anymore, are you?"

"I—"

"Right?" he says louder, shaking me a little.

"Right, right."

"That's right."

He lets go of me, leaving behind a thick sense of emasculation.

"It's all fine and dandy. Besides, you were the one who convinced the second guard just to take it on the chin. I still can't believe he went for it."

He lets out a chuckle.

"You're a natural at this," he continues. "Trust me. You just need to stop overthinking things. Come on. We'll drop that crate off at my place and go have a drink. I'll buy it."

He turns to walk away, and I fall in behind him. Our dynamic has shifted in those few moments. He rarely had to make use of his form like that. Perhaps once or twice when we were young. But to have it creep into adulthood.

"I suppose you're right," I say. "But please don't manhandle me like that again."

"What do you mean—" he says, turning back around. "Oooh, I guess I did, huh?"

Genuine bewilderment flickers across his face.

"You got it. Won't happen again."

"Good." I smile a bit and nod. "So, where are we drinking tonight?"

"Well"—he turns back around and keeps walking—"it ain't gonna be like that café if that's what you're hoping for. I'm no prince. I know a place that gets you two drinks for the price of three silvum."

"Ah," I say, wincing. "Those brews must be rancid."

"Just you wait, Fey. Just you wait."

Gren's reassurances make sense, or at least I must want them to. But it still doesn't feel right. I can't shake it—this sense of shame or guilt.

It hurts even to ask, but am I ready for all this?

CHAPTER 6

Rivulets of sweat descend from Gren's thick brow onto the dining-room table. He leans as much as he can into the crowbar that's wedged into the crevices of last night's prize. With every heave, the metal crowbar slips and occasionally chips off more of the dark wood onto the floor, getting lost in the wool-lice-eaten rug.

He pushes once more, and the crowbar flies from his grasp, dully thunking onto the floor.

"I'm telling you; this box has got no give!"

"It's gotta be dwarven-made. Holding out like this. Has to be. Maybe the crowbar isn't getting into a deep enough crack."

Like a frustrated child, Gren charges the box and tries to pry it open with his bare hands. Once that fails, he slams the crate back onto the table.

"That's it," he says, walking over to the crowbar. "I'm smashing this open."

"No, nononono." I rush over and step between him and the crate. "That would destroy the value of whatever's inside. Let me try."

"Fey, I'm twice your size."

"Then we're about to find out if the brain beats brawn."

"I have both, but whatever," he mumbles, dropping the crowbar into my hands.

I pull up a chair and lean in to get a closer look at it, wishing I had any clue of what I was about to do.

This three-by-three hands-width timber citadel is barren of any sort of marking save on one side: a square helmet with a skull in place of a visor and a few runes below it. They're definitely Highrock Dwarven, but unlike anything that I've seen. The runes stop and start at acute angles, very unlike the broad, square sides that the language usually has. The gap between the lid and the crate itself is about as wide as a few strands of hair. The spot where Gren was heaving and hoeing has barely splintered.

"I don't suppose lockpicks work on nails, do they?"

"Shut up."

A knock sounds off to my left. I turn to look at the door. A visitor? Gren doesn't get visitors. I think.

"Are you expecting someone?"

Gren shakes his head in response and drops to a crouch, his long legs stalking toward the door. He slides up it, peeks through the spyglass, and shrugs toward me.

"You two better open this door before I kick it down," a low guttural voice says just past the door, raspy and tired like a stone eroded by time. So, my assumptions about the crate were right.

Gren cracks the door open slightly and brings his foot up to the base of it.

"I'm sorry, sir," he says, "but we was just leavin' shortly."

A tree trunk of an arm shoots at the door stomach-level and steadily presses. The hinges whine in agony and the wood buckles before Gren finally relents.

"Alright, fine," he shouts, throwing his arms up in defeat. "Please, do come in."

A dwarf steps in and inspects the two of us. He is a little taller than the table but is almost three heads wide, his broad shoulders framing his barrel torso. His beard is clipped short and gray, and he has a deep, cragged scar that runs across his left cheekbone and up his nose. His head is bald, with a large tattoo lining the side of it. In deep-blue ink, a serpent is winding around itself, with its head on the outside of the circle. Its mouth is open, and fangs are bared, ready to strike. Dwarven letters line the inside and outside of it. If I had to guess from the symbols, he used to be in one of the martial mountain clans. Deathaxe or Splitskull, maybe. Martial clans don't have any holdings in mixed cities, so he's likely an exile. Keeper knows what grave crime he committed to be sent this far south.

His attire can only be described as aggressively out-of-style. He's a frontiersman, perfectly preserved from fifty years ago. He has half calf-length leather boots, a woolen button-down with rolled sleeves, and a thick, black leather vest. On his right hip is a holster, with a revolver residing in it. Unholy void, that gun is large. I can't tell if he plans on using it or not or if he even cares about the difference.

"Something I can do for you, shortstack?" Gren rebukes.

The dwarf draws his gun in a blur, flipping it twice as if it was a parlor trick, the barrel aimed squarely at Gren's chest. Although, to call it a revolver is ill-fitting. It's closer in size to the sawn-down shotguns from evidence photos featured in *Ophidian Gossip*. The cylinder of the gun is holding rounds big enough to blow clear through a dozen men without stopping. I don't even think I would have time to feel it without dying first.

"Sure can, half-breed," he says, "I hear you have something that belongs to my boss. I'll be taking it off your hands now."

His gaze turns to the crate.

"Ah, that should be it. Out of the way, brat."

I skirt clear of his warpath. The dwarf's gun arm pivots on a swivel, staying right on Gren even when he isn't looking. He rubs his free hand lovingly across the surface, whispering foreign syllables to the inanimate object.

"I can hear the ring of the metal inside there," he coos. "You boys gave it your best shot, eh? This here's Deepcore Mahogany." He raps his knuckles against the lid. "Can withstand a thirty-floor drop with no problem. You were gonna bash it open, weren't you, tuskie?"

Gren nods begrudgingly.

"It would have bent the crowbar."

He hefts the box under his left armpit and turns back toward us.

"Right, so you two are coming with me," he says.

With seven words, my heart falls into my stomach.

"W-what? Why?" I stutter.

"Because I said so. And you'll be dead if you're feeling defiant. Tell me, Arthur Fey, are you a rebel?"

He knows my name. Just my luck that the dwarven exile psychopath knows my name.

As the gun slides from Gren to me, a cold wash goes down my neck.

"Not at the moment," I say.

"Good. And you, half-breed?"

Gren has a deep scowl across his face. He's been shown up in his own home. I'm not sure his pride will allow for that.

"I don't know, stuntie. I'm feelin' awful brave. There's two of us and one of you."

The dwarf drops the box, draws a handaxe from somewhere behind him, and slides the blade across his own cheek, scarlet running down his face.

"Let's have it then."

"Now, now gentlemen," I interject, "I'd rather not see any death today. Or ever, if I can't help it. Gren, let's just go with—" I trail off, motioning to the gunman.

"Bjorni," he states.

"—Bjorni, and hear him out."

"Fey, he's going to take us out back and shoot us," Gren says. "If I'm dyin', it's in my own home."

"No, I'm not, you fool," Bjorni says, spitting out the last word. "If my boss wanted you dead, I wouldn't have even bothered to knock."

"Tryin' to get my guard down. Classic manipulation."

I've moved directly in front of Gren, leaning the entirety of my body against his. I don't even think he notices.

"Get your gun," he whispers.

"What? No!"

"You even try that, and both of you will be unrecognizable," Bjorni commands.

"I'm not going to get the gun. Could you please holster your weapons? I'm trying my best to defuse this."

The clock on the wall ticks once, twice, and twice more, the only thing moving in the room. Bjorni finally sighs and puts his implements away.

"There. Happy?"

"Big mistake," Gren laughs, shoving me out of the way.

He swings his bull-like arm at Bjorni's face, who sidesteps it as soon as I blink, already getting behind Gren. Bjorni punches him in the pit of his knee, forcing him to stumble over. Gren blindly shoves back his right hand to pull in Bjorni, but swings just over his head again. Bjorni grabs this wriggling appendage and wrenches up before the half-orc pivots on his knee and faces the bald visage of our house guest. Gren tries to lift the dwarf into the air, but his feet keep their roots to the rug floor. The tattoos on Bjorni's head flicker for a moment before he releases his grip, spins behind Gren again, and forces Gren's large body flat onto the floor with the force of a collapsing building.

In the space of two heartbeats, Bjorni is victorious, holding Gren in a chokehold and wedging his arm between his shoulder blades.

"Don't make me disappoint her, whelp," Bjorni grunts.

Gren stops struggling for a moment. "Wait, her?"

"Yes."

"Is she pretty?"

Bjorni narrows his eyes.

"Sure."

"Wait, wait," I say. "So, who is it you're taking us to see now?"

"You'll find out soon enough," Bjorni says. "What does it matter? Both of you out the door. Now."

We newly discovered prisoners-of-war march in single file out of the apartment into the hallway, with Bjorni in lockstep behind us. He's kind enough to allow Gren to lock his door, although it's so cracked that a strong gust of wind would force it open. Bjorni keeps his gun holstered, although I'm not sure if that's due to the gentlemen's agreement or because he's already shown how capable of violence he is.

It's all I can do not to scream and run. We two amateurs have immediately drawn the ire of an actual player in the Ophidian underground. There's never been a shortage of *Gazette* articles on idiots like us. Pictures of dead men shot and stabbed and beaten and choked and drowned after they inevitably made the wrong move and angered the wrong person. Now, that's us, and we didn't even get to profit from our first score yet. It's too exasperating to even quip about.

As my heart falls to my stomach in defeat, another impulse rides just below it. Amidst the fear and dread, sitting on an isle lapping the currents of the two, is genuine curiosity. Just who did we cross? And why do they want to talk with us?

We amble down the steps of the front entrance, and a black automobile is parked on the side of the street directly ahead—rear door open and waiting. Gren and I stop and wait for permission to do anything. Bjorni walks past us, stops by the door, and points into the interior.

"If you go."

We clamber in, and the dwarf joins us. The back seats are like that of a carriage. Two sets of seats facing one another, with a small window peeking into the driver's portion, heavily tinted and obscuring any details. The other windows are rolled down, begging for a breeze to wash out the humid blanket that's laid across the city.

The engine kicks and sputters to life, and we are off. Rows of patchwork tenements pass by on our drive. Planks of wood are nailed into crumbling brickwork, protecting the numerous holes and patches. Windows on the first floor of most buildings have wrought-iron bars affixed to them. Most of the denizens out and about are the homeless and children committing truancy, chasing one another with sticks representing either swords or rifles, depending on the imagination of their wielders. Fabric flows and flutters from the laundry lines on the roofs. Blankets, and shirts, and underwear, worn and riddled with holes. The flags of the impoverished. As we pass one street, a distant mandolin hums from the open window of a higher floor.

After some time spent passing along these sordid streets, a stone-cut wall five stories in height juts out of the road in front of us, with a raised gate in the middle of it. As we pull up, an officer with a rifle disembarks from a toll booth and approaches the driver's window.

"Why are we entering Founder's Square?" I ask.

"We're just passing through," Bjorni answers.

So, the mystery woman whose ire Gren and I have spurred has the resources to just casually pass through Founder's Square should they wish to. This means one of a few things: she's a blue-blooded aristocrat or business owner who has a manor in this district, or she could be a criminal who's so good at forgery she can falsify papers to fool a Founder's Officer. Lastly, she could be a New Colonian official, likely Security Affairs, the ones that catch and hang enemies of the state. None of these propositions are any less dangerous than the others. Delightful.

As we drive into the area, cramped stacks of apartments are replaced with sweeping estates of elaborate fencing, manors the size of small hills, sculpted topiary taking the shape of animals both real and imagined, and statues of people both alive and dead. Ornate iron gates are barred shut in front of every beautifully manicured driveway leading up to these grand estates. A bright glint of something on the road blinds me for a moment, causing me to wince and look down at the offender. Nullification powder is spread so liberally, it piles on portions of the concrete street, and the tires swish it aside like waves, pushing the scent of dry chalk up into the air. If a sorcerer tried to cast something here, they'd probably drop dead from cardiac arrest.

"Remind you of home?" Gren jabs.

"Somewhat. Can't say I miss it."

"Now's not a good time to lie, you know. Baldy here might be takin' notes."

I turn to look at Bjorni, and find him reading today's paper.

"Anything interesting, Mr. Bjorni?" I ask.

He doesn't respond.

We pass through another guarded gate, and we pass out of the Square into Downtown Snap. The buildings here are packed together but not enough to make one claustrophobic. It's as if one enters an amphitheater that has a set littered with lovely distractions to entertain them for the night. The banners that stand atop the theaters and dormant cabarets are less commercialized here. More abstract and artistic. One that has a humanoid shape leering at radio waves with three eyes catches my attention. It's become a game for some to go to the Snap and guess what some of the ads are promoting. We pass by a bakery, and the scent of fresh bread awakens my stomach.

The car stops on a street corner, and we disembark. Bjorni points us toward an aged metal door wedged in the corner of the structure in front of us.

When I open the door, I'm met with a sparsely attended affair. A dim bar with flaked countertops holds up a handful of bodies leaning over glasses, with only one or two more at the tables scattered around the establishment. Bjorni pushes past me toward the counter. I follow with Gren behind me. I'm at once bewildered and disappointed. I was expecting either an office high atop a tower with a grand view or a decrepit dungeon filled with blood and viscera. This is just utterly banal.

"How goes it, Bunk?" Bjorni asks the barkeep.

"Oh, not so bad. Who are these two?"

"Some new friends of mine. Going to take them down to see the vintages you have in the basement if that's alright with you."

"Of course. Go on in."

Bunk lifts the counter flap, and we walk past the array of spirits on shelves and down a stairwell into a cellar. Who would meet us in a cellar? Bjorni must have lied, and he's going to put us down after all. After he got my hopes up. What a brute. I'm split between running or praying to the Keeper for a quick death. I heard when one's shot in the head, they don't even hear the gunshot.

When we reach the bottom of the stairs, the dwarf walks all the way to the back wall without saying anything and stops in front of it, turning back to look at us.

"Listen, stuntie," Gren shouts, "If this is a lie and you're actually gonna do something, why don't yo—"

"Enough, you buffoon," Bjorni interrupts. "The two of you walk in there. Now."

I'm the first to move and inch toward the wall. What does he mean, walk toward it?

Somewhere deep in the back of my mind, a connection reawakens. Where have I heard about something like this? A shove at my waist pushes me through a viscous membrane, and the dark bricks morph into the blurry image of moving dresses and satin tables. I tear through the wall and find myself in a club, with a dissipating grease in every crevice of my body. The silence of aging barreled wine is shattered with a cacophony of fluttering woodwinds, breathy brass, and stringed instruments playing in a heated crescendo. From the music comes a pulse. Like an external heartbeat that stays to the rhythm of the music and bumps beside my own. The room is large and dimmed, with soft balls of orange, lavender, and pink floating around in silent patrols. To the right is the stage where a band is playing—some fifteen members strong. The rest of the room is tiered into three levels. On each level are staggered rows of tables, filled with people of every race. Humans, elfbloods, and a few orcs and half-orcs. All commiserating and enjoying one another's company. Even a few dwarves took the time to break away from their insular clans to attend. A few tabletops have a smoking apparatus set up on them. A nearby table has one billowing out a kaleidoscope of smoke that smells at once sweet and bitter. Waitresses walk about with trays of exotic foods and drinks, some I haven't seen since my family was at the New Colonial Embassy ten years ago.

This assault on the senses leaves me in a tailspin before a large, familiar hand rests on my shoulder and reorients me.

"I think this is on a' them conjurers' hideaways that the *Gazette* talks about," Gren says close to my ear. "They're smokin' chimera over there. Crazy stuff. They say enough of it'll knock your soul right out of your body."

"Very tempting, but the drink is good enough for me," I loudly reply.

"I think that woman up there wants to talk to us."

Gren's pointing to a figure waving at us from a table on the uppermost platform, near the back of the club. Bjorni is already going toward her.

When we approach, an orc in a black suit holds his hand up to stop us before turning to the woman, who gives permission to let us through.

We sit down, and I'm able to make out that the woman in question is an elfblood. She's stunning, with bright blonde curled locks of hair laid across the left side of her head, long, pointed ears protruding outward. Her cheekbones are sharp, jawline defined, and eyes green. When she turns to look at me, I'm certain she can see right through my clothes, right at my palpitating organ. She doesn't even need to hear it. What else can her kind sense? What else does she know of me?

"So, these are my chummy little *thieves*," she begins, raising her voice above the club's noise with no effort. "I must admit, you two have some stones on you, stealing from protected territory like that."

She brings a pulpy red drink up to her stained lips.

"Actually, it's not protected at the moment," Gren shouts. "Hvinyar died a week ago, and there's still some disputes." He casts a side-eye in my direction. I can't tell if he's trying to jest or wants me to chime in. Neither will be helpful.

"Very cute. Have you been waiting long to break out your street knowledge?"

Gren opens his mouth to speak again.

"Be quiet, for now. Both of you. I don't care why you did it, and I never want to hear excuses. You will wait until I tell you to speak, understood?"

We turn to look at each other before curtly nodding.

"Good. I'm Astraea, and you've already met Bjorni." She motions over to the dwarf, now whittling a small figurine with his axe. "We gathered reports and testimonies from those who saw your little stunt last week, including the poor watchman you hospitalized. I could use them to lock you away until you're halfway through your lifetimes. Theft of an Arcane Item and Greivous Bodily Harm are punishable by a combined twenty years in a penitentiary or Wayward Industries mining complex, you know. But I do not wish to do such things. I'm not a tyrant. I'm an opportunist, and I see such a thing right here in front of me. Arthur Fey, I liked what I heard from the guard that was conscious when you confronted him. It's difficult to persuade a man to get assaulted by a half-orc willingly. You're convincing, and that's very useful."

A server comes by our table and drops off two drinks for the both of us. I pick it up and consider drinking it before deciding against it. If only my stomach wasn't in knots.

"Gren Halfborn, you're a mountain that moves with the speed of a beastkin, and that's also very useful."

She takes another sip from her drink and gazes slowly around the room.

"I would like the two of you to come under my wing as employees for my business venture." Her eyes return to us. "Bjorni here is head of security, and you will be his underlings."

"Uhh," I drone, still processing what I heard.

"This isn't an offer, but a command. If you refuse, you will either become a prisoner or a corpse, depending on how I feel. You may now ask your questions."

"What's the gig?" Gren asks.

"Whatever Bjorni asks of you. Typically it's approaching businesses we have contracts with and enforcing the terms we've agreed upon."

"Extortion. Hm. Not much different than the Yard then."

"I knew you'd be familiar with it. And what of you, Mr. Fey?"

My eyes focus back on the table, then look up to her.

"I'll pretend I have a choice and say yes."

"Excellent. Don't worry. You'll be well compensated for your efforts and will accompany me on a journey unlike anything you'd ever see otherwise. Now, enjoy yourselves! Drinks are on me."

"One last question," I submit.

"Yes?"

"Is Astraea your real name? That's the name of the elven archer that assassinated Sigesar."

"Very astute of you," she smiles. "I'm glad the Oxlen education didn't go to waste. And whether or not I'd tell you my real name as soon as I met you is for you to decipher."

She rises from her seat to go to another table and immediately hugs some other woman as if they'd known each other for years. I turn back to the drink on the table and down it in two gulps. The sting is dry and bitter. Most likely gin.

The speed at which that all occurred leaves behind an impression of whiplash. In the span of an afternoon, we've gone from hunted animals to shadowy employees. Keeper above, one measly theft into my career, and I'm already in over my head.

I look over to the dwarf again.

"Say, Bjorni," I begin, "is it alright if I ask you a few questions, too?"

He stops whittling and looks up at me. I wait for him to answer, but he doesn't.

"How about a few yes or no questions?" I ask. "Like, will we be breaking the law as your underlings? And if so, are we expected to live long? Is this a 'use us until we've outlived our purpose' sort of deal?"

He chuckles and goes back to whittling.

"Cool it, Fey," Gren whispers to me. "You already know the answer to the first one. And no one answers the second one."

"Yes, I suppose you're right."

"Who cares about that anyway? Look at us. We do our first job and are immediately drawn into all *this*."

Gren sweeps his arm around, motioning to the party.

"Nowhere to go but up. You're my good luck charm. Always have been."

He slaps me on the back and downs his drink in one go.

"I'm goin' to go find some of that chimera to smoke," he says, grin on his face.

He struts off toward the lower tier of tables, leaving me with the exile. I can't help but cross my legs and lean away from him to people-watch and drink. Not that he likely cares.

To be immediately shown to an incredibly illegal cabaret, just as an introduction and job offer. By some elfblood who fashions herself after an ancient assassin. There's something off about her, too. It's like when she looks at me, she's looking down at me the whole time. But not due to height or angle. Like I'm smaller than her, and always will be.

Grand moves are being made this night, with Gren and I being but small pieces on the table. A natural starting point for two-bit criminals, I suppose. But a point bereft of any guarantees of safety or sanity.

I flag down a passing server and grab a full glass of something blue off of her serving dish.

If we've been cursed, at least the drinks are good.

CHAPTER 7

Someone pounds on a wooden door nearby, pulling me from another formless dream. It takes a moment, but I realize that I am, in fact, alive and still staying on Gren's stained sofa. Where was that pounding? It comes again, from the front door. Oh, right, naturally. Astraea said she'd fetch for us when it was time, but two days is a bit soon.

I rise up, stub my toe on the short table beside the sofa, and eventually, open the door to Bjorni's upturned face.

"Get Gren. It's time to earn your keep."

I nod, rub my eyes, and turn back inside, leaving the front door open in case Bjorni wants to make himself at home. We're starting bright and early today. The midmorn bell hasn't even rung yet. Beneath the slumber of my activating mind is a waking unease. The memories of that confrontation in this very apartment are still fresh. Bjorni's pistol threatening death stays behind my eyes. That moment brought with it a vivid reminder, stooping down and peeking through the blinds to restate its existence: at any point in time, this will all end, and there's nothing you can do about it.

A quick peek into Gren's room reveals his meaty assembly tangled in a snare of blankets, snoring maw agape. I approach, put my hand on his chest, and nudge.

"Gren," I coo. "Wake, up. It's time to go."

And when he inevitably doesn't respond:

"Gren," I raise my voice. "Wake up, you lummox. Gren!"

His snoring abruptly stops, and one eye opens to look at the intruder.

"The midmorn bell hasn't rung yet," he mumbles. "Go away."

"Bjorni's waiting for us. We've got to go."

"Just a few more ticks," he shifts his body to face away from me and into the wall.

"Fine then, I suppose I'll do the first job myself, and Astraea won't have a need for you anymore."

A rough groan echoes from his chest, and he starts to rise. "Can we at least stop somewhere for mornmeal first?"

"I'm sure we will, now get up."

When I return to the main room, Bjorni is still in the same spot in the hallway, puffing away on a wooden pipe. I gently close the door on him for privacy and turn to the bathroom to change.

While putting on a shirt, I catch a glimpse of my face on the dingy wall-hung mirror. A few spots of small red blemishes here or there. Weak stubble that I could shave if I had a razor.

"Hey Fey," Gren's voice calls through the door. "Can you hurry it up? I gotta go."

"Hold off a moment," I call back. "Say, why do we do this to ourselves? Just judge our appearance like this, first thing in the morning?"

"Do what to who? What are you— You know what? Whatever. Hurry up with the reflectin' and let me know when you're done."

I grin to myself. It's only fair to confound him, too, some of the time.

Hung up along the bathtub rails are the new suits Astraea had the two of us fitted in. Gren's boxy tweed suits almost entomb my slim cotton ones. His are all the same pattern, too—a row of slim green lines on brown suits running the lot of them.

In short order, vest, trousers, and shirt are slapped unto my skinny form, and I commit the mistake of looking at the mirror again. And with that casual glance came the wanting of memories.

The rosy times of father's cufflinks needing to be put on by a younger Fey. *Where are we going this week, father?* I'd often ask. How I enjoyed our little getaways.

"Ech," I bemoan to myself. "Enough from you."

Once the rest is put on, I open the door and am pulled out the rest of the way.

"You take forever," Gren huffs.

"Beauty takes time, you know."

He slams shut the bathroom door, and I go out to join Bjorni. He never moved from his spot in front of the apartment door.

"Gren would like to know if we can get mornmeal first," I say.

"'Course. I'm starving, meself," Bjorni replies.

Even though he continues to be as wordless as possible, Bjorni's immediate demeanor is a grand shift even from the time of Gren and I's suit fittings.

"You seem to be less—" I begin. "Ah…"

"Intimidating?"

"That."

"Because we work together now." He turns his gaze to the length of the corridor. "No sense in keeping you scared stiff."

"So, that was all an act?"

"No. If you two refused to come along, I'd have put you down. You know that."

That casual remark drags a cold scrape along my spine. Keep the bald dwarf happy, and I will live. Noted.

Gren eventually joins us, yawning as he locks the door.

"Gentlemen," Bjorni bellows. "If you come with me, I know of an establishment that serves excellent sausages."

There's no vehicle escort today, so we follow Bjorni out into the crowds of the docks. I do my best to follow the tattooed skull through the meandering crowd, but dwarves have a tendency to disappear into the masses. At one point, he dissipates behind a man with a yellow trench coat, and Gren and I are stuck looking around in vain. Just then, a sharp whistle shoots through the steps of the wandering folk, and we saw him standing at the entrance to the tram station, waving us over.

Workers for the steel mills stand about waiting, dressed in faded denim jumpsuits and holding lunchboxes. Past some stubbled, withered face, a murder of children prance about and imagine the benches of the station are the parts to some fanciful castle.

The Thirty-Six tram bound for Lagiagwop Row grinds to a halt, and we board. As it jostles back to life, my worries about what the job even is glide alongside it. Since it's our first job, it can't be anything too dangerous. What are the most reported crimes of the city again? Robbery, breaking-and-entering, and what was the third one? It escapes me. This has to be a simple little thing to keep the two of us complicit.

Bjorni leans back further into the padded seat, crossing his arms and lowering his head. It's a little frustrating; he usually looks like he's one drink away from falling asleep, but flashes of his ferocity in my memory do most of the intimidating for him.

As we pass into the Row, streets of lofty apartments sit alongside empty, rundown lots. The opinion pieces of the *Gazette* talk of how the middle class is shrinking. Each year more and more bankers, telephone operators, and traveling salesmen disappear into the background noise of the country, leaving their homes behind to die a slow death of abandonment.

Our stop is at the main station, and Bjorni then takes it upon himself to make as many twists and turns down the boulevards as possible. In a short while, I have no idea where we are. The architecture starts to blend into one messy mural, with one facade looking similar to the last.

Finally, a small café appears at the mouth of an alleyway. We take our seats outside the door and are met with overly eager staff. I order whatever Gren does and don't really notice the taste. Thoughts of what crimes I'm about to commit possess me. Surely we're close enough and out in the open enough to discuss it all. At least enough to free me from this ambiguous torment. Finally, the whine of inner questions explodes out.

"So, Bjorni…" I halter. "What— What are we, namely…"

"What are we doing?" Gren finishes.

"Was beginning to think you'd never ask. You see that place over there, across the street?"

He points a greasy bone at a windowed business with a fine lacquered door. A sign hung atop it reads *The Last Tree*.

"That," Bjorni continues, swallowing the last of his meal, "is the domain of one Ronny Stenton. A money lender. Likes to bring in sob stories that are about to lose their houses and offer them a loan with extortionate rates. He always winds up with taking everything because the families can never afford the payments. It's been a while, but it's time we collected from Mr. Stenton."

He takes a deep draught from his morning ale in true dwarven fashion.

"And Fey, you will be our negotiator. Gren and I will step in should you fail."

"What? Me, negotiate? That's what I'm here for? But I've never done anything of the sort."

"Nonsense, boy. You did it back at the docks just fine. Besides, you don't get a choice anymore."

"What do I even say?"

"Something along the lines of 'you failed to pay my employer, and they're not happy.' Keep it vague. They'll know what we're talking about."

I nod and finish the rest of my blackbrew, and a thousand plans buzz and dart about like mental insects. Keep it vague? Wouldn't knowing the name of the extortionist strike fear in his heart? I finish the rest of my pipe before lighting another. Of course, I'll just assume the role of an experienced extortionist, as one is apt to do. Shouldn't be a problem.

Gren leans in toward me and whispers, "Your hands are shakin'. Try and keep a lid on that when you go in."

"*How?*"

"A buddy of mine always bit his tongue. That might work."

"That sounds painful and not beneficial at all."

"Just try it, trust me."

Bjorni pays our tab and gets down from his seat.

"Right. Off we go."

I get up and try Gren's advice. The pain of biting sears all along my tongue. Almost instantly, I give up and feel my hands still tremble.

"That didn't do anything, Gren," I whisper.

"Too bad, that," he smiles. "Can't ask for tips from him anymore. He was shot a few seasons ago."

Once we cross the street and stand in front of the building steps, they leave me to ascend them on my own. I stop halfway up and turn back for a sign of what to do. The two have already turned away from me, acting as if I'm inside. I take a deep breath, flatten out my tie a few times, and walk in.

Pictures and writs line the walls of the long and narrow room. The building is more like a wide hallway than a proper lobby. There's no real furniture to speak of, besides a few uncomfortable wooden chairs to sit and wait on. At the other end, a counter with an opening awaits, similar to the ones banks have, with a door beside it, the silhouette of a frumpy woman in front of it. I slowly press on.

What should I say? How should I say it? What was that one moving picture called again? The one with the highwayman? What did he say, his opening line? Void, it was so suave. Keeper above, what am I doing here?

As I get close, the woman turns and struts toward the door in a huff, showing the worry lines on her face.

"You have a few more days before payment's due, so don't be too sore, Mrs. Galvaire," this Stenton character calls out to her. "What can I do for you, young man?"

I take a few moments to stare at the man, hoping it counts as intimidation. I also keep my shaking hands as far below window-level as socially practical. He's a head shorter than me, with an underdeveloped chin, small, curved nose, and a pair of thick glasses. His receding hair is combed to the sides and parted down the middle. There's a smirk on his face like he just achieved something worth gloating about. So the money 'lending' is a power trip for this man. Quickly and quietly, righteousness replaces fear.

"I've come to talk payment, Mr. Stenton."

"I'd imagine. It's the reason I'm in business."

"No, that's not what I mean. Rather, I've come to talk of your payment. To my employer. You're late, and she's not happy."

"What? No, I'm never lat— Wait, did you say 'her?' Who are you talking about?"

"Let's not be coy, Mr. Stenton. I'm keeping things civil for your sake."

"No, no. Answer my question. Who are you talking about?"

I simply snicker and smirk and let that be the answer.

"Alright, wise man. If that's how it'll be, then you can go to the void. How's that for payment?"

"Is this how you wish to play it?"

"We're done here. Please leave."

I raise my shoulders and hands in submission.

"As you wish."

I cross the room, open the front door, and emit a whistle from between my teeth. Once the two enter the room, Stenton's demeanor swivels on its heel.

"No, no," he stammers, "I'm not letting this happen again."

"Too late, widow's peak," Gren sneers.

Ronny disappears from the clerk's window as we cross back to his side of the lobby. Before we reach the door leading into the office, two latches click, and some sort of wooden beam thunks down into place.

He reappears in the window.

"Good luck now, gentlemen," he grins.

"Did you lock the door with a crossbeam?" I ask.

"Indeed I did. Good luck now. Last time four of your orcish pals couldn't make a dent."

"We'll see about that," Gren says.

Gren braces his shoulder and rams into the door at great speed. The door buckles a little but bounces him back, almost knocking him off of his feet. This causes him to grunt in annoyance and bash the door again. After a few great pounds on the door, the result is the same.

"Having trouble, boys?" Ronny sneers.

His glasses slide down the bridge of his nose as he grins at our impotence. With such a cowardly play, he must feel as if he's won.

For a first job, this is a strange and mischievous one.

"Enough of this," Bjorni says.

He draws his hand cannon and takes aim at the door with one hand.

"Wait, wait, wait," Ronny pleads.

Five shots boom forth from his gun. Two tear through the hinges, one shot hits the latch, and two more where the crossbeam is affixed to the door. The velocity of the third round sends the door off of its seat and landing it squarely on the ground.

I can't help but wince from the deafening volume of the shots. No weapon I've been near was loud enough to make me feel dizzy, in addition to making my ears ring.

I blink and press on the spots under my ears to ease the slight pain. By the time I look back up, the two pass into the office and turn into a force of nature. Gren goes straight over to Ronny and lifts him off of the ground.

"Bet you wished you played nice by now, don't you, little man?"

Before Ronny can beg for forgiveness, Gren slams him into the bank window twice and throws him across the room. Ronny flies through the air and thuds against a bookshelf. His glasses fly from his body and break on the hardwood floor.

Bjorni starts ripping out drawers and clearing off desk tops. Soon enough, Gren joins him and does the same. Although, Bjorni's violence is more measured and ambling compared to Gren's blind, screaming ferocity. Books, glasses, paintings, and electric lamps fly onto the floor. Ronny is struck utterly powerless and tears up over the loss of his ill-gotten gains.

Eventually, Gren flips up a rug, and his face brightens.

"I think I've found somethin', lads," he says, pointing to a crack between some floorboards.

Bjorni stoops down and grips a loose plank. With one heave, the piece of wood splinters free and reveals a safe.

"Care to tell us the combination, Mr. Stenton?" I inquire. His eyes are wide and shaking, failing to focus on any one thing.

"I don't like to be kept waiting," I continue.

Bjorni walks up and seizes one of Ronny's arms with both of his. Bjorni's iron grip shrinks the diameter of his meek forearm to half its size. Slowly, Bjorni twists both hands in opposite directions. Ronny's arm immediately starts to turn a deep shade of crimson, and he can't help but let out a small yelp.

"Alright, alright," he whines. "It's 53-13-97."

Gren turns the dial, and a loud click comes from the safe. Once he heaves the door open, stacks of silvum dollars and coins are revealed.

"How much does he owe, my grizzled friend?" I ask.

"Oh," Bjorni says, "the principal sum is about 3,000 silvum. So with interest, it's about 9,400 silvum, give or take."

Gren takes the stacks from the safe, and Bjorni shoves Ronny aside before the three of us make for the door.

"Pleasure doing business with you," I shout as we leave. "Oh, and you have a some time until the next payment, so don't be too sore, Mr. Stenton!"

CHAPTER 8

I f I were to change one thing about drinking, it would be the spins. After a few glasses, the world boards a carousel and slowly wobbles on its axis, and feeds a nausea that tends to sour the mood.

I turn on my barstool and look past Gren into the cabaret at large. A few weeks of Astraea's jobs have paid off in spades. In some bizarre twist of fate, Gren's dock heist worked. The jobs have been uniform in occurrence. We visit money lenders, pawnshops, and liquor stores dotted around the city and run our gambit. Usually, the two showing their force is enough. Once a man challenged Bjorni and made the grave mistake of insulting his lineage and found himself out a window and a few floors down on the sidewalk. Strange how when you see a man be violent a couple of times, your mind starts to normalize it. After the third job, my nerves quieted down a little. The targets are always hives of scum and villainy, men of greed and avarice, so it's not as if they don't deserve it. In a way, we've become a balancing weight in the urban ecosystem. Little rats that find their way around the law face the ire of a skinny academic invalid and his two lumbering non-human friends.

The Keeper always corrects the tales of life, as they say.

I've also rented my own studio apartment in the Acre, overlooking a wide city street filled to the brim with shops and moving bodies. In the mornings, I ready some blackbrew and look out the window at the lines of ants. It's oddly calming how I've found a way out of the humdrum of civilized life, striking out on my own with my best friend. Crimes aside, life isn't too bad at the moment.

Although, Astraea has been tight-lipped about what we're taking all this silvum for. Bjorni always gives the two of us our cut and then disappears with the rest, telling us he'll fetch us for the next job. Natural enough for a line of work like this, I suppose. Less risk for her as a leader. This could just be a simple extortion racket. Stealing and threatening to avoid the harsh realities of the working class and play at our own version of opulence. The *Gazette* writes about them often enough for that to be the truth. But it's a truth too simple to make sense. Something tells me there's a bigger game at stake. It has to be. Still, we never even see who else is working for her.

That "fatal curiosity" you always warned me about, Caddock. Cropping up again. I don't know if I'll ever be able to kick it or even resist it.

Perhaps one night, I can work up the courage to follow Bjorni and see where the silvum goes. Tailing someone can't be that difficult, right? Another time, perhaps.

"Hey Fey," Gren says, slapping his drunken limp arm around my shoulders. "What do you say about us findin' some gals tonight? I'd wager there's plenty of fish to catch."

"If you wish to, sure. But I'm not in the mood for that tonight."

His eyes fix to mine with raised eyebrows, but he decides not to challenge it.

"If you say so, your majesty," he jabs, rising from his seat to enter the shifting crowd.

I tip my drink toward him and let him set off to find his bounty. It's far from the first time he's chided me so, but it's not even worth fretting over. There's no excuse for it. It could be cowardice to confront the fairer sex or some deep-seated psychological issue involving my parents. But who cares? The women who entice me are few and far between.

The band is playing notes with a relaxed fervor, speeding and slowing as the rhythm permits. Men and women lock hands and face one another, sticking their legs out in unison. The soft orange lights and drifts of smoke eddy and swirl above the mass of heads. Reminds me of the balls I was dragged to in childhood. I was just as awkward and out-of-place on the outskirts back then, too. There's been one considerable improvement since, however. Martinis.

The crowd has been frantically dancing for some time now, and the heat from all those bodies is enough to make even those of us at the bar sweat. I need to step outside. The swoon of the band muffles with the closing doorway, and I light a pipe. Along the boulevard, giggling groups hustle to the next party, and drunken louts stoop over and vomit into the gutter. Ah, the Snap. My home away from home.

A whistle comes across to my left, and I turn to see the waving body approaching me. It takes a few moments, but I recognize the smiling face of Wolfrind.

"I haven't heard from you in a spell," he says.

He reaches to shake my hand.

"I've been a busy little boy, Wolfrind," I say, sticking out mine as well.

"Busy, eh? That's good to hear. With what?"

"I've entered a private enterprise with Gren."

"Oh no, don't tell me that brute got you mixed up in something bad."

"Quite the opposite, actually. We're doing pretty well for ourselves."

"That's great! What are you doing?"

I feign to take a deep breath of my pipe, rushing for a polite way to say "I'm an extortionist now."

"We deal with business acquisition," I contrive. "Help one of the big companies snatch up smaller companies. It's all rather secret, though, so I'm afraid I have to be vague."

"No need to say more," he grins. "I admit, I was worried about you for a bit. Glad to hear you've figured your life out."

"For now."

"Ah, yes. For now."

I offer my pipe to him, and he pinches the paper to take a drag for himself.

"I'm on my way to an event. Care to come with?"

"Not tonight, sorry. My brute is in there, warming up to some ladies."

"Women around here have a thirst for the exotic, that's for sure. Well, don't be a stranger, Fey. Give me a ring sometime."

I nod and blow some smoke away, and he continues down the sidewalk.

I feel guilty that he hasn't entered my mind since that party, but there's nothing to really be done about it. That life did end, in a way. 'The death of an aristocrat.' Maybe some part of me knew what was going to happen all along.

I stamp out the pipe and return inside. Gren has returned to where we sat, with two women in tow. The three of them keep throwing their heads back in laughter. It would take some time for me to catch up to how many they've had, so I decide to turn back around and check my watch. This week's episode of *Coast City Cases* plays in a short while, and if I hurry home, I'll be able to listen. Some scotch and fictional drama sounds like just the thing for a hermit like me.

CHAPTER 9

"These suits will draw eyes, Bjorni."

"That's the point."

I turn away from him to gaze behind Gren's head and out at the passing mural of city life gliding past the tram window. Brick, mortar, and streets fly past below the tracks.

The jab of the pistol in my shoulder holster feels out-of-place, no matter how many times I adjust it. Bjorni gave it to me to wear for "intimidation purposes" but he loaded the thing, so I'm starting to wonder if it's some sort of test.

I've taken to biting my nails again. No matter how many pipes I pull from the pack and light, a heated ball of anxiety stays behind my ribcage. The casual violence of these jobs has become more routine, but something about this one feels different. Far more dangerous. For one, we're going into Dikun's Culvert, the northern stretch that caps off the realm of poverty on the other side of the Grengara. We've stayed on the western side of town until this point, and for a good reason. Men in suits are likely to get mugged and killed on this side of the city.

The jobs have been relatively safe. As soon as they're done, we walk back outside and fade into the background. But it'd be impossible to fade here, where our suits are about 1,600 more silvum than anyone else's. It's as if I'm going onto a battlefield.

As the tram car becomes more deserted with each stop, the bundle of fear grows. I need a distraction to get my mind out of itself. Anything.

"I don't believe you've ever told me who we're after today."

"That's because I don't want you getting cold feet."

He's chipping away at another wooden effigy with his axe. The way his thick hand grips the axehead with such precision is a calming sight.

"Well, we're past that point now. So, who is it?"

"A man who runs a scrapyard. Goes by Ghozek the Wicked."

The anxious bundle within stretches until it pokes out of my pores.

"Hold on a moment. Are they a human or an orc?"

"Human."

"What?"

"You heard me."

"A human that runs a scrapyard in the Culvert?"

"Yes."

"Filled with orcs, I presume?"

"That's right."

"And his title's the Wicked?"

"Enough. Repeating it won't make it any less true."

My hands become possessed by shaking, and I can hear a clacking against the steel floor. Turns out it's my loafers.

"That fear is what will get you killed," Bjorni says. "Get a hold of yourself."

"Besides," Gren says, "if anyone tries anythin', the two of us will try anythin' faster."

"Yes, yes, my gallant heroes," I say, "I'm never tire of being the damsel."

I light the fourth pipe of the trip and press my hands into one another until the ends of my fingers turn white. Nothing can stop the shaking. The void-damned shaking.

The tracks lift and fall again after a few moments, denoting our passage across the river. The modest apartment buildings have fallen in height, a few floors shorter on average compared to Gusilp Cross.

These scant stacks of bricks are surrounded by monoliths of crooked metal and piles of detritus. Anything that's been used again and again until it's past the point of worthlessness winds up in the Culvert. Every worn-down cargo truck and household appliance is piled on top of one another until the little shapes are incomprehensible and make one steel-wrought mountain. Old worn clothes dangle from broken machines, our urban scarecrows. Dikun's Culvert may be the biggest district, but it's not the most populated. Society deemed it fit to let orcs "take out their natural aggressions" in the scrapyards, ripping apart worn-out appliances for the prized scrap within.

All these thoughts don't distract from the dread.

"Fey," Bjorni says, "look at me, boy."

I turn back to Bjorni and notice my jiggling leg again.

"You ever hear of the Turavuhri, the passage of adulthood for young Dwigne in the mountain clans?"

This is the first time Bjorni has used the tongue of his kinsmen around me. The dusty syllables of the accent almost sound like they're coming from a different person.

"Can't say I have," I say.

"For mine, I had to leave the solitude of the peaks and enter the morphing woods, with nothing more than flint, tinder, and an axe. I was not to come back until I had done my part in culling the wild menace. I was a pup back then. Horrified by the wide-open sky and all the trees."

His usually uncaring gaze goes off past the other end of the tram, ages away from now. The three of us aside, the car is desolate.

"My first time was a beastkin that stopped for a drink at a pond. Soon as he saw me, he was frozen stiff. Just a babe still, his legs shaking from the hardship of learning to walk. Wide-open eyes that probably never saw my kind before."

"Then what happened?" Gren asked.

"Isn't it obvious? I'm still here, and it isn't."

His gaze returns to the car and turns to me.

"That weaker part of me died that day because it needed to. Today will be the same for you, boy."

A few moments pass.

"I think I had one 'a them passages too, Bjorni," Gren pipes up. "For a gang, I had to fight two men at once, in the dark."

"Doesn't matter what you fight. It's all the same."

The rails of the tram screech to a halt and our stop awaits us. So, am I to kill whomever we're meeting? Is that what the gun is for? Keeper above, I was never ready for any of this.

The tram starts to kick back into motion, forcing me onto the platform. The two lead the way through the cracked concrete walls and grimy tiles. I lose my pipe somewhere in the journey and reach for my pack to find it empty. We exit the station into the realm of castoffs. Burned-out carcasses of cars and pages of old newspapers litter the street. Eyes filled with hate look to us from cardboard boxes and gutters. A hooded man spits on my leg as we walk past. I fold my arms tight over my chest to feel the reassuring press of the pistol.

The smell is no more pleasing than the sights. Body odor and mold. It's as if we entered the Garden of Decay from the old legends. Too bad I haven't been knighted.

The backs of Gren and Bjorni are the most assuring sight of the scene. By counting the stripes of the jackets, I can stop focusing on the supposed murder I'm to commit. Someone calls for our wallets from a window, and a bottle shatters nearby.

Eventually, the voices fade away, and the noise of grinding metal and whirring buzzsaws replace them. Brick walls transform into chain link fences, splayed and broken in places from holding in the bounties of the scrapyards for so long. The two stop walking and turn toward an open gate. A steel sign hangs off of one of the posts *Ghozek's Yard. NO SOLICITORS.*

Past the opening is a score of large gray bodies ripping and hammering at broken amalgamations of metal. Dismantled automobiles, construction machines, and anything else manmade can be found here, at its final resting place.

"Go to that tuskie and ask where we can find the boss," Bjorni commands over the noise, pointing to an orc peeling a door from a small car.

Why can't I move? My heart pounds in place, pulse screaming in my neck. Is this it? Will I die here?

Gren walks over to talk to him. The orc tears the door free and throws it over his shoulder, narrowly missing Gren. Once Gren taps his back, the orc's shoulders tense, and he adopts a wide stance. Then, Gren pulls out a bundle of silvum, and the act drops. He points to the upper portion of the large warehouse and speaks for a moment before returning to work.

"He says it's up the stairs at the back, and it's the first door on the left," Gren shouts, walking back to meet us.

He takes one look at me and approaches.

"Fey, you alright?"

"Y-yes, yes, I'm alright," I reassure, running my hands down my suit to smooth out some wrinkles.

He approaches me and grabs my head and brings it toward his until our foreheads are touching.

"Get outta your head. It ain't doin' you any favors. 'Sides, you got a piece on ya if things get real bad. So man up."

"Your breath is foul."

"More than usual?"

I chuckle and start to loosen up. I have two of the most violent men in Ophidia on my side. What's some scraplord going to do, really?

I hate it when Gren's platitudes work more than they should.

Orcs turn and look at us during our march, and some reach for tools to intimidate with. Spikes of fear continue to run through me, and to be honest, I'm starting to get annoyed with it all.

We enter the building, and the echoes of grinding gears and blades make me wince. At the back of the building, a set of stairs is set into the wall and leads upwards into the offices.

Atop the stairs, a door awaits on either side. A label beside the one on the left reads *Office*. Gren pushes me to the front. I take a deep breath and open the door.

Inside is a desk and behind it a tall, broad man. His chest is wide as a barrel, with arms to nearly match. His ears are crimped and swollen. Behind him is an assortment of filing cabinets, and a closed window to the left looks out onto the warehouse. He looks up at us for a moment before returning to his paperwork.

"Leave."

I look at Bjorni, and he doesn't return the gaze. So, the usual gambit. Got it.

"I'm afraid we can't do that, Mr. Ghozek," I say. "Not until we receive my employer's payment."

He looks up from his papers, eyes narrowed.

"Payment?"

"Yes, that's right."

He drops his papers and rises from his desk.

"So, they sent you three misfits to collect from me?"

He lets out a wry chuckle before walking up to me, stopping one step shy of running into me. He's two heads of height above myself. The power dynamic cements immediately.

"How about this?" he grabs the end of my tie, running his thumb up and down the fabric. "I'll let the three of you turn around, and I won't have my twelve orcs tear your limbs off. Would that be good enough 'payment?'"

"I'm afraid that won't be enough, and you know it, Mr. Ghozek," I yank my tie free from his grip. "Just pay the normal monthly amount, and we'll be on our way."

In a flurry, he rushes forward, grabs my collar, and lifts me from the floor. Gren steps to intervene.

"Stop right there, half-breed, or I'll toss your friend from the window."

Gren stops a few steps away.

"Now, could you run that by me again, fairy?"

"We…" I begin, feeling the crack in my voice. "We will not be leaving until you pay us, Ghozek."

He releases his grip on me with his left hand and uses it to slap me. The side of my face stings, and my ear rings; my gaze off and to the right. A hot burn washes over my face. I'm dangling helplessly in the air, being manhandled by some large oaf. How embarrassing.

"Fine, here's your payment, you little imp."

His hands go for my throat and squeeze, a meaty vice choking the air right out of me. My legs kick helplessly in response. I can't even turn to see if the other two are helping me.

Memories really want to be confronted now. This scene is a rehearsed one, save with you instead of a scrapyard owner. I was an unruly child back then and needed such lessons. With every slap, I was supposed to become more dignified. A hearty slap whenever I dropped something or spoke out-of-turn. A hearty slap whenever I didn't listen or needed to be 'disciplined.' Echoes of times where bruises throbbed behind locked bedroom doors. As much of a failure as I was, at least I got the rebellious part right, didn't I? You've always talked about how worthless I'd become if I failed all of that. And it looks like you were right—a choking end for a defective man. My vision starts to dim from lack of oxygen. He's about to collapse my throat, I think.

It's always been just so embarrassing.

Keeper above, I'm so *sick* of always feeling like this. How much more will this go on for? I kick helplessly at this man, and my two comrades think too lowly of me even to stop it? With death as the only other option, this all needs to change.

Arthur Fey, enough is enough.

Slowly and gently, as my head pounds in pain, my right hand reaches into my jacket and unbuckles the holster.

As I start to draw it, I'm flung free from Ghozek's grasp. I land squarely on my seat and look up to see Gren tackling Ghozek to the ground. After a brief scuffle, Gren punches him once, with a thick crunch coming from Ghozek's face. Then Gren's fists crunch into his face over and over and over. By the time I stand back up and dust my suit off, Ghozek's blood and teeth are scattered around the space in front of the desk.

"You like that?" Gren screams. "Eh? You like that, you miserable bastard?"

He raises his fist again.

"Half-breed!" Bjorni yells. "Gren, stop! He's no good to us dead!"

Bjorni and I run over to pull off Gren, and he almost turns to swing at us. But once he realizes we're his friends, his normal self returns.

"Sorry, I just..." he says, "He, he was—"

"It's alright," I say. "Thank you, Gren. You saved me. My gallant hero."

I try to chuckle and lighten the situation, but there's too much violence here. It doesn't work at all.

A necklace lies on the ground, between some of Ghozek's molars, red jewel gleaming.

"I do hope you're more agreeable now, Mr. Ghozek," I sneer. "That's a nice amulet you have there. A family heirloom, perhaps? I'll be taking that."

I amble across the office while his groans pervade the room and lean down to snap it up.

"I'm a little curious," I say. "Where is your safe, pray to tell?"

Ghozek grunts and rises to his feet. His swollen eyes are filled with a vicious hatred. "I'm... gonna kill... you."

"Gren," I begin.

Gren steps in front of him and punches him in the face once more, winding his whole body before leaning into the blow. Ghozek moans and falls to the ground. When Gren's foot presses onto his head, he relents and gives us the location and combination.

While Gren and I sort through it, Bjorni peers out the window.

"You've really gone and done it now, boys," he growls. He draws his pistol from the holster and aims it at the door. Footsteps pound on the floor up the stairs.

The office door flies open, and Bjorni responds with a thunderous boom from his hand cannon. The orc breacher immediately falls backward and stumbles away from the doorway, scarcely believing that he wasn't hit.

"Consider yourself lucky, you tusked abomination," Bjorni screams. "First one to enter the door loses a head."

Shots break the glass of the window and ricochet around the room. I drop to the floor and fumble drawing my pistol. Somewhere behind me, I hear Gren yelp. The orcs at the door decide to opt for a tactical retreat, as their loud footsteps thud back down the hallway.

Years pass in those few moments; the only sound is Ghozek's moans. A standoff settles over the scrapyard.

"Fey," Bjorni whispers. "Aim your gun at the door. Shoot anyone who comes in."

I obey his command and look to Gren to see what happened. He goes to peel a bullet from his forehead.

"Ach, those are hot," he winces. He pulls a handkerchief away from his pocket and holds it to the wound. I catch his eye, and he smiles.

"Bounce shots. Wouldn't pierce fresh bread," he says.

If I wasn't so afraid of dying, I would've laughed.

"Focus, boy," Bjorni harshly whispers beside me. He pulls a photo from the top of the desk and ducks across the room toward the window. His back flush against the wall, he holds the frame at an angle. After a few seconds, three shots answer and force him to pull down his hand.

"We got you lot surrounded," a voice calls. "How about you give up and avoid all this mess, eh?"

"We got your boss here, bleeding out," Bjorni shouts back. "The longer we stay like this, the closer he gets to the void. I count four of your boys down on the factory floor, and only one of 'em had a gun. He's not too great of a shot, either. So unless the rest of you want to run in with pipes and hammers, I suggest you back off, and we'll be leaving."

"Only one gun, you say," the voice jeers. In a few moments, footsteps charge back down the hallway toward us, and a blur of a body appears in the doorway. A snub—nosed barrel crosses the threshold into the room. My hand refuses to respond and pull the trigger.

Another boom and Bjorni's weapon blows the body backward. The small revolver it held skitters into the room.

"Alright, alright enough," a second, high-pitched voice screams. "We're backing off. Just get out of here!"

"Not until your man on the floor drops his weapon," Bjorni responds, picture frame at an angle again.

"Hvengar, drop the gun, will yas? He killed Ben."

Somewhere far below us, metal clacks on concrete and scrapes away from its owner. Bjorni drops the picture and crosses the room, drawing his axe with his now free hand. He aims his gun into the hallway and slowly steps into it.

"Down the stairs, before I make your short lives even shorter," he bellows. His eyes turn to Gren and me, and he beckons us out with a nod of his head.

I get up and step over Ghozek's barely breathing body. When we enter the hallway, the last orc is walking backward down the stairs. One slow, measured step at a time, we go toward the stairs. When we clear the hallway, Bjorni steps forward and swivels to the right, aiming at where the lone gunman was before.

"Don't even try it, grayskin," he says.

The tension is so thick, it's almost visible. As we descend the stairs, a step at a time, my aim swivels from the crowd at the base to the crowd off and to the right. I glance quickly behind to see if Gren is following and find him padding his forehead wound with one hand and holding a sledgehammer with another. My throat is too dry to ask where he got it from.

The orcs break apart when we reach the last step, and guilt starts to seep through the adrenaline. I pull some silvum from my coat pocket and throw it at the crowd for some desperate grab at recompense.

Eventually, we exit into the yard. The few orcs outside stopped working to look toward the commotion. Us three swiveling turrets march as quickly as we can to the gate before holstering our pistols and rushing down the street into safety.

When we reach the station and run onto the leaving tram, I remember to breathe and take in a large gulp of air. Gren lets out an ecstatic screech, and Bjorni sighs to himself.

"You almost turned to stone in there, Fey," Bjorni says.

"I'm sorry," I say. "I— I just…"

"And Gren," he continues, "were you too angry or too stupid to avoid almost getting us all killed?"

"He was choking Fey. The void was I supposed to do?"

"You were supposed to let him handle it!"

"Boys, boys," I shout. "Enough. Please. I'll handle it next time. It won't happen again, Bjorni. You have my word."

"Your word and your life," he says. "I'll be damned if I let some amateur get me killed. The void was Astraea thinking with you two?"

Gren turns away from the two of us, anger radiating from his body.

The sun sets below the city skyline, and the tram rocks along its tracks, the sound of creaking metal being the only sound in this empty tram car. The adrenaline leaves as soon as we cross the Grengara again. As soon as it does, and I have no tobac to ease myself with, I just want to vomit. Vomit until there's nothing left in my stomach or my mind. This job was cursed from the beginning, and I was a fool to even continue along with it. Bjorni supposing this as some rite of passage, what an idiot. What idiots the three of us are. In that way, I suppose we're a great fit for a crew—a crew of delusional morons.

Just what have I gotten myself into? Risking life and limb for some plot that I know nothing about. To the void with this constant nose-leading. I'm following Bjorni and seeing where the silvum goes.

If my life is on the line, I'm going to know what for.

CHAPTER 10

I t's going to rain soon.

Smudgy gray clouds overlap each other until they form an unending blanket across the sky. The large-cut stones of the buildings in Xaggik West match the monochrome of the sky. The edges of some buildings are built in the style of castle towers, with rough-hewn dwarven faces jutting from the edges instead of gargoyles. For a race that's responsible for several technological advancements, dwarves are quite nostalgic. Smoke from a dozen nearby refineries and smithies belches from smokestacks and leaks into the sky, leaving the scent of burning coal behind.

Dwarven nostalgia, at least at the collective scale, is only outdone by their industriousness. If an aristocrat wants a custom car, a self-cleaning stove, or a replica broadsword, they find someone in Xaggik: home of all machinations, both legal and not.

No matter how much I think about all this, yesterday still won't leave my mind. Once I returned home, and my nerves decided to stop being frayed, the totality of how close I was to death seeped in. The cold press of the wooden bench below me barely registers.

So, this is who I am now. A man who can't even draw when his life depends on it. Too cowardly to defend myself in my dying breaths. Actually, no, that's not all of it. It's too one-dimensional. I was choosing inaction in addition to merely freezing up. It's got to be something else. Something inside of me that's choosing to hold back.

Enough of this. Ruminating and ruminating. Today's going to be the day I at least get some answers. After all of this, before he disappears, I'm going to tail Bjorni. Just for a little while. Once at least one question of mine gets answered.

"Quite the sight today, aren't ye boy?" a familiar voice calls to the left of me. I look up and recognize that tattooed skull.

"I did my best to freshen up." I rise from the bench and stomp out the pipe on the ground.

"No matter. We're only going shooting," Bjorni turns away and starts down the road, expecting me to follow.

"Alright, here's the first question of the morning. Why is it that you never tell me what we're doing on the phone?"

"Phone lines could be tapped."

"Tapped? What does that mean?"

"Someone else listening."

"People care enough to listen to us?"

Bjorni scoffs.

"I know you're not that daft, boy."

I laugh to play it off as a joke. At first glance, Bjorni's answer seems alarming, but it carries an unintended assurance: Astraea isn't an agent from Security Affairs. So, instead of being some sort of informant, I am actually working with a criminal. If that's better or worse is up to those who aren't as closely involved as I am. But at least it means I won't be bagged and dragged away once New Colonia decides I've outlived my usefulness.

In his usual taciturn fashion, Bjorni leads me through blinking traffic lights and blurting car horns. Deep in the heart of Xaggik, the merchant and manufacturing clans are out in full force. Dwarves dressed in suits or thick leather aprons make their way along the road. The stout folk tend only to wear muted colors as well. The sea of bobbing heads dressed in grays, blacks and browns mix into the stone-cut architecture and sidewalk. If I squinted my eyes, it would probably morph into one great and faded mural. A few humans and elfbloods sidle past the two of us as we go on our way, but there are no orcs or their half-breeds. Some habits from the World Before still stick around.

Suddenly, he leads the two of us into some nondescript alleyway. I should have a leash by this point, with how closely I'm always behind him. As we crunch along the gravel, he stops by a dumpster and slowly wheels it away, revealing a manhole. He squats down to heave the slab of metal upward.

"Uh, Bjorni?"

"Hmm," he grunts, popping the lid free from its resting place.

"I thought we were going shooting."

"We are."

"I meant, I thought we were going somewhere sensible to go shooting."

"Boy, if you want to get caught shooting a firearm you have no license for, be my guest."

Once the metal cover is free, Bjorni begins his descent down the rust-flecked ladder. The stench of raw sewage flows freely into my welcoming nostrils. With a stiff handkerchief pushed against my face, I descend the ladder after him.

The dark is flung back by Bjorni's electric torch, revealing perfectly aligned rows of brickwork forming into a smooth transition from walls to ceiling. We stand on a stone walkway with a shallow canal between us and the other side of the sewers.

"My, my," I say. "The craftsmanship that lies below our very feet."

"My kin to thank for that. The earth could split in half, and these sewers would hold just fine. Come now, follow me."

Our echoing march comes to a halt at an ancient wrought-iron gate barring entry at a break in the brickwork. Bjorni pulls something from his pocket, holds it to the door, and the door pops open with a click.

When we enter, he pulls on a nearby rope, activating a string of electric lights along the far wall, illuminating the room. A wooden chair sits in the nearby corner, and to my right, the room stretches into a corridor. At the far wall, tires are stacked to hold up bottles, cartons, and other detritus. Pockmarks heavily deface the bricks behind the tires. Hundreds of rounds have flown through this room.

"You needed a trinket to unlock this?" I ask.

"Keeps the sanitation workers out. You'd be surprised what else is down here."

I amble in and find a rock on the floor. When I pick it up and toss it across the shooting gallery, the clack against the brick reverberates throughout the room.

"Well, let's get started, shall we?" I suggest.

"That we will. But before I hand you back your gun, we need to talk about something."

"And what's that?"

I look down at Bjorni, and his face is grimmer than usual.

"When I hand this back to you, a lot of feelings are going to come rushing back. Steel yourself now."

I scoff at the notion, but he is unmoved.

Bjorni strides over and hands me back the pistol from yesterday. By the Keeper, the dwarf is right. Vivid, repugnant snapshots of Ghozek's blood and the corpse in the hallway pass my eyes at a blinding speed. The dizziness almost knocks me off of my feet.

"It'll pass. Just give yourself a moment."

He offers me a puff from his wooden pipe, and I accept heartily. Dwarven tobac is much stronger than what I'm used to. The rush from it combats the dizzy spells.

"Your fear winning over and almost getting you killed can only be a one-time thing if you learn to stomp it out."

"How do I do that?"

"Learning to fight back. I should have taught you this first, but I thought you'd handle things fine. Today we correct that. With repetition comes ease, as my clansmen would say. Now, take up the gun."

I rise from the seat and weigh the heft of the pistol, staring at it for a long time. When I look back up, Bjorni has set some bottles on the tires.

"Keep your arms straight, but don't lock your elbows." Bjorni puts a hand behind me and guides me into position before stepping back. "This is probably the greatest distance you'll have to worry about, so get used to it. Three-ring caliber is a bigger round, so prepare for the kick of the recoil."

With both of my hands holding it, I bring the sights up. The trembling starts to set in once more.

"Put your left foot forward a bit more. Focus on the end of the sight, then squeeze the trigger."

I take a deep breath, aim for the green bottle of Hughman's Finest, and squeeze as instructed. The shot goes wide and to the right.

"That's fine for a first shot," Bjorni says. "Do it agai—"

I pull the trigger again, and the bottle explodes into pieces.

"Argli Gwagnta. What a shot, boy!"

For the first time, I see a slight grin on that cragged face.

"A good thing that scum Ghozek caught you before the practice, else he'd really be dead," he laughs. "A few more times, then we'll be done for now."

I nod and turn back to the gallery.

During the afternoon, I crack several of those bottles. Those feelings of fear and being small slowly dissipate and are replaced with something more… More powerful. Something I can get used to. No more of that scared, sniveling child that I used to be. His era has come to an end. These games we play now are more for men.

And this man will seek the answers he wants.

...

The expected rain is more erratic than usual. Sheets of droplets fall unevenly all over the city. There's no uniformity to it at all. Right now, a cluster of pattering falls onto our tram as it coasts to a stop in the East 45th station.

With the sun setting on the Row, I feel a great sense of relief. With every shot fired, more and more of the day's stresses were stripped from me. Bjorni is an excellent teacher, as well as a strong-man. His first impression was a lot grimmer and more menacing than the dwarf I'm finding him to be. That trope of the strong and silent type having a heart of gold may have some truth to it, after all. But even if it does, there's no way on the Keeper's dry earth that I'd say such things to him.

Here's hoping that catching a tail is one of his weaker skills. I'm incredibly stupid for wanting to do this, obviously. But the canned routine of Gren and I's jobs need another layer of explanation. At the moment, it feels like we're parts of a cuckoo clock, coming out and receding as the clock dictates. What's the reason behind all this?

Bjorni is finished whittling whatever effigy he's been working on for the last few days and sharpens his axe instead.

"Looks like my stop," he says. "You've done good today, boy."

"Thanks, I'm glad I have worth in some aspects."

"We'll be calling you in a few days."

He drops from the tram seat and passes through the doors. A gentle male voice calls from the tinny intercom in the station.

"Attention passengers, the 35th tramcars that are eastbound to Gusilp Cross are experiencing a slight delay. We apologize for the inconvenience."

It's a phrase that's been repeated so many times, the voice becomes part of the background noise of the tram stations. As natural as the squealing brakes and ringing tram bells. I probably wouldn't have noticed it if I wasn't so nervous.

After counting the passing ticks. One, two, three, four, and...
five. I spring from the seat and pass through the tram car as well. Too
long, and he's as good as lost among the moving bodies.

He's just passing out into the street. A thick drop of rain lands
squarely on his bald head and drips down it, and he doesn't even
react. Just a moving statue, that old dwarf is.

I wait and count a few more ticks before exiting the station and
following him. He's already begun melding into the crowd, bald head
bobbing and disappearing behind notch lapels, dress skirts, and tin
lunchboxes. He has a way of moving that is unique, however. The
amount of times Gren and I have lost him just to catch sight of him
once more has made this plainer to see. A slight limp in his left leg
has a slow and steady rhythm to it.

The break in rainfall is a welcome one. Glimpses of the setting
sun coming through the clouds and catching on windows and light
poles is a calming sight. Everyone's in an equal rush to be somewhere
dry and warm. This also helps in keeping eyesight on that old dwarf.
He's never in a rush anywhere. I wind up bumping into people more
often than usual as a result, trying to keep a decent distance.

There's no way he'd be this slow to get somewhere important,
right? For all I know, I could be risking all this to see where he stops for
a drink. Wouldn't that be its own kind of poetry? Casually endanger-
ing myself to find what a dwarf considers a quality hole-in-the-wall.

He never looks back once, either. As we cross the streets, take
cuts through alleys, and break back out onto sidewalks, I take the
time to dip and stay hidden in door alcoves and dumpsters, but he
never checks if he's being followed once. There's no way he'd be so
reckless. He has to know then that it's me and only me. That's the
only thing that makes sense. Unless I'm better at all this than I think?

No, there's no way that's right.

Thin drops of rain return to pattering from above. A few
moments later, they turn into thick beads, drenching all of us pedes-
trians in turn. The glimpses I catch of Bjorni show that even these

developments mean nothing to him. Streams fall down his scalp, and he doesn't even so much as bring up a newspaper to cover himself. The ocean could come crashing down, and he'd likely be the same.

A motor car roars past on the street, splashing a puddle right up into my face. A few people nearby are also hit.

"The void's your problem, you fool!" an old man shouts at the passing driver, fist in the air.

I pull up the ends of my jacket and try to wring out the filthy rainwater, but not much comes out. Not that it matters since the sky is still leaking.

I look back up to the street corner where Bjorni is heading to, and he's not there. Disappeared. Of course. Fey, you idiot. I rush toward where I last saw him and pray that some hint of him is shown once more.

Then, in a break between two liquor stores, he's just entering an alleyway. Good fortunes, after all. I run as politely as I can and get up against the wall, peeking just barely into it.

He's unwrapping a tobac stub as he continues on his way. A strange choice as the rain meekly continues its onset. Once he reaches the bend to the right in the alley, I skulk in and continue following him. The street lights have been lit by now in this section of the city but do little to combat the dimness of these back streets.

As soon as I reach the break, he's there, waiting for me.

"Yeah," I say. "I assumed as much."

"At least you're not that dumb then."

The rain intensifies once more, and Bjorni puts his stub back away.

"Little too optimistic, eh?"

"Stop talking. *Now*. Void, you're so lucky she needs you."

I have to fight the urge to ask what for.

"Here's what you will do. You're going to turn back around and go home. Immediately. And pray to your good Keeper above that you still breathe."

I nod and turn around to leave.

"Need to realize the tightrope you're walking, Fey. Death's waiting for you if you don't."

I start to leave but stop in my tracks. There needs to be something that resembles an answer here.

"I'll leave. Okay? I will. But I need something, Bjorni. Something that resembles a notion of what we're all doing this for. How much longer will I be led around by the nose like a dog? I *deserve* to know something."

I turn back around to face him, and his eyes are cold and emotionless. Half-closed and bereft of any empathy.

"Right," I eventually mutter. "Right, right. Of course. I'll be on my way then."

"Are you Bjorni?" a voice calls out from the opening in the alley.

A man with round-rimmed glasses and a briefcase stands a few paces away from Bjorni. He's half-turned back toward the street as if he's one bad reply away from sprinting away.

"I am," Bjorni says.

"Who's he?" he asks, pointing to me.

"A worker of mine, who was just leaving."

"Ah, I see," he says. "Hello there."

He waves to me, and I nod in response.

I turn and walk away but keep my ears keen to catch anything.

"You said you'd be alone."

"I am now, aren't I? Now, hurry up before I decide you're wasting my time."

"Right, right. I know how your employer feels about idealogues, but hear us out. Just this once..."

The voices lose their clarity once I round the bend and get far enough away. But there's no way he wouldn't know if I stayed and listened. His rotten dwarven ears can probably hear me cursing his name in my apartment, halfway across Ophidia.

Something was gained from all this, though. Idealogues could mean a lot of things, but knowing this city, they're of the political variety. Dissidents and/or politicians are trying to get Astraea's help. The eternal spat between the poor and rich is nothing new, although it has been taking on a new face these last few seasons. Labor strikes and protests have become more of an occurrence. It's probably linked to all that. I'm going to need to know more, though. And trying something this aggressive again would be suicidal. So, the patient route is the only way to go. Keep looting and extorting until new things develop.

CHAPTER 11

The way that steam rises from sewer grates at night always captivates me. Some nights nullification powder is caught in the wafts as well. Electric street lamps catch the sparkles of dust in the swell of little clouds of transformed water.

Above the grate and across the street is the stone foundation of the Gusilp Cross clocktower. The grand wrought-iron hands of its face tick away. Not the likeliest place for tonight's reverie, but the change isn't unwelcome.

"Mr. Fey," a servant's voice calls from the alleyway. "We're having some difficulties with the um… device, but you'll be let in as soon as it's ready."

His suit and bowtie have a dull sheen to them, and his white gloves have a kaleidoscope of colors on the fingers. I nod at his reassurance and inhale some smoke from the amber burning point of my lit pipe. He turns and disappears behind a stack of water-stained crates and wooden pallets.

The affectations of this conjurer's hideaway are more complicated than usual, apparently. Astraea is going to be with me for this job, although she assures me that it's more of a celebration of recent efforts than a job. My guile and wit are more necessary tonight than Gren's brawn and Bjorni's skill, she instructed earlier today over the phone. But odds are we're going to be mingling with some blue-blooded old folks, the kind that are as xenophobic as they come.

Tonight marks the ending period of the Harvest, a Pre-Exodus event from the World Before. A time to celebrate the food brought in from the peasants, or to give more modern context, a time to celebrate our escape from the Great Undeath. Not that many care about the history of events like these, however simple. They like excuses to drink and be merry, and I can't say I'm any different.

"It's ready, sir," the same voice breaks into my thoughts. I turn to see his smiling face beckoning into the alley. His suit clashes oddly with the puddles of grease and filth on the ground. I follow his lead and eventually face a brick wall.

"If you would be so kind as to make a lunging motion," he instructs. "And put out your pipe, please."

I follow his instruction in the anxious manner of a schoolboy and lean into the wall. The echoing beeps and dins of the street morph as I pass through the portal into the hushed mumbling and gentle violin work of an affluent dinner party. Film from the passage finds its way into my mouth and leaves behind the tangy taste of a nosebleed. I tap below my nostril and find no crimson. In one piece, it seems.

The soft light of dozens of lit candles fill the room from atop the covered tables and sconces on the wall. At the far end, beside a modest stage, is a bar with a few men and women seated waiting for cocktails. The suits and dresses that adorn tonight's guests give the slight shimmer of enchanted fabric, a textile that's valued in the thousands of silvum. The convoluted nature of getting here shows the lengths the rich will go to to be left alone.

A familiar female form spots me and rises from a table to approach. She has the ears of a half-elf, but her hair is a deep auburn.

"There's my promising young man."

"Here I am, Astraea. Your hair looks different than last we met."

"You like it?" She gently pushes the bottom frocks of the hairstyle and looks to the right coyishly. "I'm going for something more earthy."

"It's very grounded."

"And how are you, Fey? Bjorni tells me that recent events have unnerved you."

"I'm fine, thank you for asking."

She takes hold of either side of my upper arms with her hands and looks into my eyes. She has the expression of a worried caretaker, but the way she does so gives me an inkling of it being a facade. It's too forced. Something closer to an shepherd evaluating her livestock than a friend that's looking after her own.

"You sure?"

"Yes, mother."

"If you're being facetious, then you're doing alright."

She relinquishes her grasp and takes a step back.

"I must say, you've taken to this lifestyle rather quickly."

"Well, you know how the saying goes: The right men chase success."

Another of your aphorisms. Hope you don't mind me stealing it, Caddock.

"What confidence," she giggles. "Come now. There are some friends I'd like you to meet."

She takes me by the hand and leads me back to her table. Two men reside there, with an age difference of a few generations between them and me. They puff on fat brown stubs of tobac and lean back into their chairs; their gray hairs combed back and tightly to their scalps. Their body types cover both ends of the spectrum. One is corpulent, while the other is wiry like myself.

A scene I've been in a hundred times. All they need to do now is pinch my cheeks and call me a strapping young lad.

"Now, now, who's this?" the large man on the left booms.

"Sirs Vandernam and Kelhiem, this is Arthur Fey," Astraea responds, subtly waving her hand to motion for handshakes. Their grips are stereotypically aggressive.

"Arthur Fey, a pleasure to meet you," the man on the left responds. "I'm Vandernam, and he's Kelheim." He points with the end of his stub of tobac.

"Fey, Fey, where have I heard that name before?" Kelheim ponders. His face is familiar as well, likely from ages long past, when I was a few heads shorter.

"Are you related to the late Caddock Fey?" he finally asks.

"Indeed I am. He was my father."

"I knew I detected a hint of that Venerian accent. You've done a good job of hiding it," Vandernam guffaws.

I take my seat at the table and resign to having to be dragged through whatever scheme Astraea has devised.

"What a long history your family has. I'm honored to have you here," Kelheim gently bows before sitting back down.

"Glad to be here," I say.

"Terribly sorry about how your parents left us. Zeppelin accident. Nasty way to go," Kelheim dotes.

"I'm sure they're in a better place," I say, eager for the subject to be changed. The mental sting of the events looms in the distance. I need a drink.

"Can I get you something, sir?" a waitress asks from behind, on cue.

"Yes. Whatever cocktail is in fashion right now, on the rocks," I reply.

"My, he's got a wit," Vandernam wryly smiles.

"Indeed he does," Astraea giggles. "One of his many talents, and partly why he and I are business partners."

That's one way of putting it.

"Oh? Ms. Huxlei has brought you into her little gambit, has she?" Kelheim asks.

"That's right," I lie. "When she told me about the possibilities of..."

I look at her.

"Of district expansion," she finishes. "He saw the promises that my business would bring into Chimeg Acre, and he saw a way to bounce back his estate, shall we say."

"Bring back his estate?" Vandernam says. "I didn't know things were so bad in your neck of the woods, Mr. Fey."

"Yes, my father put us in dire straits, so to speak," I say, feeling a dull ire at the gall to parade out my lineage like that.

"Times are a-changin', aren't they?" Kelheim says.

"Ms. Huxlei here has already serenaded us with her business pitch," Vandernam says, "but I want to hear it from your mouth: What exactly did you gain so far?"

"Ah," I say, "well, if I were to look at last season alone… I'd say the few business ventures she's convinced me to invest in have had at least a twelve percent increase in returned investment."

Vandernam whistles. "Twelve percent? Just compared to the previous season?"

I look at Astraea again and simply nod.

"We've already been booming this entire year," Kelheim says. "Even so. Such a number."

"Indeed," she says. "It's due to the fact that most investment firms are overlooking a few key industries and missing out on hundreds of thousands of silvum."

"Oh, yes?" Vandernam says. "Such as?"

"Second-hand arcane pawn stores," I say.

The two stop and look at me, mouths slightly agape.

"Second-hand what now?" Vandernam asks.

"Arcane pawn stores," I repeat.

I don't even look toward Astraea; I can feel her polite glare.

"Think about it," I continue, "Ophidia's on the mouth of a major river leading into the rest of the country. Immigration and tourism the world over pass through here both ways. Add to that the amount of busted or semi-useless arcane items that spill out of the mountain clans and picked-over abandoned settlements, and you have a small but incredibly robust retail industry. Especially since most people let go of said items for coins on the silvum. People the world over go prowling through the Acre looking for such places. I've seen it myself."

"That so?" Kelheim says.

"Yes," Astraea says. "Yes indeed. You see, Mr. Fey here is a bit of a more eccentric investor and wanted to put his money somewhere more obscure. But the returns don't lie. And with such passion, he speaks of it all."

"That's a fact, at least," Vandernam laughs.

"Well, say no more. If your ventures are so promising that some of the old blood is so willing and passionate to back it"—Kelheim shrugs—"I don't see how I should be any different."

"If you're in, so am I," Vandernam bellows.

The two rise to shake my hand.

"We're glad to have you," Astraea smiles. "You'll be sure to hear more from me about our proposals."

"We have the same accountants, so reach us through them," Kelheim replies. "If you'll excuse us, our better halves are starting to get restless."

They look to a far-off table full of occupants. They both slightly raise their hands as a casual goodbye and leave the two of us alone.

"Second-hand pawn stores, eh?" she says.

"It just came to mind," I say. "And they looked like they needed convincing."

"They did, and you caught it so quickly."

She brushes a hand across my face.

"I'm so fortunate to have caught you, Fey," she says.

Feigned affection and closeness. I have to stop myself from wincing away from her.

"Either way," she says, "Tonight was a success. See? I told you it'd be easy."

"Oh sure, and all that was needed was my family name. The nobility is a commodity like anything else, right?"

"Watch it," she hisses. "Easy or not, tonight was still a job for you, and I'm still your boss. Leave the facetiousness for the dandies. It doesn't suit you."

Such sudden harshness. A gentle reminder of how dangerous she can be should she choose.

"Where is that waitress with my drink?" I ask to change the subject.

"Good question," Astraea adds. "You're done for the night. Go ahead and go to the bar. I have a tab open."

I nod and rise from my seat.

I file away toward the end of the room. This is the second time she's interacted with me, and it's to use my name like a lapel pin to feign prestige. Something about all this nauseates me. It feels cheap. I prefer the nights where my life is on the line. Far less mundane and disappointing.

An open chair awaits at the bar. I take my place and order my drink under the name of the illustrious Ms. Huxlei. I want to ask her if it's her actual last name or yet another false one, but being that curious is probably a terrible idea. I wonder what other pieces she's moving around in whatever scheme all this is for.

When the drink arrives, I swivel the chair and gaze about the room.

At some tables, men slap one another on the back, laughing about some joke or story. At others, the tables are filled with those too dignified to appear so uncouth. Some faces I recognize from *Gazette* articles regarding Parliament bills and elections. Others I remember from billboards in the Snap and Acre. So this is one of those get-togethers where business and politics intermingle. All for the good of New Colonia, I'm sure.

"Excuse me," someone calls from my right.

That someone is a bespeckled man with balding hair. The slight age lines under his eyes hint at him being in his early forties. He wears the patterned tweed jackets that I've seen on many of my professors during my time at Oxlen.

"You seem to be in no rush anywhere," he suggests.

"No rush into anything but this," I say, holding up my drink.

He smirks. "Don't worry. I don't usually laugh. I've been called 'humorless' many times."

"Noted. What can I do for you?"

"I'm somewhat of an academic. A historian that is fascinated with Legaciary Theology and Post-Exodus Country Formation. And my studies have brought me to something of a quandary that I'd like to have a stranger's opinion on."

"Now, this is unexpected, in here of all places."

"I can imagine. A friend brought me here as a 'date,' but I fear it was more for an act to impress her friends."

"In that"—I turn my face toward him, raising my glass—"we are comrades."

While I gulp down my drink, he pauses and tries to come up with an appropriate response.

"Right. So, as you can imagine, in my readings, I've hoped to find a hint of the Keeper and his workings. If you're learned in Pre-Exodus events, his divine intervention was rather literal and up-front, through miracles performed by the paladins of old and what-have-you."

I swivel my chair back around to order another drink.

"And now," he continues, "I was hoping to find out how he maintains the Legacian, or book of reality, in the strange new land we find ourselves in."

"I've been to church before. I'm aware of these basic concepts."

"Right, sorry. I just prefer to be thorough. So, anyway, I was close to a breakthrough until I came across one fateful journal. It belonged to one Lilyath M. She was one of Sigesar's statesmen and trusted advisors during his realm of conquest. She mostly kept to herself, at least according to official records. If you remember from class, Sigesar had many enemies and was victim to many assassination attempts, and no one really knew how he stayed alive. Well"— he smiles, eager to share his discovery—"I found out how."

"It was due to her," I flatly state.

"Glad you're paying attention. So, over the last month, I've been reading through this and cross-referencing it for legitimacy, and it all checked out. And I felt I was closer and closer to finding out how the Keeper writes out our lives. With each entry, Lilyath told of the conquests they all made and how their oracles told them of how they were destined to found the realm of a new civilization. She would topple schemes and conspiracies, and together Sigesar and his council spread their dominion for years and years."

With the finishing of this second drink, that familiar gentle spin starts to set in.

"Then, on one fateful day, they spread as far west as they could back then, and their gaze turned toward the mountain clans. She spoke more and more of how the trade sanctions and military actions would set up for the greatest siege the New World has ever seen. And then—"

His face sinks for dramatic effect.

"And then what?" I ask.

"That's precisely it. Her last entry was on some economic election she took part in. And when I looked into it, it turned out she died in her sleep the next day. After that—"

"The siege failed, and the Civilized Empire fell into civil war,"

"Exactly. So, my question for you is this: How can our god write such nonsense?"

I look toward him, taken aback at the abruptness of his existential quandary.

"I'm not sure. Sometimes I wonder something along those lines."

"Yes, no one can really answer it. I just didn't understand the point behind helping those fateful few along just to let them fall apart into nothing at the end. Kingdoms rise and fall, it's true, but not as sporadically as they do now. Sometimes I can't help but agree that the Keeper was left behind in the World Before."

"What I think, my good man"—I get up and finish the rest of my third drink—"is that you're in one of the most exclusive places in Ophidia, sipping the best spirits silvum can buy, and you're torturing yourself with notions that you'll never find the answer to."

"Hah. I suppose I am doing that aren't I?"

A nice quiet settles between us, and I get to enjoy my drinks.

"I am prone to fits of melancholy," he says, breaking the silence. "Your words are cutting but have some sense to them."

"I hope so. But I'm just an academic dropout who's an embarrassment to his family name, so what do I know?"

"It sounds like we're kindred spirits then, in a way," he pleasantly pushes some air out of his nose, as a sort of gentle laugh, and sips more of his brandy.

"Maybe so. But I've got the spins, so I'd like to return home. See you around, good sir."

"And a fine night to you. May the Legacian house your memory well."

I nod to him and make my way between the rows of tables, bumping into the shoulders of older men and women and quietly apologizing for doing so.

As I stumble through the portal and out into the street, the echoes of his words bounce around my mind.

Maybe such things are not meant for mortal men to ponder.

CHAPTER 12

"When I imagined the dark market," I say, "I didn't think it'd be so literal."

"Out of sight, out of mind," Bjorni says. "Far as the state is concerned."

Yet another journey into the sewers awaits us on this fine day. Gren is with us this time. When I asked him what he did in the last few days, he simply said something along the lines of "oh, you know," and gave me a wink, as if that was supposed to mean anything to me.

Bjorni finally pops open the manhole, and we begin our descent down the weathered ladder.

This job is different from the ones we've been running these last few months. Our prize is information instead of silvum. We are looking for one, Ms. Julie Fullows, an informant for the state of New Colonia, that has some information Astraea would like to get her hands on. Apparently, Ms. Fullows also knows that people like us are looking for her, so she's taken to hiding in the sewers. According to Bjorni, a whole new world awaits us in these stinking halls, something far grander than a bullet-holed closet for shooting bottles. I hope for this informant's sake that it's true.

Once my head dips below street level, that old familiar stench surrounds me. It's stronger here than at the other spot by the shooting range. Waste from bodies and rotten food slowly trickle along the canal, and it's oh so intoxicating.

When we reach the base of the ladder, Bjorni wrestles an electric torch free from his satchel and guides us along the narrow brick-laden path. The brickwork of the tunnels is just as impressive in this section. The symmetry of each brick laid perfectly aside one another is hypnotizing when watching them slowly pass by.

"How could these not be laid by machines?" I mutter.

"My kind studies their craft for 60 years before they lay one brick, that's how," Bjorni says, with a hint of pride.

"Sounds boring," Gren says.

"To a half-breed that can't sit still, it would be," Bjorni says.

I look to Gren and can barely make out his features in the darkness, but he doesn't seem to take offense. That's something I've always admired about him. He never seems to care when people insult him or his kind. It's its own sort of innocence.

The twists and turns of the sewer take us some time to navigate. Once or twice we've had to take a detour because of a blockage that overflows onto the passage. Eventually, Bjorni stops us at a dead-end.

"This should be the spot," he says, pulling out that one trinket he used before.

It glows a faint blue and starts to vibrate. He nods, then takes the electric torch and starts to study a spot of bricks at his head level.

"Which one was it again?" he mutters to himself.

His hand hovers between a set of three bricks before he finally grabs the face of one and pulls it slightly to the right. Something behind the wall falls and clicks, and a ticking starts afterward.

"Alright boys, same as the cellar, you know the drill," he says.

He takes a step to the right and walks into the wall. His body blurs and fades into the wall itself before he fades completely.

"So, that's how it looks," Gren whispers. "Looks more painful than it is."

He follows suit, and I right behind him. At once, the smell of sewage dissipates like kerosene. The film that usually covers my body during these transitions is more like silk than grease. The dead-end morphs into a thin corridor. The echoing drip of drying sewage is replaced by a different sound, some distant reverberating humming that sounds almost human. Like a choir but more machine-sounding. Bjorni puts his torch away as some light source seeps in from the opening at the end of the corridor. Bjorni and Gren's silhouettes solemnly going into this light is a strange sight. I pace quickly to fall into step with them.

The choir reverberates more and more the closer we get until it finally washes over us as we exit the corridor. A wide pit lies ahead of us, with a passage branching off to the left and right. A few floors wind around the pit, with figures milling around them.

Soft light sources illuminate the area, but I'm unable to pin where they are. The place has the atmosphere of a library.

"What is this?" I whisper.

"The Dusk Guild and its inhabitants," Bjorni replies, "built this place ages ago, with help from the Arcane Society."

"The society that was exiled from the country?" I ask.

"The very same."

"So, what is all this for?"

"Anything you can't buy above ground."

"Something so grand lies right below our feet. I don't know what to say."

"Good. Less you speak to these people, the better."

Bjorni sets off once again, with Gren and I in tow. The cobblestone path absorbs the sound of our footsteps, so all that can be heard is the choir and echoes of far-off conversations. The scent of some pine incense pervades the space. Timber doors with an arch and thick metal hinges identically line the walls to our left, styled after the castle gates of the olden times. Bjorni stops in front of one seemingly at random and slowly pushes it open.

We enter into some sort of shop, with sconces lit to give the room the same soft orange glow that was in the main area. Its ceiling is shorter than usual, and the dimensions are particularly narrow.

The counters are lined with mundane items: jackets, dinnerware, hats. Anything that could be found on the first floor of a well-to-do home. Behind the counter is a passage into the dark void of another room. The shop keep is nowhere to be found.

With what will the Legacian be written, a thin voice says inside of my mind.

"With the passages of days come and past," Bjorni says monotonously.

"What can I do for you, gentlemen?" someone says behind me, giving me a good start. When I spin to face him, I see a robed figure whose face is obfuscated by a hood with an impossibly-dark space where the face should be.

"We're after the location of someone," I reply.

"Don't speak. I know nothing of you," he commands.

I nod and turn away so that Bjorni can take care of it. Gren does the same, and the other two pair off and go through the passage into the other end of the shop. Gren and I slowly amble toward a counter and look at the items on it. Soup and chowder spoons with the dull sheen of weathered silver. Tea kettles with veins of gold running through them. If mother was around to see all this, she'd be in a state of ecstasy.

"Looks like all the stuff we stole back in the day," Gren whispers.

"I was about to say," I whisper back. "It's like we're at a royal dinner."

Further down the counter, handkerchiefs and pocket squares of wildly different patterns and textures lie neatly folded beside one another. One with a plaid pattern catches my eye. It reminds me of something father would wear when we went hunting. The aching nostalgia rushes over me, and I reach to touch it.

Please don't, the same thin voice says inside of me. *Once it feels your soul, it can track you to the ends of the world.*

"Ah, very well," I say out loud, retracting my hand.

I turn and look at the passage behind the counter. Just what strings did Bjorni have to pull to get help from these folk? What debts are being repaid? Can that voice also hear all these thoughts as well?

I tiptoe closer to the passage until I'm touching the counter. I can hear Bjorni's gravelly whispers and the mutterings of the robed person. Their voice is so thin, like the one of a person who's still recovering from sickness.

Then comes the sharp grating of nails on chalkboard. Keeper above, what a horrid racket. I put my hands over my ears, but it does nothing to quiet the noise. It slowly builds in pitch and volume. Until I want to rip my ears out and be done with it.

Finally, Gren pulls me back and spins me around to face him.

"Fey," he says. "What's going on?"

"You didn't hear all that?"

"All what?"

"The… The grating. Void below, it was the worst."

Gren looks over into the passage, past my shoulder.

"Whatever it was," he whispers, "it was probably because of…"

He doesn't finish his sentence but points at the passage and raises his eyebrows.

I nod and reaffirm, "You're probably right."

I hear footsteps come out of the doorway and see Bjorni walking toward us. Gren and I take a few steps away and pretend to look at some dinnerware.

"Consider the debt repaid, Exiled One," the figure says.

"Yes, yes, yes it is," Bjorni frustratingly replies, waving his hand. "Let's go, boys."

As we leave the shop and the door closes, Bjorni says, "Can't stand these shamanic types. So excessive."

While we return to the corridor and back out to the sewer, a question weighs on my mind.

"Bjorni, why did you bring us along here?" Gren asks.

"In case you need to come down here, so you know the way."

"Isn't this rather… Exclusive for the likes of Gren and I?"

"For now, but without the waystone, you can't get in anyway. And if you give the location away, they'll know, and you won't be around for very long."

He steps through the arcane passage and melts back into the brickwork, with Gren and I right behind.

"Place is pretty stuffy, you ask me," Gren dismissively says.

"I thought it was serene," I say.

"You would," Gren chuckles.

"Alright boys, we're off to the Culvert. Our squealer is there," Bjorni cuts off.

"How we doin' this, boss?" Gren asks.

"Same as the other jobs. Fey tries to be nice, and we're there if it doesn't work."

CHAPTER 13

Bjorni and I stand atop some old tower in Dikun's Culvert, taking turns sharing a decrepit monocular with lenses that must be a day away from cracking completely. We focus its warped sight on a flaked tenement building's entrance, an old wooden door waiting atop a few brick steps. Stone steps lead up to the door, with a few emaciated people sitting on them, nodding off from whatever chemical they could find to forget about reality.

"Where did you get this monocular, Bjorni? It's better off being melted down for scrap."

"Mind your tongue, boy. It's older than your grandfather."

He strides over and snaps it from my grasp. I look down at the insulted dwarf with something like mirth. As he brings it up to his eyes once more, I look down from the rooftop again onto the stretch of the Culvert.

This district is the twin to the Yard, only less offensive in smell. Where the Yard is filled with the tawdry castoffs of Ophidia, who are often orcish and in gangs, the Culvert takes care of the folk fortune has even less time for. The inhabitants here are too tired from overworking to bother with violence. Apartments all over these streets are full of generations of a family, tens-of-tenants over capacity. Grocers open in the morning with the few scraps of fresh produce that they can manage to get in stock. All of this and more awaits the awestruck adventurer in Dikun's Culvert. The tenements and dilapidated warehouses lean into one another on long avenues, all the way until they are at the shores of the Grengara River. The building we're on top of used to be some sort of watchtower in ages long past and stands a story or so above the other buildings.

Our quarry is shacked up with a smaller orc-run gang in a spot deep in the district. Since they would bristle at the sight of me, a wealthy human, or Bjorni, a dwarf, Gren has taken to staying at street level to make the grab, with the two of us arriving later on as backup. Government types are said to be overly paranoid, so she won't be leaving the building until her schedule dictates.

Luckily, according to another "friend" of Bjorni's, she's going to be moving somewhere else soon, as her former employers have found her out and aren't too kind to turncoats.

Something about this job has me sweatier than usual. Bjorni wanted me to tackle it in a similar fashion as the previous jobs, but as soon as we got to the street, he muttered something to Gren and motioned for me to follow him, and we made our way up to this perch. For a while, I didn't want to second-guess Bjorni because of how wizened he is to this type of thing, but my curiosity has gotten the better of me.

"So," I begin lighting a pipe. "What happened to 'I'll be nice, and you'll be there if it don't work?'"

"She's shacked up in an orc tenement that you wouldn't come back out of alive. That's what happened." He sets the monocular down on the concrete parapet. "All your big words would just make killing you easier."

That statement is like a cold shock to my system, making me face an obvious fact I've been willfully ignoring since we got here. Violence is imminent.

"So, we're going to be killing her entourage then when she exits."

"Probably not. They likely won't have guns as we do. Besides, you won't be hurting anybody, so quit shaking."

I look down at my hands and see that he's right. I turn away from him and close my eyes, focusing on that familiar sense of power that emanates from the holstered pistol under my left shoulder. All else fails, it'll always keep me alive.

"Someone's leaving," Bjorni interrupts, handing me the monocular as I reapproach.

A bald orc in a sleeveless workshirt is kicking at the people on the stoop, warding them away to make room. His frame is twice the size of the wretched junkies he's shoving down the steps. Another orc shortly exits after him, a full head shorter than the first. He's dressed in a similar fashion to his friend: ratty slacks and a sleeveless workshirt. However, he's wearing a hole-ridden stovepipe hat to differentiate himself.

"A few generations too late to be wearing that, isn't it?" I mutter.

The hat-wearing orc puts his arm out in some sort of defensive stance as a third form exits: a human woman.

"Is that our Ms. Fullows?"

I hand the monocular back to Bjorni. He brings it up to his eye for all of five heartbeats before deciding.

"That's her. Let's go."

He collapses his monocular and sets off toward the stairwell in a hurry, with me quickly behind. The crisp open air of the outdoors gets stuffed into the stairwell with us as we go down the flights, the noise of distant vehicles replaced with muffled conversations and smells of mold. The five stories take longer than necessary due to Bjorni's shortened gait and my reluctance to bypass him and wound his pride.

Eventually, we exit onto the street and don't see the three anywhere. Across the road and in the opening of an alleyway, Gren waves us over. Bjorni emits a frustrated grunt, and we cross to meet with him.

"They went this way, lads!"

"Why didn't you slow them down?" Bjorni asks, teeth gritted.

"How was I gonna do that?"

"I don't know," I say cheerfully. "Words maybe?"

"Save it," Bjorni says, "Come on."

The three of us pace into the alleyway as fast as dignity allows, ducking under collapsing fire escapes and stepping over suspicious puddles. The cool breeze raises the nauseating smell of rotten food and fabric. Destroyed wooden pallets are strewn haphazardly in eclectic piles across our path. I hear a dull pop and look down to see that a nail from a small wooden beam has pierced my shoe. After pulling it out and finding that it missed my extremities, I thank the Keeper for not getting a shot of steelrot and continue to watch my step for any further traps. The buildings we are between slowly start to get closer to each other before turning into a fork sharply to our left and right. Ms. Fullows and her guards have all but disappeared.

"Great. Good going, Gren."

"How was I supposed to know I needed to con them? That's your job."

"Quiet," Bjorni hisses.

Fear shoots through my back in a juvenile manner, like I'm being scolded by a school teacher. Gren's back is as rigid as mine.

Bjorni slowly walks over to the far wall, stopping by a dumpster to hold a hand to the crumbling brickwork, slowly feeling over the individual bricks. While he does this, his gaze nudges bit by bit, scanning the scattered pebbles on the ground. After looking at the left fork for some time, he gently turns his body to face the right fork and lightly steps to the other side of the dumpster to repeat the ritual. I worry that the pounding of my heart is upsetting his investigation and will further draw his indignation. After quite some time, he breaks away from his work and points down the alleyway to the right.

"Stones say they went that way," he flatly states as if it's a fact.

I'd laugh if he wasn't so intimidating.

"I didn't know the stones could talk," Gren murmurs, like a dumbfounded child.

"Vibrating all the time. Your kind just can't hear them."

," Bjorni sets off in the stated direction, and we're close behind. As ludicrous as it is, his words reveal themselves as true the further on we go. Rodents skitter away from us as we pass over the knocked-over trash bins they are raiding. Greasy puddles are splashed around with wet footprints leading away from them. These folk aren't just moving hideouts. They're running from something.

Bjorni's walk degrades in speed the more we press on, his gaze moving around more quickly and looking up above us more and more, at the fire escapes and rooftops themselves. Soon the alley turns at a sharp angle to the left, and he draws his hand cannon from its holster on his hip. A slide of steel-on-steel rasps from the other end of the alley. After that, Gren and I follow suit with our own handguns.

At the lead, Bjorni sidles up against the wall itself, and Gren and I stack up behind him. The wash of my blood flow thumping in my ears makes it hard to hear anything else. Bjorni waits a moment and then peeks his head around the corner, aiming his pistol at him. All I see is the slight widening and then narrowing of his eyelids.

"Hello, boys," a dry voice calls from the other side. "You can all come out now, nice and slow."

Bjorni steps out in full into the entryway, hands raised above his head. He keeps stepping to the side and quickly nods his head to the side, signaling us to do the same.

When I reach his side, I turn to see who called for us. The alley opens up into a larger square, with more dumpsters and detritus stacked up against the walls. Our quarry is on their knees facing the left-most wall, with a gunman to each of them aiming at the back of their head. The gunmen have flat caps casting shadows on their faces, obfuscating everything from their nose upward. Three more of them aim pistols in our direction, with the third not wearing a hat and having more wrinkles on his face than the rest. The silhouette of the firing squad causes my heart to fall into a pit in my stomach.

"Guns on the ground," the older man commands again. "We knew we weren't the only ones looking for Ms. Fullows here," he gestures toward the three with his pistol.

The two orcs are farthest, with a frustrated look of repetitive impotence; it's a familiar dance they've done far too many times. Ms. Fullows is trying her best to appear calm, but since her eyes are darting back and forth so rapidly, I think she's doing about as poorly as I am.

"Eyes back here, boy," the older man threatens, pulling the hammer back on his pistol.

When my eyes run between him and the gun, a malicious grin spreads across his face. The way he's relishing this moment fills me with a burning hatred. A small man made powerful with the swing of a handgun. How pathetic.

He takes a few meandering steps closer to us, eyeing us up like prize cattle.

"A skinny human"—he begins, pointing the barrel at my chest—"a half-orc, and a tattooed dwarf," he ends, aiming at each of us as he prattles on. "So, you must be the three knights that've been stealing from our folk these last few months. How the Keeper smiles on me this day. Ol' Bregario will give me my stripes over this haul."

He lets out a wry laugh and looks to his underlings as they hesitatingly do the same.

"What's your name, kid?" He looks to me, pressing the barrel into my ribcage.

I look to Bjorni for guidance, but he's gazing ahead of himself through half-shut eyes. As helpful as always.

"I asked you a *question*," he yells, jabbing the barrel.

My lightning-fast heartbeat and a rising sense of powerlessness bring forth that scared little boy again, hiding in the recesses of my mind. Too much fear for dry wit.

"Tim Halen," I eventually mumble.

"Tim Halen," he eyes me up and down for a moment. "Never heard a' ya."

He looks to Gren and spits at his feet and doesn't even turn toward Bjorni.

"Oh well, doesn't matter. You're all coming with me, and my boss will sort it out. Renny, Hal, Wolen, get those three up and get 'em moving."

The gunmen behind the trio crouch down and dig their free hand into the armpits of their captives, dragging them to their feet. Fullows yelps in response.

"To the void with this," the stovepipe orc states before turning and headbutting the gunman behind him.

The crunch of the gunman's breaking nose causes the rest of his friends to turn and look at the scene before a thunderous gunshot to my right makes me wince and dive to the ground, scrambling to retrieve my own pistol. A strong grip yanks at the back of my jacket and violently pulls me to the left, back behind the wall. As I whirl helplessly, time distorts into a crawl. Bjorni becomes a slowly moving statue, eyes and tattoo glowing a deep indigo as he aims and fires his hand cannon. Kicked-up old issues of the *Gazette* flutter past his barrel as it booms shot after shot. A few shots are returned his way, flying just barely past his head. And true enough to his character, he doesn't even flinch. Somewhere far to the left of us, screams fumble over one another until the resulting sound becomes biological noise. Bjorni's death-herald shoots once, twice, thrice more before he moves back behind the wall. I look up and see Gren letting go of my jacket, with a manic smile on his face. He's screaming something, but I can barely hear it over the ringing of my ears.

This instant assault of stimuli in these last few, eternal moments sends my mind screeching deeper within itself until I'm hiding beside that scared little boy. Some foreign impulse causes my hands to pull back the slide of my pistol and aim it at the corner, over Bjorni's head, should some intruder come rushing around it. A few more shots knock pieces of brick off of the corner before stopping altogether. Something drags me back onto my feet, and Bjorni is pressed up against the wall, shooting one more time. After that, he thrusts his arms down in frustration, muttering something in dwarvish. When he breaks away from the wall and rushes around the corner. I follow as close behind as I can. In this alleyway lay some humanoid shapes crumpled on the ground. I can only bear to see them in my periphery, and when I do, I feel myself on the knife's edge between life and total annihilation. Bjorni steps over them, emptying the cylinder of his revolver as he does so. So careless when surrounded by death. This dwarf is horrifying.

When we empty back out onto the boulevard, masses of people are shrieking and running as far away from us as their legs will allow. Automobiles and horses are tearing down the street to find safety, honking and neighing in collective fear. To our right is the squealing of tires. A car that's trying to escape holds the familiar form of Ms. Fullows. The small car is packed with the gunmen, with one still trying to enter as he's losing his footing. When the car breaks into the street, he's sent careening back onto the sidewalk, pistol skittering across the concrete.

Bjorni rushes out into the chaos of traffic and aims his gun, and I turn to see Gren has disappeared from my right. When I return my gaze to the gunman, Gren's already on top of him, fist smashed into the gunman's face.

A boom comes again, and I dive for cover behind a parked car. Moments later, I hear the pop of a tire. I inch my head to be level with the car window, and I see the escaping car rendered immobile by Bjorni's bullet. Three men exit from it and aim their guns in our direction. Only one word roars inside of me: Fire.

My hands aim the pistol in an instant, and I fire at the vehicle with impunity. Recoil be damned, I pull the trigger until the steel beast goes silent. Somewhere in the chaos, Fullows falls and screams, and two of the gunmen grab their chests and stumble. Whether I or

Bjorni hit them, I do not know. Once my gun is empty, I fall back down behind the car and pray that Bjorni and Gren do the rest. With each beat of my heart, a shot echoes down the street.

After a few minutes or hours, an awkward silence settles over us. My hands become unable to hold the pistol, and it clacks against the sidewalk. My entire body is shaking and it can't stop. Whatever fueled my retribution was burned to nothing, gone as swiftly as it filled me. Gren and Bjorni talk to one another nearby, but I can't hear them over the ringing. A wave rises into my throat, and I shoot back onto my feet to take a few steps to vomit. With the expulsion of liquids comes a sort of catharsis, and I slowly return to something resembling my senses. A heavy hand pats against my back, and I snap away from it.

"Easy, Fey," Gren yells. "You did good."

"That you did," Bjorni adds. "Good shooting, boy."

"Where's Fullows?" I groan.

"She didn't make it," Bjorni says. "I knew we couldn't do this sort of thing alone anymore."

"Keeper above, did I hit her?" I shout. "Did I kill her? Did I kill any of them?"

"Arthur!" Gren yells. "Arthur! Look at me."

"I can't," I whimper, "I— I— I—"

Gren pulls my head in close to his.

"Them or us, buddy," he says. "Them or us. You didn't kill the lady. One of them finished her off. You're fine. You did good. Alright?"

"A-alright."

"Boys, we gotta run," Bjorni says. "Before the lawmen come."

Bells ring in the distance, cueing us to sprint in the other direction of the street. I stop and rush back to pick up my handgun before surging to return to my friends.

As I pant, the consequences of what I've done slowly sink in. I'm going to need a drink.

Now more than ever.

CHAPTER 14

Another evening dinner and another suffocating event with the aristocracy. Although, this one is an improvement, as Gren and Bjorni are allowed to come along. After a few weeks of hiding and letting the police forget about us, we're at some sort of fundraiser. It's in the name of some long-perished war hero—a public event with no need for some arcane gateway. Earlier, Astraea pulled me aside for her little dog-and-pony show, and I obliged as begrudgingly as I could without drawing her ire. She kindly released me from duty after that, and I've been left once again to enjoy some drinks on her tab. Gren and I are sitting at a table in the dimly-lit theater. Some woman on stage is speaking candidly about the shortage of nullification powder that's starting to take its toll on the city. The spice of this mulled cocktail has my primary attention, however. My efforts are on accelerating the warm buzz that's beginning to seep into my brain.

"Oh, drink, how you're always a comfort to me."

"Are you talking to that glass?" Gren asks.

"Yes. I am. Gren."

"Easy, princess. What's got you so wound up?"

"Oh, nothing. Just my family name being used as a glittering trinket once again. And now here we are, sitting around in this self-aggrandizing nonsense," I hiss, motioning around the room. I notice some heads turn toward me and welcome the judgment.

"Fey, remember when you told me to stop you from going down these 'temper spirals' of yours?" Gren haltingly says, scrunching his fingers to emphasize the term.

I look into his eyes, and his gaze is one of familiar worry. I'm becoming a child again, aren't I?

I down the rest of my drink and sink into my seat, grimacing at the spice

"You're right, dear boy. You're right. This week has just been… Trying. That's all."

"I know. You ain't as used to this sort of life as I am. You're just settling in is all."

Months upon months of this, and I'm still settling in? The statement seems a little incredulous, but who am I to debate such things?

"I suppose you're right," I say, to put a cap on the topic.

"Say," Gren starts, eyes shifting to that recognizable mischievous gleam. "What's keepin' us here?"

"What do you mean?"

"I mean, Astraea's done with ya, ain't she? There's nothin' keepin' us at this gig."

"Yes. Yes, I suppose you're right," I say, feeling the bubble of excitement rising from within. "What do you have in mind?"

"I'm not a planner, you know that. Never have been. Let's just go on out and see what the night'll do to us."

"Say no more, you've convinced me." I rise from my seat. "Should we bring Bjorni along?"

Gren looks around the room and responds with a shrug. "Don't see why not. Let's find him."

We push in our chairs and weave between the tables of dimly-lit geriatrics toward the bar. Behind me, Gren keeps bumping into the backs of those around him and apologizing a bit too loudly. Sure enough, once we reach the counter, the old dwarf is there, sitting on a plush stool and bringing a stemmed glass of something murky to his lips.

"Bjorni," I say, tapping his shoulder. "Do you have a moment?"

"Leave me alone, I'm no—" he says, turning to see me. "Oh, it's you two. What do you want?"

"What do you say to ditching this place and having a morale-boosting night with your subordinates?" I wave my hand between Gren and I.

His gaze flicks between the two of us, with our mischievous grins, and downs the rest of his drink.

"Oh, why not."

Gren makes a celebratory grunt, then muffles his voice when he realizes he's being too loud. While Bjorni swivels down from his stool, I get the attention of the barkeep.

"Excuse me, madam. What was my dwarven friend here drinking?"

"Firebeard Stout, sir."

"Could I get a bottle of that? On the tab of Ms. Filuxous."

"Let me check the tab first, sir."

She goes back toward the till to look over the tab's limit, and I steal a glance behind me at my fellow bandits. Bjorni is pulling on his jacket, and Gren is picking the flaking scab of that ricochet wound again. What an unlikely trio the three of us are.

"Here you are, sir," the bartender says, handing a thick bottle to me. "Will that be all?"

"Yes, thank you."

With a tap on his shoulder and the simple gift of dwarven stout, Bjorni emits a chuckle and cracks something that resembles a smile.

"You're alright, Fey," he says.

It's probably the spirits talking, but as we swagger out of this charity dinner, I feel three times larger than usual. The spins are even manageable. Soon enough, hushed tones and the aroma of smoked meat are replaced with the shouts of street criers and the smell of horses and motor oil.

"You boys have an idea of what to do," Bjorni asks, uncapping the bottle.

"Uhh," I say.

"We were thinking," Gren says.

"I'm not scolding you two, out with it," Bjorni says.

"We were just going to see where the night takes us," I say.

"Yeah? And where is that? A cabaret? Another dinner? Please. I'll show you boys where the real fun is."

Bjorni takes one more swig of his stout and approaches the curb, whistling loudly for a carriage. When we board it, he tells the driver to go to some location in Xaggik West. I find it hard to stay still in my seat. Going to that district this late always gives a mix between excitement and nervousness.

"So, what awaits us there, Bjorni?" I ask. "Some abandoned refinery?"

"Cute. No, something other than what you're used to."

The chill night air breezes through the open windows of the carriage and the mural of electric signs and drunk denizens passes by in slow succession. The warm, sleepish feeling of the spirits starts to settle into me, and my eyes can't help but start to close.

"Hope you're rested, sleeping beauty," Gren says, waking me. "We've arrived."

I stumble out of the carriage and stop short of the entrance to some sort of pub. The door is a little shorter than usual, and a large engraving of a dog's head knocking back a dwarven beer stein sits to the upper left of it.

"Ah, my second home," Bjorni says, spreading his arms to his side as if to give the building a hug. "In we go, lads."

The thick door slowly budges open despite my best efforts, and the opening explodes with a wash of music. Creaking woodwinds and antiquated string instruments play along in a jaunty melody. The ceiling of the place is shorter than most establishments, so my head brushes against it. Dwarves fill the place, drinking at the counter or sitting at the myriad of round tables. Near a roaring fireplace at the other end of the room and down a few steps, two dwarves man a mandolin and hand-drum and play for a receptive audience.

"Come. I'll get you something to drink," Bjorni shouts. Gren and I cling near him out of social apprehension. He's the only familiar thing in this hospitably foreign place.

A corpulent woman serves drinks behind the bar, and her eyes widen in recognition when she sees Bjorni.

"Ay, there's my young'un," she says, reaching over the counter to shake his hand. "Hva Gaehelim."

"Hva Gaehelim," Bjorni responds, smiling as he returns the handshake. "I need something for my boys here. Nothing too strong."

"Aww, look at the two of ya's," she says. "Remind me of my own. They look just as nervous, too, whenever they come in."

"Sorry if we're intruding, ma'am," I say.

"Nonsense, we love to have ya's. Your lot doesn't come through this district too often."

"Because we think dwarves don't like the likes of us," Gren says.

"Nah, just a nasty rumor," she responds. "Except for the martial families. They might not like ya's."

She pulls two wide stone-made steins from somewhere below her and starts to fill them with something from a keg.

"Here, drink up," she says, handing Gren and me a stein. "Hvangar is here, Bjorni. Playing at the table over there, if ya like."

"Thank you, Gwyn," Bjorni replies.

I bring the stein to my lips, and the acrid smell of the spirits is enough to singe off my eyebrows.

"Phew. This stuff smells right strong, Bjorni."

"Good. Have a sip. It doesn't burn as bad as your kind's stuff."

One cautious mouthful and I find he's right. Even though the brew is very dark and hoppsy, there's no burn from the distillation and no nauseous response.

"I could get used to this," Gren says.

"Come with me. I'll show you a game I like to play," Bjorni says, motioning us to follow once more.

He leads us to a large table with only a few empty chairs. Dwarves fill the rest and are playing some sort of gambling game. They use small stone tablets with icons marked on them and stack and file them in odd configurations. Bjorni takes a seat and motions for Gren and me to join. The rest of the dwarves don't seem to pay us any mind, save for one.

"I was wondering when I'd see your tattooed mug again," a graying dwarf with a short manicured beard says to Bjorni. "Who are your friends?"

"My students, shall we say," Bjorni says.

"Uh oh, that's not good," the dwarf laughs. "I'm Hvangar. Nice to meet you, boys."

"Arthur Fey," I say.

"Just call me Gren," Gren says.

"Would you like to play?" Hvangar asks.

"I'll have a seat, but I won't be playing, thank you," I say.

"What's wrong, Fey?" Gren says. "Never seen a game of Feftunal before?"

"No, Gren, I haven't."

"Just watch your mate play, and you'll get the hang of it," Hvangar says. "Basically, whenever he gets cornered, he'll have to drink, but he may pass it off to a friend if he wishes."

Oh, good.

Bjorni is handed a stack of tablets and gets into the game right away. Turns pass wordlessly between the dwarves as they stack a tablet or two, reconfigure the stack, or just move a stack from one spot on the board to the next. In all my years, I've never peered so directly into something so foreign. I might as well be watching two trees on the frontier changing shape and becoming one, over and over. After a few turns, Hvangar lets out a laugh and pushes a stack of tablets toward Bjorni, and Bjorni grunts in defeat.

"Fey, take a drink," Bjorni says.

I look between him and his friend and capitulate soon after. I take a small sip, savoring the taste.

"Aww, come now, what sort of midwife's drink was that?" Hvangar jeers.

"You expecting, Fey?" Gren laughs.

"Fine."

I exhale quickly before taking a large gulp from the stein. The punch of inebriation comes on quickly.

The game continues, and Bjorni and Hvangar exchange blows, I think, with the other dwarves slowly losing and filtering out to do something else. Gren and I are pressured into taking a few more drinks, and the spinning of the room and distortion of time welcomes me soon after.

"Fey," Gren says, already slurring his words. "When's the last time we had a good test of strength?"

"B-before puberty," I say, involuntarily burping.

"Too long, I say," he bellows. "Meet me at the arm-contesting table if you ain't craven."

"At the what?" I ask.

"Follow me," he says, leading us to a small table nearby.

"Gren, you're almost twice my size," I say, taking a seat.

"Don't worry. You'll get a handicap."

If he wasn't being so jovial, I wouldn't indulge him. But what friend would I be if I didn't feed his self-esteem once in a while?

Gren and I take off our jackets, roll up our sleeves, and set the elbows of our right arms on the table, locking hands.

"I'll give you the count of 10 to try and wrestle me down. Loser takes a drink," he says.

"Fine, if you want to get me drunk so badly," I say.

The contest only goes one way. No matter how much I grunt and heave, his massive forearm stays still as a pillar. Then he immediately pins my hand, and I take a drink. So much so that I find the stein empty.

"Oh no," I mumble, "the stein's empty."

"Let's solve that," Gren says, finishing the rest of his stein as well.

I rise from my chair and almost fall to the ground. My legs have become a lot heavier.

"This is… Sooner than I thought," I say.

The countertop finds its way in front of me, and I order another stein. Somewhere in the noise, I hear a feminine voice. I turn and look down to see a female dwarf asking me something.

"I beg your pardon?" I shout.

"Would you like to join us for a dance, long-legs?" she asks.

"If you'd like to see me fall, sure," I say.

She takes my hand and leads me to the front of the fireplace, where a spinning circle of dwarves is gyrating and moving far too fast for me to keep track. She brings me into the circle, and I'm lost in the revelry. Their big smiles and happy-like faces make me feel like I belong, and it's something I haven't felt in forever. The pipe-thing the musician is playing makes a flutey, melodic sound and guides me right along, even as I stumble.

"Closing time," Gwyn calls from the bar, ringing a bell. "Come close your tabs, you hooligans."

"Aww, already?" Gren says beside me in the dancing circle, slowly breaking apart as dwarves filter out.

"Where's Bjorni?" I slur.

"Dunno," Gren says.

We turn and yell for Bjorni.

"Right here, you children," Bjorni says. He's as serious and sober as ever.

"Did you drink too, Bjorni?" Gren asks, one eye half-closed.

"Yes, I did," he smiles.

"Let's go then, chaps," I say. "The night ain't over yet."

Bjorni pays our bill, and we walk out into the cold night as I bump my head on the top of the doorway. Gren turns away to vomit, I think. One of them leads the way down some streets. I'm not really sure where we are. Some people look to us like they're scared, but who cares? Just leave, if we trouble you so. Ha!

Bjorni keeps drinking from a bottle that I think I got him sometime back. Then we sit on a bench, and I close my eyes.

When they open back up, I feel a bit more sober and turn to see the two sharing a tobac stub. We're seated in a small plaza at the top of a hill. Way out in the distance, barely lit by streetlights, is the deep blue expanse. I think.

"Thanks for the date, Mr. Bjorni," Gren says.

"Don't mention it, lad," Bjorni says.

"Keeper above, I love you guys," Gren says, wrapping his arms around us and tightening in an aggressive hug. "Nights like these are the best."

When he lets go, his eyes wander around a bit, and something in them changes.

"Sometimes moments like these make all of it worth it, don't you think?" he asks.

"They sure do, Gren," I say.

"Still," he says, eyes looking far off at the expanse, "I can't help but wish sometimes things were different, you know?"

Bjorni turns to look at him, and something about Gren feels more sullen.

"What do you mean, Gren?" I ask.

"Sometimes. I just wish I could get another try. See if I'd get it better the next time around," he says.

His head goes slack and rests against the bench, and soon his eyes start to close. Then comes the snoring.

I turn toward a gray form that's a ways beyond us and walk up to it. Turns out it's a statue. A human man in full plate mail, one foot triumphantly planted on the corpse of some beastkin; the body of a man with the head of a goat. His unhelmeted face is so familiar, it's annoy-ing. Strong cheekbones. Full beard. Circlet holding back his billowing hair. Then the familiarity finally pierces my slowly sobering brain.

"Sigesar," I say, pointing to it. "That's who it is."

"Took you that long to figure it out?" Bjorni says.

"Well, sorry, Mr. Older-Than-My-Grandparents, I'm still a lit-tle inebriated."

I pivot back to him, and his face is of solemn anger. Fear drops in my stomach, reminding me that he's still my boss. Just then, a smirk cracks on his face.

"You're lucky you've given me ale this night, boy."

I laugh away the awkward tension and sit back down on the bench. Gren's slumbering form is still between us. Something about his drunken, stumbling words sticks to me and makes me want to say something myself. Something intimate and frightening. I can't help but speak.

"Bjorni?"

"Yes," he says.

"When do things feel… right, in life?"

"What do you mean?"

I already regret the wretched vulnerability, but something forces me onward.

"For a long time," I continue, "for most of my adult life, I'd say, things have always felt off."

I look over to him to see his eyebrows raised in confusion.

"You don't have a clue what I'm talking about, do you?" I ask.

"Not really," he says.

I let out a sigh and pull a tobac pipe from a pack in my breast pocket.

"Let me say it this way," I try again. "When did you feel like you were successful in your life?"

Bjorni sits on the question for a moment, lets out a quiet grunt of amusement, and looks back down the boulevard.

"Ah. That. Can't say I've ever felt that, Fey. At least, not that definite. Just did what I felt needed to be done, and here I am."

"How reassuring."

He waves his hand, gesturing toward the city itself.

"This. Fighting for all this. Is all my people know."

"Dwarves?"

"Not exactly. Just my gwaergna. My sect."

"Your clan?"

"A more sentimental way to put it, sure."

"Is that what your tattoo is from, too? Your 'sect?'"

"No."

He traces the tattoo on his head—a rugged serpent surrounding an axehead—with his thick pointer finger.

"A gift from my father," he says, "as well as my axe."

He takes a swig from his bottle and offers some for me. I wave it away.

"Strange time to be young," he says. "Right now. Things are changing."

"They always say that," I reply.

"Yeah, because they're scared of what's different. But this time, they should be. Back then, all you needed was to look after your kin. Make sure they're safe. Anything else was a bonus. Nowadays, there's too much distraction. Folk are more concerned with what to buy and how it suits them. Using the craft of others instead of crafting something themselves. Silvum's gotten too important."

The dawning light washing over the deep wrinkles and craggy ridges of his face gives his visage the look of a stone effigy, with parts of it eroded away from time.

"That's rather grim, don't you think?" I ask.

"Maybe," he says, taking another swig. "Maybe my age has just come and gone. I've been around for too long. Seen too much. Could just not be meant to be around anymore."

He sets down the bottle and starts to pull a tobac stub from his vest pocket.

"Well, I've done alright," I say. "Silvum-wise, I think. I just. I just, still."

A sudden well builds up inside and forces a tear out of my eye, where it has no right to be. Weakness has no place in front of someone like Bjorni. I turn and feign a cough to recover my dignity and wipe my eyes.

"Just feel like I'm missing something is all," I say.

"You are. You're young. It'll come with time, though. No need to fret."

The first fringes of the sun start to peek out over the bay. I look over to Gren's peacefully slack face.

"Time to get us all home, don't you think?" I say.

"In a bit. You go on back. I'll phone a carriage for this oaf after I finish this draught," Bjorni says.

As I rise and walk down the street, my vision settles onto the distant waves of the Great Blue Expanse. For the first time in a while, my mind is trapped with itself. Somewhere in my emotions, this uncomfortable ball of something settles in. For a bit, I find it foreign, only to realize that it's something too familiar. Something I've been willfully looking over and ignoring for a long time. I can only describe it as that noise that lies in between the radio stations. That irritating crackle that embodies emptiness. Its volume ebbs and flows, but it's always there.

But this, this hasn't always been there. Upon closer inspection, I think it arrived at a precise time. Some time, a few years back, when you and mother were forced to leave. I ignored it when I saw that despicable iron contraption in the hospital. That disgusting mass of pipes and valves that gave mother a few more days of life. I told myself that I was fine, that this isn't that bad. It was a lie. She couldn't even wake up to say goodbye. You didn't get that luxury, either, did you, Caddock? Dead on impact, they said. The two of you left me with nothing. Only some musty portraits from your earlier years that don't even look like you. Every time I looked at them, I always thought that mother was too short and you were too tall.

So fickle are the supposed Keeper's writings. His Great Book of Reality is a sordid mess of suffering and heartache. Nothing worth keeping at all.

I regret this discovery. It's an infernal find. The traumas of those nostalgic days, and only now consciously remembering them, is an awakening of a latent psychic pain I've clung to out of desperation. Clung to so tightly that they're no longer simple memories. In the back of my mind, they've been repeating endlessly, being relived over and over again. Each time they're replayed, the visions of the past warp a little more until they're nothing more than decayed and aching replicas that barely sound and feel the same as they once did. What a terrible thing clinging does to the psyche.

This cyclical ache. This inner agony. When did it become a part of me, and when can I let it go?

CHAPTER 15

We're gathered around in a bright hotel room, with two beds and one of the new electric furnaces underneath the table adorned with a radio. We're somewhere deep in the Acre. Bjorni fetched Gren and me in his usual fashion, routine by now, and we arrived without incident. What has me nervous is Astraea being here and the two new faces relaxing on the second bed. I take out a pipe to light, so my hands are busy.

"I do hope you boys are feeling sociable," Astraea says, fluffing her coal-black hair. "We've got some business partners."

Every time I see Astraea, her hair has changed. Elfblooded women are known to be aggressively fashionable, but even so, this feels to be a bit much.

The two men lazing on the bed are dressed more casually than Gren, Bjorni, and I. Their slacks are held up by cotton suspenders, with worn long-sleeve shirts underneath them. Their faces have the flush skin of youth. They can't be more than a few years older than me. One has a pronounced hook nose, and the other has long brown hair, slicked back with pomade. The lighter I'm using to light my pipe won't catch.

"Need one that works?" the hook-nosed one says, pointing to my lighter.

"I suppose so, yes."

He pulls a small metal rectangle from his pocket and tosses it to me. I catch it and inspect the insignia on it. A crudely etched fist sits in the middle of the lighter, with the letters "NCLP" below it. Something familiar about those letters. I've definitely read about them or heard about them. There's a connection here, but I can't place it.

It lights on the first try. Bjorni goes to lean on the first bed, with Gren sprawling himself across it as well.

"Thanks," I say, tossing it back.

"Where are your manners, boys?" Astraea says. "Introduce yourselves."

"Sorry," I say. "I'm Arthur Fey, pleasure to meet you."

"Bjorni."

"And I'm Gren."

"Cillian," the hook-nosed one says.

"James," the long-haired one says.

Astraea picks up the radio and drags the cord from it, and hands it to Bjorni.

"Set this by the door."

Bjorni does as commanded and turns it onto a station playing some Old-World style stringed music.

Astraea gestures toward the foot of the beds and pulls a chair in between them for herself. We all cluster close into a tight circle, with the two strangers on their bed, us three on ours, and Astraea sitting in the wooden chair.

"So starting tomorrow morning," she begins, "You all are fetching something very important and very rare, and you will be going quite far to get it. And if you want to ask any questions, don't. That could prove to be a fatal inclination. Understood?"

We all nod, and I bite my tongue.

"You're all to spend the night here. Then, at first light, you will be joining the travel caravan at Kleman's Gate, westbound to Traitor's Pass."

I feel a sharp lurch in my stomach at the mention of leaving Ophidia.

"Don't worry, you won't be talking to anyone else on the caravan," she continues. "Or even leaving your carriage for that matter. Once you reach a certain frontier village, a guide will lead you out of the trading post to where you need to go. Eventually, a pair of soothslayers will arrive and hand off the package. When you have the package: *Don't*. Under *any* circumstances. Open it. This item is too important to give to any no-name courier, hence why you're all responsible for it."

So soothslayers do exist. I merely assumed they were narrative fodder for pulp novels. Bounty hunters that track down and kill magical monsters for their body parts. Something that sounded too fantastical to be true. Once she's done speaking, her gaze moves between all of us. Her eyes stop on me.

"Don't be so nervous, Fey. The New World isn't as bad as the papers say. Usually. And try to keep your drinking under control out there, darling."

She gets up from her chair and tucks it back against the table.

"Get some rest, lads. You're to leave bright and early."

She reaches the door, moves the radio aside with her foot, looks back at us, winks, and leaves.

I let go of a breath I didn't know I was holding.

"Leavin' Ophidia," Gren says. "Never in my life did I think I'd get the chance."

"Don't get too excited," Bjorni says. "It's a mess."

"I'm with you, half-orc," Cillian says, scratching his nose. "This is gonna be incredible. I didn't think I'd get such a job for my first gig."

"You're new blood, and you're already doing this?" Bjorni asks. "How'd you manage that?"

"Nepotism," James says, scooting back against the bed until his back rests against the headboard.

"If you bring up my father one more time, James," Cillian grimaces, balling his fists.

"What? It's true."

Cillian's brows furrow but then release.

"Whatever. Once we get there, I'll show you all what I'm capable of."

I sit down at the foot of our bed and pull my pistol out of its holster, to inspect it yet another time, for a feeling of safety more than anything.

"Wait a second. You guys are packing?" Cillian says.

"You aren't?" James asks.

Cillian shakes his head.

"There'll be tools when we get there," Bjorni says. "Now stop talking. You're all giving me a headache. Gren, Fey, ask for some blankets at the reception. I get the bed tonight."

"Yes, sir," Gren says.

I put my pipe out in the ashtray and follow Gren out the door.

Gren's grinning from ear to ear as we stalk past the row of doors to the stairwell. If only I was full of so much optimism.

"Let me guess," Gren says, looking over to me. "You're all mopey now that things are changin' up again."

"Sometimes I regret being around you so much."

"Oh, come now, sulky," he wraps his arm around my head and constricts it. "I'll keep you safe. Always have."

"Alright, alright," I say, muffled against his chest. "Let go!"

Once free, I brush some wrinkles out of my shirt.

"We're only going into bedlam incarnate. How bad can it be?"

C H A P T E R 1 6

The change in temperature once I exit the spirits shop into the bleak morning is jarring. Blisteringly hot one moment, near-freezing the next, I wish the arcanosphere would make up its mind.

I pull a flask from my jacket pocket and start to fill it with the mulled-spice brew from the slim bottle. It won't be enough for the whole trip, but it should be enough to get to Traitor's Pass. My eyelids ache due to the miserable night's sleep I had. Such a cramped hotel room was never meant for five snoring adult men.

The monolithic wall that encompasses Upper West Grove casts a long shadow over me; our carriage is one in a long line of vehicles crawling their way to the gate. Ours is more of a moving metal crate than a traditional carriage, with riveted plates covering the walls and metal shutters on the inside over the window openings. The driver is in some sort of wide cylinder, with a slit around the top for him to see out of. He looks at me, and he winks. With a slow pull, I open the door and clamber back inside of it.

The hot wash of the electric furnace beneath the seats welcomes me with open arms. For a horse-drawn vehicle, the interior is fairly spacious. Two rows of seats face each other, with a small table in between them and a wooden crate right below it. Gren's wide frame only leaves enough room for Bjorni on his side, so I wedge myself between Cillian and the steel-slitted window. Gren is absently looking at a newspaper with Bjorni whittling right beside him. Cillian and James have books open, but they aren't really reading them.

"No fancy car for the likes of us, eh?" I ask.

"No car would last outside the wall," James says.

"Get any for us?" Gren says, pointing to my bottle.

"No, I'm not so benevolent," I say.

His innocent frown forces me to capitulate, and I hand him the fifth that remains in the bottle. The frown upturns instantly, and he uncaps the bottle for a drink.

"Gah, this is taking ages," Cillian grunts. "How long does it take to get through Customs?"

"When I last came through around this time of day," James says, "I didn't pass the gate until at least the midday bell. Bjorni?"

"They didn't have passports when I came into the city," Bjorni says.

"You've been in Ophidia for the last *century*?" I ask.

"No. Just when I came in from the wild country," Bjorni says. "Going through the ports isn't so stringent."

"I've never left Ophidia," Gren says, beaming. "This is excitin'."

Gren pulls on a string to the right of him and draws open the slits of metal beside him to be able to see out the window.

"Bye-bye, stuffy rich land," Gren says, waving at the tall apartment buildings. "Can't say I'll miss ya."

The notion of setting out into the actual New World is frightening, although that should go without saying. There are a handful of publications that have made their wealth on reporting the insanity of what happens to the frontier fortresses, trading towns, mines, and Wayward company towns that struggle for survival every day. The nullification powder that restored sanity and safety to Ophidia was only successful after several iterations, the first of which failed to keep places like Fort Eri'dahn from getting turned into a fiery sinkhole by beastkin shamans. The mix of rum and no breakfast makes the anxious pit in my stomach all the worse.

"So, tell me, those who have been to the other side," I say, "Is the wilderness as bad as they say?"

"Sometimes," James says.

"Depends," Bjorni says.

"On what?" I say.

"How it feels," Bjorni says.

Oh, goody. Keeper, if you haven't written this story out yet, let me stay alive, please.

I take a few more drinks from my flask to calm my nerves and to try and retrieve some lost sleep while the cart judders and stops on its quest to get us out of safety. Things get quieter and calmer in time. Soon enough, nothing is going on at all, and it's relaxing.

...

Someone mutters, a familiar voice off in the distance.

"He's gonna miss it," a friendly voice says.

"There's plenty. He won't miss much," another retorts.

A violent shake wakes me back up, and I turn to see everyone peering out the right side of the carriage.

"Fey, look," Gren says, pointing aggressively over Bjorni's head. "That tree over there—it's changing!"

I follow his finger, and out in the distance, a large dark tree is slowly and subtly changing. The tint and grain of the bark gently swirl and brighten, while other parts darken and start to form branches. It's as if the tree is in a painting that's melting and reforming itself, with the trees around it acting as normal.

"So, all those stories from the *Gazette* are true," I say.

"The frontier is always changing," Cillian says.

"Why's only that one tree doing that?" Gren says.

"Because it's more potent," James says. "Someone will get sent to chop it down soon. It'll become more frequent the further we get from Ophidia."

"Potent? What's that mean?" Gren asks.

"What he means is chaotic," Bjorni says. "My people call it the wild country for a reason. Beastkin and feral-elven tribes thrive in this mess."

Things such as these are so alien, yet so close to home? The forests back in Veneria were never like this. Everything was so calm and stable. I remember my father talking with some scholar way back in the day, and he said something about this. How Veneria is such an old country, and the beastkin tribes were dead for so long that civilized kind managed to beat the "wild" right out of the wilderness. There's some sort of connection to be made between the tribes and nature itself, I suppose, but that conversation is for people that have graduated from Oxlen. The way the tree shifts and morphs, so slowly yet so determinedly, is equal parts graceful and chilling.

"I think it's beautiful," I say.

"Wait until whatever it's hiding tries to kill you," James says.

Bjorni emits a short chuckle in affirmation.

I can't take my eyes off of the strange phenomenon. When heaps of stories write about the morphing woods, it starts to lose its significance. But when those words transform into a shifting reality, it becomes something ethereal, almost. The way the leaves blend into one another and slowly become one with the bark is calming to watch.

How can such beauty be dangerous?

CHAPTER 17

Bjorni and his wealth of knowledge are proven correct once again. As we follow the main road down the wide hills of the landscape, the shifting trees multiply over and over until the entire forest seems alive, moving as one big organism. The rocks, boulders, and ground stay the same, but every tree, shrub, flower, and sapling are always in gradual motion. We're forced to keep the windows shuttered in case any of the nearby beastkin tribes decide to attack. Apparently, the feral elves aren't anywhere near civilized land, so we aren't going to see any of them.

The setting sun shows that we've been on the road for quite some time. Stretches of New Colonia aren't that far apart, although that's to be expected from a country that's barely three centuries old. We passed through a small military encampment and a palisaded town that was home to the miners in several nearby mineral and earthblood quarries.

The clouds hang low above us, with a break of sky far off in the distance, near some mountain range. Drizzles of rain came and went during the morning, but now is just the wet aftermath, shimmering on moving leaves.

"How come we ain't seen no animal yet?" Gren asks.

"What do you mean?" James says, putting down the paper.

"We ain't seen any of the beasts the papers talk about. No jack-anapes. No deerbison. Nothin'."

"They're deeper in the woods," James says. "Years of hunting parties made sure of that."

"Aww," Gren says. "That's a load a' brash."

A break in the woods appears, with a clearing that is devoid of any type of flora, instead replacing them with cut, still tree stumps. This sight was familiar at both the military post and the mining town.

"We must be close," I say.

Gren points somewhere behind me, and I turn in my seat to see a wooden palisade. Logs sharpened at the top with meandering human forms behind them. A glimpse of the gates is visible before the turn in the road completes, and it's too far in front of the carriage.

As we get close to the gate, a voice shouts, "Halt! Open your top, driver, and hold out your papers!"

In the front of the carriage, a squeal of metal is followed by creaking hinges and the rustling of documents.

A few moments pass and the voice yells for the gate to open, and we pass through.

The buildings on the other side of the palisade are squat and pressed up against each other, like the tenements in the Culvert. They're only one or two stories tall, with small shuttered windows. People of every race are walking between the buildings and crossing the wide street. The suit and longshirt attire of the city is replaced with leather vests, long shawls, thick blue pants, and knee-high boots. Similarly to how Bjorni dresses himself. Clothing that places function and warmth far above fashion.

The carriage driver calls to the horses, and the carriage slows to a stop in front of a large building rife with foot traffic.

"Here's your stop, boys," the driver calls out.

We get out one by one, and the comfortable warmth of the carriage is again replaced with a nipping cold. Bjorni goes to the driver's side and climbs up the ladder at the side of it until he's near the driver's hatch. The driver opens the hatch and sits atop his pod in the meantime. Bjorni says a few things to him, gives him a stack of silvum, and drops back down.

"Gren, get the crate from the carriage," Bjorni says.

While Gren pulls the crate out from under the table, Bjorni leads us into the large building. A pair of steps lead up to it, with horses tied to a horizontal post near it, drinking from a wide trough.

"Oh, this is amazing," Cillian says. "We're finally out here, on the frontier, where *real* life happens!"

"Settle down, boy," Bjorni says. "These people don't enjoy city folk that act like tourists."

"I'm no tourist," Cillian says. "I'm as much of a citizen here as they are."

"Right," James scoffs.

The town's lack of running water becomes evident in smell as soon as the building's door swings open. The smell of body odor is baked into the walls and floorboards. The counter is on the other end of the bar, underneath a walkway to the rooms on the second floor. Next to the bar is a doorway into a kitchen, judging from the oven that's visible. Off to the right side is another door out of the building, beside the large fireplace. Between us and the bar is a wide array of tables, with only a few having occupants in one cluster near the front door, talking among themselves. Or at least they were until we came in.

"Pretty spacious for a bar," I say.

"It's that and a hotel," James says. "Places on the frontier are multipurpose."

"Well, Bjorni," I say, "what next?"

"I'll find out who has what room," Bjorni says. "Do what you like."

I pull out my flask from my coat pocket. The trip rode out the last of my rum, so my quest has revealed itself. People around the room cast baleful eyes in our direction, and the rural versus urban disdain rears its ugly head once more, something I haven't seen in a long time. Cillian bumps his leg against the shoulder of a woman, with her slight whisper of discontent in response. The man next to her shoots up from his chair onto his feet in a matter of seconds.

"What's your problem, street boy?" the man says.

"Nothing," Cillian says, balling his fists. "Unless you want to change that."

"No fighting in the bar," the bartender shouts. "You know that better than anyone, Leeroy."

"He didn't mean anything," the woman says. "Sit back down, would you please?"

I decide to go the long way around Leeroy and his ilk, weaving between the empty tables to get to the bar.

"Sorry about that," the bartender says. "Leeroy's family are troublemakers. Get antsy since they can't leave the walls this time of year."

Keeper above, I don't care.

"Fill up this flask, would you?" I say. "And give me a shot as well, please."

"Of what?"

"Whatever is the finest brandy you have back there."

"Alright. Thirty silvum, please."

I pull the stack from my other pocket and place a few bills on the table. As he's filling, the rest of my group find a table to sit at, and a woman far younger than the bartender comes out from the doorway behind the bar to serve them. Bjorni is the first to talk to her, although his deep tones blend in with the background noise of the room.

"There you are, sir," the bartender says. "Would you like anything else? Something to eat, maybe?"

"Not right now, thank you."

I take the flask and make my way back to the door outside.

"Where you rushin' off to, Fey?" Gren says.

"I'm going outside to have a smoke," I say. "Please don't join me."

Once outside, I stop and lean against the logs that make up the outside walls and try to rub out some sore muscles from the bumpy ride over. The thin cushions did nothing to mask the hard metal that comprised the entirety of that carriage. With a sigh of relief, I pull a pipe from my pack and light it.

The carriage we arrived in is parked beside the bar, the carriage driver desaddling and caring for the horses. The sun has almost completely set, and the cold is getting a little more unbearable. The majority of the town looks to be along this main strip, with a few slim alleys here and there between the squat houses and a small square where the town well is located. Lanterns are lit in every window, and a few more are hanging from a building that looks to be the general store. Its windows are filled with tipped-over boxes presenting packaged goods. There's also a white-timbered building, which is the sign of a practicing doctor's establishment. There's only a handful of people crossing the muddy street or hanging around the well. One of the human shapes looks to be an older gentleman with a worn jacket and long, gray beard, is walking toward me. Here's hoping he doesn't feel like talking.

"Less lively than you're used to, eh?" he says. His cadence of speaking has a drawl. Even his speech has slowed down a bit in age, it seems.

"What gave it away?" I sigh.

"The overcoat. Folk around here don't wear that nice a' clothing. I'm Lang."

He sticks his hand out to shake as he stops halfway up the two steps, and I respond in kind.

"Arthur."

"Town's not usually this dead. It's the middle a' trapping season. Most able-bodied folk are out in the country. The woods don't move as much in this cold."

"Isn't it too dangerous for that?"

"No. Not right now. Most tribes are too far out from this passage. We don't see any of 'em unless the military did something to draw their ire. You and your buddies probably won't see them either."

He must have seen us all come in earlier. Still a little creepy to comment on it.

"Don't really feel like talking, do you, kid?"

"No. No, I don't, sorry. It's not because I hate people. I was just trapped in a small box with a few of them for the majority of the day, and I'd like to be left alone. No offense."

"That's alright," he says, with an upraised tone of gentle mirth. "I spend months away from everybody, and I always feel great. I'll be with your lot tomorrow anyway."

"How's that?"

"I'm your guide. Don't worry. We'll have plenty to talk about then. Good night."

"Good night."

He turns away and takes a leisurely stroll back to wherever he came. His total lack of being in a rush is somewhat relaxing to see. Now that I notice it, it looks like most of the people outside are like that. The sounds of insects and lack of electric light add to the feeling of... Something. I can't quite put a word to it. It's a feeling I hadn't felt since early childhood, when I lived back in that rural villa, somewhere in Veneria. My being both enjoys and is revolted by it, on different levels. How odd.

The silence is something entirely calming on its own. I never noticed how loud living in a city is.

This sort of serenity is something that a drink could perfectly compliment. The flask in my jacket pocket sloshes in agreement. I take a few more moments to indulge in this idle fancy, spinning off the top of the flask and taking a couple of drinks.

Back inside the bar, I can hear Gren's roaring laugh. He's probably just as happy to be out of the carriage as I am. The complete lack of something to do must have killed him.

Once I finish smoking the pipe, the warmth of the shots refills my ability to socialize, and I turn to reenter the bar.

Leeroy and his gang have left, giving my group free reign over the place. Cillian and James are playing some sort of card game, with Gren talking to the woman that came out of the kitchen earlier, com-

pletely oblivious to the bartender's open disapproval. Gren's ignorance of racial politics is as active as ever. I go and sit beside our two
new compatriots, opening my flask once again.

"No need for that," Cillian says. "Here, we bought a bottle."

He passes a bottle across the table, and I oblige.

"What's this?" I say, gesturing at the cards.

"Killer's Hand," James says.

"You've never seen it?" Cillian asks. "People all over Ophidia
love it."

"Not the people I was around."

"Who's that?" Cillian says.

"Aristocrats."

"You're a nobleman?" Cillian says.

"Used to be. Haven't been in that sphere for a while."

"Good riddance," James says.

"Hear, hear," I say, taking one more drink from the bottle before
setting it down. "Did Bjorni ever say what town we're in?"

"Fallund," Cillian says.

"We're that far west, huh? Ruins of Fort Eri'dahn aren't much
farther."

"Past that is madness," James intones.

"That's what they say," Cillian smiles.

I look up at Gren and his efforts, and the spinning room starts
to settle in. Finally, something I can sit back and enjoy.

"I'm going to head up to my room," I say. "Call it a night.
Which one's mine?"

"Second on the right," Cillian says.

"See you tomorrow, boys," I say, rising from my seat.

My newly found lack of balance makes me go at a slower pace
than usual, stumbling into a chair once or twice. Gren and his friend
look to me, and I wave to show that I am, in fact, sober and in no
need of babying. Once I go up the stairs and into my room, a bed
with thick furs awaits me. I strip off most of my clothes in record

time and nestle in between the blankets, and the immaculate comfort that settles in as I sink into the mattress is second to none. My aching back and shoulders sigh as they're surrounded by the feather mattress. The spirits do their job and relax my body completely. This must be how babies feel prior to birth.

Maybe I should keep my eyes open, try and enjoy this a little more before I—.

CHAPTER 18

Once I hear the chirping of morning birds outside my window, I realize I fell asleep. My bleary eyes dread opening to the morning sun. For every comfort the spirits give, they take away two more. My sore back and shoulder muscles have spread into a dull ache, and I wish now, more than ever, to stay in this bed until I pass by natural causes. Sadly, I'm pulled into the waking world by a pounding on the door.

"Fey," Gren's muffled voice says. "Mornmeal is ready. Come on, get up."

I release a whispery groan in response.

"I'm opening the door, chum. You better be decent."

The door cracks open, and he stoops his head to peek through the opening.

"My, look at this lovely sight. You're so precious, Arthur."

"Gren. I may be incapable of violence, but I will break your neck."

"Look at this; the cat's got claws. You may be intimidatin' yet. Come on, let's get some grub in ya."

He walks in and reaches under the covers to pull me from my intimate home, and I put up no fight at all. With no exertion on his end, I'm on my feet. He motions to lead me out of the room.

"Yes, yes, that won't be necessary," I say. "I'm not a baby, as much as you'd like it so."

"More than anythin' in the world," Gren smiles. "Food's downstairs. We brought in a box for you last night while you slept. It's over there. Join us once you're dressed."

I look to where he's pointing and see a small crate at the foot of my bed, covered by some furs that I must have cast off in the night. He turns to leave the room, and I take a few more moments to enjoy my temporary sanctuary before it's lost. With a rub of my eyes and a bit of willpower, I'm at the box. When opened, it has a thick winter longcoat, a pair of long undergarments, a scarf, long knee-high boots, and some sort of lever-action repeating rifle. So, that's why Bjorni told me to leave the pistol at home.

Once I change my shirt and pants and put on the lavish outfit from the footlocker, I lock the footlocker, leaving the rifle inside, and turn to leave the room.

The smell of cooking bread and syrup wafts from the kitchen below, mixed with thin clouds of tobac smoke that hang around the ceiling. There's hardly an empty table; most are filled with people in dirty wool jackets and thick scarves, eating their fill of today's mornmeal. The sounds of a dozen conversations inundate the room. Gren is to the left, stepping off the stairwell toward our group, dressed similarly to me and looking ready to travel. Despite the fireplace, the nip of morning cold is still in the building, and my nose is already starting to run.

I go down the stairs and join my table of comrades, and an empty plate waits at my seat. A stack of flatcakes sits in the middle of the table on a wide plate, and the others have already begun eating.

"Get your beauty sleep, Fey?" Cillian asks. "You were out cold when we brought in the box, thirty minutes after you went to your room."

"You have no idea, Cillian. I've added years to my lifespan."

"You missed a riot of a time," Gren says. "We got Bjorni to show us a dance from when he was a kid."

"That right," I say, smiling at the mental image.

"Drink out here is stronger than I remember," Bjorni says. "Haven't blacked out like that since... I don't know when."

"I've never seen such a spry old dwarf," James says.

"And you never will again," Bjorni says.

They all have a fun laugh at the memory, and the happiness makes me bitterly regret missing out on such camaraderie.

"That's what I get for wanting to be alone, I suppose."

"Ah, don't fret, Fey," Gren says. "There will be plenty more nights like that."

"Once we're back behind nice big walls," James says.

"You boys finish eating," Bjorni says, "I need to go speak with our guide. Get a good bellyful. We ain't eating again until midday."

Bjorni wipes his lips and beard with a handkerchief and drops from his chair to head toward the front door. The flatcakes aren't particularly tasteful, but they're more filling than I expected, along with the draught of beer that accompanies them. Slowly, we start pushing our plates toward the center one by one, until Gren is the only one left still eating.

"So, that's why you're so large," Cillian says.

"I'm going to go outside and see what awaits us," I say.

Once past the cluttered tables and out the front door, the gentle chill on my nose intensifies into a full cold, and I fold the scarf up closer to my face. The muddy road has hardened and crunches under the feet of multiple people milling around the town, going from building to building and packing horses to travel out into the wild. Wives kiss husbands goodbye, and children chase each other with sticks. Farther away, a carriage similar to the one we arrived in is unpacking some provisions for the general store.

To my left, Bjorni is next to a horse talking to that old man I met last night. Four more horses are lined up near them on a hitching post, packed and ready to go. The guide looks up from Bjorni and smiles at me. I take it as an invitation and join the two.

"You sleep good last night?" the guide asks.

"Wonderfully so. I'm terribly sorry, but I forgot your name."

"That's alright. It's Lang."

"The boys close to being done?" Bjorni asks.

"Everyone except Gren is," I say.

"Hope they don't eat too much," Lang says. "Horse riding can be dreadful to the stomach."

"Time to go anyway, so fetch the boys, Fey," Bjorni says.

"Yes, sir."

Once I'm back at the door, I wave my hand to get their attention, and James is the first to catch the motion, tapping the other two and pointing at me. I wave them over to me, and they rise from the table and start heading over. Gren stops and pays the bartender for the meal, but soon all of us are outside by the horses. Gren stops and hands me a rifle.

"You almost forgot this," Gren says.

"Ah, thank you, chum," I say, slinging the rifle.

Lang points out whose horse belongs to whom. Mine is a calico horse with a deep brown-and-white coat. Its eye looks at me as I approach and snorts at my hand patting its thick neck. It's a very calm beast, taking to my presence rather quickly, with no whinnying or bucking like horses I've ridden in the past. It's already saddled and packed, with a holster by a stirrup for the rifle. However, there's something odd about the saddle's seat. There's a divider with a second smaller seat behind it.

"What's this for, Lang?" I ask, pointing to the saddle.

"That's for Bjorni," Lang says.

"I'm sorry, what now?"

"Dwarves can't ride full-size horses," Bjorni says. "Our legs are too short."

Gren stifles a laugh.

"Something funny, boy?" Bjorni asks with a raised voice. "Care to share?"

"No, sir," Gren says. "Just remembering somethin' I heard back in the bar, that's all."

"Best to get moving now," Lang says. "It's going to be a long ride, and we need to hurry if we want to make it by sunset."

We unhitch our horses and mount the saddles. Years of riding as a boy come flooding back to me as I put a foot in each stirrup and get a grip on the horn. A cough below me reminds me of Bjorni's presence, and I look down at his awaiting raised hand. A dwarf that has intimidated me on multiple occasions, now in an emasculating position like this. A pity that I can't relish it. I struggle to pull him up, but once he grabs onto the saddle, he's able to get into the back seat with no problem. Cillian and Gren struggle to steer and command their horses, and James is shouting instructions at them to get them moving.

"Just pull on the reins to steer the horse around," James says. "Make your back more rigid. Come on, Cillian, Gren's catching on."

Cillian's horse whinnies in protest, shaking its head back and forth. Gren's large draft horse handles his weight and commands with minimal problems once Gren gets a hold of his balance.

"Just dig your heels into its side a little," I say. "That will signal it to start walking forward."

"Alright, alright, I get it," Cillian shouts. "Just give me a moment."

Eventually, Cillian's horse settles down, and he's able to control it enough at a slow pace.

"If you're all ready," Lang says. "Let's head toward the west gate."

While we're too amateurish to have any sort of rank or file, our group ambles our horses along toward the gate, where a man with a rifle stands near it, looking over the palisade.

"Open the gate, would you, Benjamin?" Lang shouts.

"Sure thing, Lang," Benjamin shouts back. "You guiding along more city folk?"

"I'm a man of routine. You know me."

Benjamin chuckles in response. "Be careful now, you hear? Oliver told me he saw some beastfolk out this way a few days ago."

"I heard. Thanks for watching out."

Benjamin hops down from his platform and pulls open the gate, and we slowly strut out from it out into the wilderness.

The morning and midday pass without event. We stop once the sun reaches its zenith and have a light lunch. Gren eats twice as much as everyone else again, despite Lang's protests. We pass by a few campfires and trappers coming out of the wilderness, but still no wildlife or beastkin. Just morphing plants and crunching dirt. Lang leads the pack, with the rest of us interspersed on the trail. Gren's behind Lang, I'm behind Gren, and Cillian and James are behind me.

"Keeper above, when do we get there?" Cillian says. "This is so boring."

"Howl all you like," Lang says. "We get there when we get there."

"Lang," I say, "I got a question."

"Shoot."

"Why is the countryside so… peaceful?"

Lang lets out a dry laugh. "Place is changing all the time. I wouldn't call that peaceful."

"You know what I mean. Where's all the death and danger? Why's every place we pass through walled off?"

"They're walled off because they're cautious. You read the paper too much. Folk in the cities are told the wild country is terrible. But it's just fear-stoking."

"What about places like Fort Eri'dahn?" Cillian says. "They got wiped out by beastmen tribes, didn't they?"

"Because they started it, by taking land for more mineral mines. Most tribes want to be left alone. The only kind that attack are the ones led by the elves, or young ones looking to prove themselves."

Bjorni lets out a loud sigh behind me.

"You disagree, Bjorni," Lang says.

"Yes, and I don't care enough to argue it."

"Suit yourself."

A mess of roots and vines spreads over the trail, and Lang dismounts to cut out an opening with his machete, something he's had to do a few times now. He's dismissed our calls for help the last few times, so we just let him carry out his work.

"Alright, what about magic?" I say. "Stories come up all the time about how it's a threat to society and all. Why's that?"

"The cities hate it because they can't control it," Lang says. "The land hates that powder they use to silence it, so it gets more fickle in return."

"What gets more fickle?"

"The land."

"So, wait, the land is an entity?"

"A what?"

"Like one big living being?"

"In a way. It's older than any of us know, and it doesn't like what we're doing to it."

Gren retches, and his lunch splatters against the ground. He sits back up and wipes his lips.

"I told you," Lang says.

"I'm so confused," I say. "If the land hates us, then how are we still here?"

"It doesn't hate us," Lang says. "Just what we're doing to it. It gets used to us, like in Fallund. Morphs around us and leaves us alone. Just gets irate around the bigger, newer cities, using all that powder."

"How do you know all this?" James asks.

"Well," Lang starts, "I was in the wilderness hunting one day..."

"Here we go."

"I shot a three-horned buck but didn't kill it," Lang continues, ignoring Bjorni's protestations, "I tracked it all day until I fell into a small ravine and twisted my ankle. An elf found me, thanked me for doing her hunting for her. She was kicked out of her tribe and wasn't a good hunter. While I lay there at her little camp, and got better, she told me all I needed to know, with what little of our language she knew."

"A feral elf," Bjorni says, exasperated, "Not killing you on sight? What a fairytale."

"I don't buy it either," Gren says. "Even the elfbloods I ran into back home hated all of our guts."

"You don't have to believe me," Lang says. "That's just my story. All there is to it."

A silence falls over us. Looking back at Cillian and James, they're rolling their eyes when I meet their gaze. Bjorni's expression is similar. They likely think Lang is disassociated from reality. I'm not so convinced. The way he just tells us what he thinks, so at ease, is strangely comforting. Still, there's a pre-rational response in my mind to the forest around us. Something that is constantly morphing like this just cannot be trusted. On an instinctual level. There's always that wordless doubt, more of a feeling, that a bush will dissolve itself and reveal a terrifying hunting party of beastkin and elves, and our last day in this place will be one of unending torture.

I wonder how much I'd have to see and survive to reach the level of faith that Lang has in the world around him.

As the afternoon sun starts to set, we continue past an overgrown fence and ranch stead, toward wherever Astraea wishes us to be.

CHAPTER 19

"Alright, here we are. You folks have fun."

We're all stopped at a fork in the road. To the right, the road continues through the forest, and a break is visible in the distance. It gleams with the faint light of the sun shining over a prairie. To the left is a narrow path leading off somewhere else, deeper into the woods. The mosaic of trees and bushes edge ever tighter together over the path, forming a sort of above-ground tunnel. The sunlight is significantly lessened as a result. Much to our displeasure, Lang's pointing us into the tunnel.

"You're not coming with us?" I ask.

"Your boss said I ain't allowed to. I'll camp somewhere nearby and come back tomorrow. Bjorni can find me easy enough if something happens."

Lang pulls his reins and splits off from our group, going back the way we came. The path is so narrow that we can only go in one at a time, into our very likely doom. The four of us look at one another, nervous to see who goes first.

"Oh, you babies," Bjorni says. "Fey, lead us in."

With his command comes the wash of fear down my spine. I can't help but freeze up for a moment.

"I won't say it again, boy."

I hastily jerk my reins to lead the horse's head, and she whinnies a little in protest. Gren, Cillian, and James unholster some pistols from their saddles and file in behind Bjorni and me. Slowly but surely, we make our way along the narrow dirt path.

The further down the path we go, the more the sunlight gets blocked out by all the moving leaves and branches. We're so close to the foliage at this point that the sound the plants make is audible. Barely heard above the horse's hooves clumping through mud is a harmony of moist creaking. It's as if there's a legion of timber-men quietly and slowly bending lumber within tiny puddles. Thousands and thousands of tiny pieces of wood buckling and splitting into and back out of something very wet. This is happening at different tones and tempos, all barely perceived by the human ear. How can such an oddity be a natural formation? I wonder what it all sounds like to Bjorni.

"Hey Bjorni."

"Yes?" he asks the small of my back.

"What does all this"—I thumb at the trees and bushes—"sound like to you?"

"Like whoever made it all should be shot."

"Guys, look," Cillian calls from behind the two of us, pointing ahead.

The natural tunnel breaks and reveals an abandoned farmstead. A barn and home lie dormant and decrepit, their walls cracked and fallen off in places, and windows shattered open. The barn is bordered off by a crumbling wooden fence. A few of the crops by the home still grow, stalks of rigid wheat among the morphing grass and flowers. The setting sun peeks over the changing treetops behind the homestead.

"What's here?" Gren says. "Buried treasure?"

"A dead-drop," Bjorni says. "We're going to make camp in that barn."

We go into the barn and unsaddle the horses, tying their reins next to an empty trough. James volunteers to take care of the horses, giving them water and attaching feed bags before brushing their coats. The rest of us set our saddles in a circle in the center of the barn, mimicking a campfire circle, with my saddle sitting the farthest away from the barn door. The barn is spacious, with rows of pens behind the trough itself. The roof slants and gets lower the further into the pens it goes, with a couple of rafter beams broken and fallen into the pens. On the other side, where the roof is far higher, is a pile of rotted hay with a ladder beside it leading up to the platform. A small window lies above the platform, with a small winch going through it, a metal hook catching the light of the sun and swaying in the breeze. There's only one entrance into the barn: the wide set of double doors we came in by. Bjorni gently closes said doors and takes a look around the spacious barn, peeking through cracks in the planks and pushing on other parts to test for something. I'm not sure what. Cillian unholsters his rifle from his saddle, and Gren plops himself down in front of his, leaning into it while he holds his stomach. I also take my rifle from its holster and wrap the strap around my shoulder.

"Ohhh," he groans.

"Lang warned you about overeating," I say.

"How was I supposed to know the horse would rock so much?"

"Man," Cillian says, eyes affectionately cast down at his rifle, "it's been so long since I went shooting. Anybody have some bottles for target practice?"

"Absolutely not," Bjorni says.

"Oh yeah?" Cillian asks. "Why's that, dwarf?"

"If you do," Bjorni says, looking back and locking eyes with him, "I'll split open your spine with my axe for being such a liability."

Cillian is the first to look away, eyes back down at his rifle. "I'm probably a decent shot still anyway."

"Being a bad shot is better than attracting some beast," James says. "You ever seen a mammothbear, Cillian?"

"Yeah."

"Really?"

A moment passes.

"If hunting pictures in the *Gazette* count."

James scoffs and goes back to brushing the horses.

I take a drink from my almost-empty flask and pull out a pipe from its pack to light. I expected to be far more afraid of being this far from civilization. Constantly reading about how the wild attacks and kills with impunity, about people getting lost in the woods never to be found, about entire settlements being disfigured or destroyed in the blink of an eye. I suspected we'd be disfigured or dead by this point. But the lack of wildlife or beastmen during our trip has put my mind at ease. Some of the things Lang said were interesting too. It all culminates into a feeling that I'm a part of this massive, shifting mural. The world itself ebbs and flows, pushing itself into motion like I do every day.

Bjorni stops and opens his pocket watch, checking the time.

"They're late."

"Who is?" I ask.

"The soothslayers."

There's that term again. Heaps of books have been written about those gunslinging bounty hunters, killing feral shamans and rare beasts alike for their biological components. All to be sold to the highest bidder and used in whatever arcane rituals they so desire.

"They still exist? Even after the Arcane Society's abolition?"

"Plenty do, yes. Just harder to track down now."

Cillian emits a low whistle. "This day just keeps getting better."

Something rustles and violently breaks branches behind the barn. We all draw our weapons and aim them in that direction, except for Gren. Whatever it is starts to thud its feet around to the entrance, with our barrels slowly following it. James backs away from the horses and silently stalks to the door and aims his gun toward it. As the being pushes open the door, James cocks the lever-action of his rifle.

"Don't shoot me, you swine," a husky woman's voice shouts. "I'm who you're waiting for."

James pivots his rifle downward and relaxes his arms, and one by one, we all do the same. The woman finishes pushing open the barn's entrance. She's tall with broad shoulders, with small tusks jutting from her lower lips like Gren's. Her hair is cut short and is mostly covered by a wide-brimmed hat. She's wearing a thick dark-black overcoat, with a long, bolt-action rifle and knapsack slung over her shoulder. Underneath the coat is a grimy, dented breastplate and riding pants with knee-high boots.

"Where's the dwarf?" she asks

"Right here," Bjorni says, coming up from behind a saddle and holstering his pistol.

She pulls her knapsack over her shoulder and loosens the string holding it closed. She then pulls out a crude wooden box from it.

"Pay up first."

Bjorni pulls a stack of silvum from his pocket and tosses it to her. She counts it, nods, and sets the wooden box down in front of her.

"There were supposed to be two of you," Bjorni says.

"Well, my husband died, so you're stuck with just me."

"I'm sorry for your loss," I say.

"Shut your mouth," she pockets the silvum. "And whatever you do, *don't open it.*"

"Why?" Cillian asks.

"What do you think killed him?"

"Say," Gren says. "You from Ophidia, Miss—"

"No, and you don't get my name. Don't follow me."

She puts the silvum into her pocket, slings the knapsack back over her shoulder, and marches off into the darkening evening.

"Rather curt, wasn't she," I say.

"I'm going to fetch some firewood before it gets too dark," James says. "Anyone want to come with?"

"I will," Gren says. "The stink of that old hay is makin' me gag."

The two leave, and Cillian and I sit down in front of our saddles and leave the other three to their business. Bjorni stoops down to pick up the box and walks over to put it inside our saddlebags. I catch a glimpse of the knotted branchwork and crooked planks. It looks similar to a tobac-stub box if they were made by a hermit with dementia. There's no artistry or craft to it, just a jumbled mess of wood held shut by a little ball of vine. A faint green glow comes from the breaks in the box. Bjorni looks over to me, and I snap my vision away to feign disinterest.

"No questions, Fey."

"I wouldn't dream of asking."

I lean back into the saddle and take another drink. The spirits from my flask and excitement have put me into a state of lethargy, so I sink back into the stiff leather of the saddle, put my hands under my armpits for warmth, and get some shuteye.

The cold gets more bitter once the sun sets. At least the small campfire we've made comforts the front of my body. James cooked some canned beans in a pan earlier, so our king's feast is that and some dried animal meat, with half-frozen water to wash it down. The barn doors are shut, but the shadows of the wilderness can still be seen through the cracks of the doors and walls, and every so often, the motion of it catches my periphery and reawakens my paranoia. This made me lean my rifle against the saddle, so it sits right beside me. Any mystique surrounding the beauty of the wild has completely evaporated. The sooner I get behind high stone walls, the better. My empty flask isn't helping things either. The night is interspersed with us feigning conversation and just sitting looking at this scant few flames. Gren is finished telling one of his gang stories, so the silence is starting to build up once again. Who knew professionals had so little to say to one another once the job is done?

"Kind of funny, isn't it? How we have nothing to really say now that the job is done."

"It's done," James says, "once we're back in Ophidia."

"This has been the dullest job by far," Cillian says. "We should have just sent the milkman to fetch it."

"How many jobs you done, kid?" Gren asks.

"Not many," James says.

"Oh, will you quit it?" Cillian says, "Always with the little put-downs. I've done six now."

"Who do you work for?" I say. "Am I allowed to ask that?"

"Can you tell us who you work for?" Cillian asks.

"Fair point," I say.

"Odds are, you'll meet them soon enough," James says.

And the silence returns.

When the night's tedium overwhelms Cillian, he takes the rifle and sets it down on his saddle, facing away from us, and looks down the sights. He does this again and again. I've even heard him make shooting noises once or twice under his breath.

Oh, here he goes again.

"Be sure to aim for the head," I say.

Gren and James laugh, and Cillian sets the rifle back down, his face turning a little red.

"Who knows?" Cillian says. "It may just be you that'll have to get shot."

"That might be preferable," I say.

"Shh," Bjorni says and turns his head to listen for something.

Oh no.

"Gren," Bjorni says. "You hear that?"

Gren raises his head and cups his left ear. A handful of uncomfortable moments pass.

"Yep," Gren says. "Footsteps. Some sound like hooves. Can't tell how many."

"The tribes?" James asks in a whisper.

"Sounds like it," Bjorni says. "Rifles, boys."

We all grab our guns and raise into a crouch, looking at Bjorni for more instructions.

"Don't let them think we know," Bjorni whispers. "Cillian, talk about something."

"Oh, umm," Cillian says. "So, I was reading the *Gazette* the other day, and hoo boy, let me tell you, the prices of fruits are really starting to... umm..."

Bjorni waves his hand toward his body at James, motioning for him to follow, and points at me, then at the window on the platform. I nod and sling my rifle and slowly creep toward the ladder.

"Guys, what should I talk about?" Cillian says.

"They can't understand you," I say in a calm tone. "They're feral. It doesn't matter."

"Just don't sound like you're panicking," James says.

Bjorni motions for Gren to keep an eye on Cillian and stay by the campfire. As quietly as I can, I ascend the ladder. The ancient wood buckles and creaks under my weight, forcing me to slow down even more. Looking back, Bjorni and James are leaning against the wall opposite of one another beside the door. Gren has his rifle aimed at the door, as well. Cillian is trying to control his voice and is swinging his gaze all around the barn. There's something about Cillian succumbing to fear that is letting me be calmer and more controlled. Us being in a somewhat secure building against a bunch of beastmen helps too.

"Umm... so those fruit prices," Cillian says. "I think they are going to spike, and I don't know if my father can affor—"

A piercing squeal violates our ears, and the barn doors shatter open. A behemoth of a fur-covered humanoid charges at Cillian. Keeper above, it's bigger than Gren. The vile sight of it freezes me in place. Four shots ring out as it takes its fifth step, and one lands in its head. Blood shoots out from its eye, and its body continues to barrel toward Cillian. Gren has to tackle him out of the way, and its hooves stomp through the campfire, suffocating it a little and dimming the room. The body finally trips over a saddle and lands near the back wall and twitches a little before its muscles finally relax and welcome death.

"James and I are going outside," Bjorni yells. "So, they don't surround the barn and kill us off. The three of you stay in here. Fey, get in that window. Shoot anything that moves."

Bjorni's authoritative yell takes the weight off of my limbs, and I scurry up the ladder. When a rung snaps from under one of my feet, my heart jumps even higher. Somewhere behind me, Cillian is saying something, and his voice sounds somewhere between terrified and excited. Gren is shouting, eager to fight once more.

"You're more orc than human, you know that, Gren?" I yell as I atop the ladder onto the platform.

He only laughs and shoots at something outside the door.

A small hay pile is in the middle of the platform, and I have to stomp over it to get to the window. The upset rotted hay smell mixes with the stink of the dead beastkin. I lean as hard against the window sill as I can and aim the rifle outside, the barrel sticking out into the open.

The window faces out along the farmstead, looking past the field at the house. It's so dark that I can't tell what is an animal and what is a plant. It all becomes one big, black, moving mass, and it wants to kill us all.

Somewhere below me, a dull thud crunches through what sounds like an egg. Bjorni's grunt follows it as his axe is pulled from meat. That means James is on the other side of the barn. Just then, on that side, a rifle shot cracks, and something brays in response. Then more evil silence.

Something steps out behind the house. I lean into the rifle and look through the sights. Just like Bjorni taught me. Aim on the inhale, squeeze the trigger on the exhale. The rifle kicks and screams. Whatever it is didn't move. Alright, it's a plant then, and now the beastkin know I'm up here.

Another squealing as something charges into the doors, and two rifle shots respond to it. It just squeals again.

"You wanna fight then, do ya?" Gren says. "Have at it, then!"

Someone tackles someone, and they land against the barn wall, breaking the wood and shaking the building.

"Stop it, Gren!" Cillian shouts. "I can't get a shot."

"Stay out of this!" Gren screams back.

The scuffle continues as punches land on skin, and scratches, and shouts, and squeals confuse me and make it impossible to tell who's winning. The hay pile makes it impossible to look into the barn as well. I'm stranded up here.

Something else rounds the corner of the house but disappears into the field. I scan with the rifle and hope it pops back up again. Another rifle shot from James's rifle, and another. Bjorni yells below me to my left, and his hand cannon booms twice.

Some sort of light pops into existence in the field pretty close to us, and I squint a little to see what it is. It's a beastkin with a crude bow and a flaming arrow. Keeper above, they can make fire?

I rush to fire a shot and stop it, but I miss. It brings the bow up and draws the string. I shoot again. Miss. It keeps slowly pulling the bow back. Go ahead and relish it, you bastard. I take a deep breath, take a second to aim at its chest. And squeeze the trigger. A thin line of blood is caught by moonlight as arterial spray erupts from its rib-cage. Its body lowers the bow, then drops it, and finally keels over.

Another flutter of movement comes from the forest behind the barn. And with it is the dull snap of a bow firing an arrow.

Ach, something stung my left shoulder. Upon looking over, a stick is jutting out of it. No, I didn't get hit. There's no way.

Instantly, every cluster of nerves on my left side is set on fire. I can't help but scream like a child. My rifle falls out of the window onto the ground below as I sink into the floor of the platform. Both of my legs convulse involuntarily, more and more rapidly. The pain is rendering me helpless. The sounds of the world are muffled by layers of pain. There is only me, my screams, and the pain. How did it happen so fast? The world is shifting. Changing. Is this it? Is this death?

"Father!" I scream. "Mother! I don't want to leave! Not yet!"

But they're not here! They're not here, you infant!

Then, the wood of the walls fades and fades. The pain fades, too. Everything gets darker and darker. Soon, the darkness is everything. Until it's nothing, and finally something else.

Where am I?

CHAPTER 20

Somewhere. Somewhere desolate. That's where I am. Buildings upon buildings, lost and forgotten. They're familiar somehow, but I can't say why. The streets and sidewalks are gone in places, replaced entirely by grass and undergrowth. Corpses of vehicles long devoured by rust and age. Big beige rectangles smattered across brick walls, peeling adhesive from advertisements of a naive age. Windows shattered, their glittering remains on the ground. The sky is one uniform shade of deep orange as if the sun has closed in on its dying days. The ages I've spent walking do nothing to change the tale, either. I can barely amble along at a reasonable rate. It's as if my legs are moving through water. My memories are something like a dream, left behind in some unreachable part of my brain. All I know is walking these streets and being hopelessly disappointed.

There is something to keep me company, though. The silence. Nothing can scare it away. There's no men, women, children, birds, insects, or even wind to dispel it. I'm not even sure I can hear my own footsteps. I've long given up calling for help. Nothing hears me, and I hear nothing. Maybe I've been kidnapped and placed in some depressive artist's painting. Not a fate totally undeserved. If this is the afterlife, the final tale of eternity in the Legacian, penned by the Keeper, then I'd appreciate it if he could erase me.

I turn a corner and find something on a wall that perplexes me—dull brown lettering on the street sign of some grocer's. A puddle of the same color sits on the sidewalk near the sign. It's hard to make out, smeared on hastily from someone's fingers. After some time, the message becomes decipherable.

The World Before Has Followed Us.

A new sensation prickles my ears. Vibrating the inside of them. Sound. Sound! Far-off voices calling for someone. I run as fast as I can through the churning invisible syrup. Sweat pours down my face. They get no louder the closer I get to them. Just then, something inside of me starts to stir. A daily occurrence, I'm now remembering. I'm finally waking from this dream.

CHAPTER 21

Ripe smells of alcohol and disinfectant are the first to come. Then the scratchy sensation of a blanket with low threading. After that, the sight of a timbered roof with splinters coming off of the lumber. Soon enough, I remember I have arms to prop up with and take a look around the room. It's small and was probably once someone's home but has now been converted into a doctor's office. A small cast-iron stove is burning at a low simmer in the center of the left wall. In front of it is a table with bottles of medicines and rubbing alcohol on it. Nearby that is a wooden counter with bowls and pans, with food bits caked on in places, now a part of the ceramic and iron. In the left corner by the door is a desk with all sorts of books and papers on it and the floor around it. On the right wall, directly in front of me, is another bed, and in front of that is a set of wide wooden cabinets. They're filled with every shape of bottle under the sun.

Someone opens the door into the room, shuddering a bit as they do so. The body shape and long hair imply womanhood.

"Winter's really setting in, ain't it?"

She speaks with a slight drawl at the end of her sentences.

"Oh, you're awake. I don't get to talk to a vegetable anymore. Sorry about the mess."

She takes off her gloves and sets them on the desk, and goes to clean up the bottles on the table. Her face has a few wrinkles around the edges of the eyes and around the mouth. Other than that, her skin is as smooth as a child's.

"That's alright," I say. "I apologize for being frank, but who are you?"

"I'm Sadie. The only doctor in Fallund. Pleased to meet you."

She stops her work to come shake my hand.

"I'm…"

"Arthur," she finishes, grabbing my hesitant hand. "Your friends told me when they raced you in here at early dawn."

Wait, that's right! The barn, the beastkin. The images race by so fast. It feels so long ago, even though there's no way it could've been. I should be dead.

"Where are they?" I ask, failing to tone down my voice.

"Easy, friend. They're probably still at the flophouse. They said they'd wait a week to see if you'd wake up."

"And it's been how long now?"

"Three days. That beastkin venom really did a number on you. I'm surprised you're even alive. The way the horse must've jostled your body around, it had enough time to get in every nook and cranny of your bloodstream. Not even the few rituals I know how to do did much."

"I suppose I'm quite lucky. Wait, what rituals?"

"Oh, just a few that my daddy taught me. They still outlaw magic back in the city?"

"Yes."

"They still use that dust?"

"What dust? The nullification powder?"

"That's right."

"Then yes, they sure do."

"What a waste," she scoffs. "It just kills the fauna and irritates the land that it's sat on. Only destabilizes things more."

"That sounds like something Lang would say."

"Oh," she says, laughing a bit. "Did he tell you his story?"

"Every outlandish bit of it."

"He's a character, that's for sure. But tall tale or not, some bits of it are true."

I nod, feigning agreement. I doubt such things about the world are true, but I don't really care to argue it.

"Can I be candid with you, Arthur?" she asks, sitting down at the foot of the bed.

"Uhh, I suppose you can."

"You ain't from normal stock, are you?"

The question lances worry down my back.

"What do you mean?"

"You're from a different type of bloodline, ain't you? What's your family name?"

"I'm not going to tell you that."

"Fair enough. Just"—she stops for a second, hands motionless in the air bracing for the explanation—"the way your body responded to the venom. At times in the night, you'd shoot straight up and start saying a mess of words about the World Before and all that. It was awful like... how should I say this?"

"The Pre-Exodus Oracles."

"*Precisely*. I've seen people stuck with them arrows a score of times, and it's never been so... Dramatic."

"I've always had a sensitive immune system as a child."

She laughs.

"No. No, Arthur, that's not what I mean. There's an educated word for that sort of response to New World intoxicants. It's... 'Threatened Prescience,' something or other 'Response.' It only happens to people who had some sort of mystic ancestry, from the World Before."

"Ah. I see. So, I'm some sort of fated hero, is that it?"

"Not exactly. You just have a different set of talents, like anyone else. You'd probably be able to hone them alright in a country that hates sorcery less."

She walks over to the table covered in bottles, unscrews the top of one, and dumps a few chalk tablets into a small cloth bag.

"Here," she hands them to me. "To keep the wound from getting infected. You should count yourself lucky. You fared way better than that boy James."

"James? What happened to him?"

"Oh. Ah..." she says, mentally reaching for the words. "I skipped over that, didn't I? I'm sorry, Arthur, but... he didn't make it."

"What?"

"He was stuck with a lot more arrows than you. He was clinging when he got here but only lasted one night."

Oh. Keeper above. I barely knew the man. But to be gone so quickly, so unceremoniously. What kind of divine tale is that?

"A veteran of a young man," I say. "Dead. Just like that."

"The wild is a harsh mistress," she says. "I'm sorry for your loss."

"That's alright. I barely knew him."

"Our town volunteered to have his scribe sheet written and his body buried here. But the dwarf turned us down."

"I can't say I blame him."

If I died, I wouldn't want my legacy written out and displayed on a headstone in the middle of nowhere either.

"Well, can you feel your legs, Arthur? Can you walk?"

"I think so. Let's try, shall we?"

The nerves in my legs tingle a bit as I move them. The skin of my feet taps the wooden floor, and I test my weight against my muscles bit by bit. Soon, I'm up off the bed, still hovering over it. My right leg is weak and wavers a little, but I can stand well enough.

"Where is my outfit, my boots?"

"Right over here," she points to a footlocker. She kneels to open it and hands me my things.

"And Arthur?"

"Yes."

She turns and opens a drawer, and pulls something small and shiny from it.

"I don't know if they're still around anymore. But if they are, this is something they'll still respect and will help you should you need them to."

She stops in front of me and holds out an old, grimy coin.

"Helped by whom?"

"The society."

The ones underground? Summoning voices to my mind to warn me of cursed trinkets?

"Safe to say they're alive and well. But why would they care about this grubby coin?"

"Tradition will force them to. It was the reason so many of their ilk volunteered to strike out with settlers and help them along. In case they needed to summon help."

So a bunch of wizards in hiding will come and fight alongside me if I show them this coin? The sooner I'm back to a world where things make sense, the better.

"No, I can't take that from you," I say, waving my hand slightly.

"Yes, you can. And you will," she says, grabbing my hand and placing the coin within it. "Because I ain't taking no for an answer."

"Uh, thank you. But why? Surely they'd be of more help out here."

"'Cus your kind is a rare one these days," she releases my hand. "Can't have anything take you out too soon."

I take the coin and stick it in one of my trouser pockets. This exchange is too bizarre for me to even quip about.

"Now, don't worry about your bill," she says. "It's been paid for. Go and see your kin."

I nod and finish dressing myself before exiting the doctor's or shaman's office. Cold wind brushes the back of my neck. Our iron carriage is sitting outside the flophouse, with the horses saddled and waiting in front of the trough. There's something wrapped and tied to the roof of the carriage. It's James. I crunch through the frozen mud and stop short of the carriage. My mind can't accept what my eyes are seeing. The complete truncation of a lifetime of experiences, sitting and rotting on top of a tin can with wheels. How close did he come to this before now? How many times did he get lucky, only for it to run out?

I clamber onto the step of the carriage to look closer at James and say my final words to a man I barely knew.

"So, this is it, eh friend?"

A loose part of the wrapping flaps in the wind.

"Has anyone said the Epilogic Litany to you yet?"

Nothing.

"That's right. You can't answer; you're a corpse. Very well, then allow me."

It's been ages since I've had to say these words. How did they go?

"Umm, the tale of many is just the tale of one, and yours has only just begun. Uhh, realms are just chapters, soon this will you will find. Something something, may the Legacian treat you better in the kingdom past death than it did in life. Keeper protect you and your legacy, James."

Memories of their funeral fill me again. Mother's body being carted away. No, not right now, not like this. It's too much. It's always been too much.

I pat James's body and wipe the tear from my eye. Descending off of the carriage, I make my way into the flophouse.

Bjorni and Gren are seated at a table near the bar counter, and Gren is the one facing the door. His face shoots up the look at the opening door, and his eyes are wide in disbelief.

"Fey," he whimpers. "You didn't die?"

"Not yet, it seems."

He springs from his chair and sprints at me, almost tackling me to the ground with an aggressive hug.

"Oh, Keeper above, I thought you'd go too," he shouts. "The doctor said your chances were slim."

"She's a bit of a loon. I doubt that's the first thing she's wrong about."

He releases me from his death grip and looks deep into my eyes.

"Glad to have you back, chum."

"I may be back, but I'm sober. Let's fix that, shall we?"

"Fix it in the wagon," Bjorni says, getting down from his seat. "We're already late. Need to get back to Ophidia as soon as possible. Get Cillian from his room, would you, Gren?"

Gren looks at me for one more moment, then pats me on the shoulder and goes for the stairs.

"Would you mind if I—."

Bjorni tosses me my flask.

"Already taken care of."

"You know me too well."

"Somewhere in your lineage is a dwarf, that's why," Bjorni says, passing by me.

"Is that possible?"

"No. It's a term of endearment."

He passes through the main doors.

"Term of endearment, the aloof veteran says," I mutter.

I slosh the flask to test how full it is before stuffing it in my breast pocket. Then I follow Gren's path up the stairs to Cillian's room. He's stopped just outside Cillian's door.

"You plan on going in?" I ask.

Gren shushes me and points to the door. I put my ear to it and hear quiet sobbing.

"James's passin' weighed heavy on him. I don't know if I can go in there."

Gren can beat people senseless just fine. But as soon as they start to cry, then it's too baffling.

"There's a jab somewhere in all this," I say. "But to the void with it. I'll handle it."

I grab the handle, but the weight of the situation comes down as soon as I start to turn it. Death and those left in its path, that's what I'm dealing with. Keeper above, what nonsense. Once the door opens, Cillian's crying stops. He's lying on the bed, his back to the door.

"I said to leave me be."

"It's Fey. Bjorni said it's time for us to go."

"Arthur Fey, the man of fortune himself."

He rises to a seated position on the bed, his back still facing me.

"Look. I'm sorry about James, but—"

"*Shut. Your. Mouth.* Don't even say another word about James."

"Cillian," I muster the softest voice I can, "I know what it's like to lose someone. I just—"

He rises from the bed and stomps over to me, and shoves me out of the doorframe. Gren takes a step back and looks at me, asking if I need help with his eyes. I hold up my hand, signaling that I have this.

"I will take no advice from you, you pitiful bum," he shouts the final words. "James, a man who's lived through and outsmarted every hardship life can muster, is surpassed by some drunken miserable lout who fancies himself a gangster."

He steps over my body and stops on the way down the stairs.

"If you utter one word about that man in the carriage, I will *beat you blind.*"

I wait until he leaves the building before standing back up.

"What a bastard, eh?" Gren says.

"No, he's right," I say. "About some things, at least. I have no business talking to him about something like this. I'm a stranger to him."

"Either way, I ain't lookin' forward to riding home with that."

"You're telling me. Come on, let's do some shots before we—"

Really? That's what I want to do, after what Cillian just said about me?

"On second thought. Let's just get home."

"You sure?"

"Yeah. The sooner we're behind big stone walls, where things make sense, the better."

Gren and I leave the building and find the horses have been saddled and attached to the carriage. We climb into the coach, palpable with tension. Cillian is fuming, arms crossed, and ignoring my existence as resentfully as possible. The driver lashes the horses and sets us on our way.

The sun starts to rise over the morphing trees. All I can do is light a pipe and keep myself from proving Cillian right. It's become such a natural movement to reach for my flask that I almost do it a few times when I'm lost in gazing at the bushes as they slowly shift into flower beds.

The third time I almost do it, frustration overtakes me. Fine, then it's time to remove the temptation altogether. I snatch it from my pocket and throw it out the window.

"Whoa, Fey," Gren says. "The void was that for?"

"Removing temptation."

Cillian doesn't react at all, still gazing out the other window.

Part of me hopes that he resents me even more for doing it. That maybe he sees it as spitting in the face of his accusation. Another little trick you taught me, Caddock. Leaning into one's accusers and all that.

However, you never taught me about dealing with misery. One great teaching that there was never time for, in between all your trips. Maybe you never figured that one out either. It makes sense. Mother was the same way. The drink was a great crutch for her, so it must have called to me too back then. When my turn came to need that crutch, I welcomed it. A great crutch for trying times. Void below, it's so obvious now that I think about it. When it comes to insight, I've always been slow on the uptake.

CHAPTER 22

"Here are your papers back, sirs," the gate sentry says. "Welcome to Ophidia."

He hops off of the side of our carriage and waves us into the city.

The horses jitter back up to a walking pace, and we pass back under the mighty Klemen's Gate. A warm sense of security immediately follows, returning behind the monumental stone walls. The setting sun comes back into view, over the distant ocean, once we're inside the city proper.

I look back from the window into our carriage, and the icy tension hasn't changed. Cillian is still just one casual insult away from killing someone. Who knows if he'll ever get over the loss of James.

"Going to get away from this life if it kills me," he mutters to himself, for the hundredth time.

Bjorni is whittling yet again. His hands can never be idle. None of us have seen the box since we killed all those beastmen for it. Bjorni has jealously hidden it from prying eyes. But the night before we left Fallund, its faint glow was visible from his travel trunk.

The metal slit between the driver and us slides open.

"It alright if I pull over here?" he shouts.

Bjorni leans up and looks out the window.

"Yes, this will do."

The driver's head turns and nods. A few short moments later, we pull to a stop near a bustling intersection and file out of the carriage.

Bjorni steps forward to face the three of us and takes three folded envelopes from his back pocket.

"Your payments," he says, holding them out. "Good work out there, boys."

Cillian snaps his envelope from Bjorni's hand and storms away. He shoulders a few passersby out of the way during his exit. I can't help but think of what he said to me. His last diatribe while standing over me in that flophouse in Fallund. The more I think about it, the more he's right. I'll turn the drinking around. Swear it off forever. Maybe that'll help things, for him and for me. Hopefully, that makes some sort of sense.

"We ever gonna see him again, boss?" Gren asks.

"No," Bjorni says. "Too weak for the trouble..."

Gren and I take our envelopes as well. I crack mine open to take a peek inside. About 6800 silvum sits inside, in neat bills. Gren's whistling implies that he has seen the same.

"We'll call you later. Like usual."

Bjorni turns and walks away, shortly disappearing into the crowd.

"So, Fey," Gren says. "What do you think? Go out for some drinks and celebrate?"

"Tomorrow night, maybe," I say. "Only thing I want right now is a quiet meal and my thoughts."

Gren blows a quick raspberry.

"If you say so, downer."

He ruffles my hair and goes to leave.

"See you," he calls back behind himself.

And just like that, I'm left alone on the busy sidewalk. The familiar smells of nully powder chalk, and motor oil envelop me. How I missed these during the rotten and earthy descent into madness. How people like Lang can be so sanguine in such a void-cursed place is beyond comprehension.

185

I pull a pipe from my pack and make my way down the boulevard, relishing the passing neon signs and busy storefronts. This city has become as much a part of me as I have of it, I've discovered. I doubt anything will ever make me want to leave. Well, anything that isn't life-threatening, anyway.

Once I get to the third intersection, I stop in front of a decent-looking café. It isn't named, but the sign has a caricature of a gnome, the long-lost race from the World Before, drinking from a great cup of blackbrew. This place should suffice.

A bell rings above the door as I enter, and a server somewhere in the building welcomes me. It's sparsely attended. A few are seated drinking blackbrew and reading the paper. An older gentleman is at the till, slowly explaining what he wants to order. I take a table and read an abandoned newspaper until a server stops by.

MILLS STRIKE TURNS VIOLENT

The worker strikes at the steel mills of Plimred Yard have reached a breaking point, our sources report, as a mill owned by Wayward Industries was victim to a sudden riot just a few short days ago. Police forces were able to contain the affair, but 23 victims were injured and sent to the Helping Hand hospital, in addition to 36 culprits being arrested. Sources say that the tensions from these strikes are only going to continue if Wayward Industries' leadership continues in its refusal to negotiate with its striking workers.

I'm gone for half of a work-week, and suddenly revolt is on the horizon.

"Can I get you something, sir?" a man to my left asks me. I look up to see an aproned gentleman with a notepad.

"Yes, I'll take a half-plate of cutter fish. sWith a cup of blackbrew, please."

"Any sweetening for the blackbrew, sir?"

"Yes, please, two spoonfuls."

"Right away, sir."

As the server walks away, the bell above the door rings again, followed by a feminine voice chirping in greeting. I look up from my newspaper and am immediately blown away as I look at one of the most beautiful women I've ever seen. She has a rich ebony complexion, with soft facial features and full lips. Her hair is thick curls pulled back into a ponytail. In that one moment, I take in as much as I can. Then she looks over at me, and our eyes meet. I can't tell if she's feeling something similar to me or if I'm offending her with my staring. I quickly bury my eyes back into the paper, feigning interest. She continues on her way to the register, orders something for herself, and finds a seat at an empty table, writing something into a notebook. Keeper above, the warmth in my chest is unprecedented.

This feeling is something I imagined I had deadened up to this point. Father had never arranged a marriage for political or material gain, and I never found anyone in my own pursuits. With all the parties and all the women I've talked to up till now, not one has truly captured my interest. I don't even think I'm that interesting; perhaps dating just isn't for me. The feeling that someone can possess me like this. It's terrific and horrifying. I have to talk to her. I have to see if she finds me interesting or dreadful. If I can just get that mystery cleared up, I could be more at ease. But what if she wants to be left alone? Most people do when they're out like this. But if I leave it alone now, I'll likely never see her again. To the void with it. Enough thinking in circles, time to act.

I check my pocket watch and rise from my seat, pretending to be at ease even though my pulse is roaring in my ears. Keeper above, give me a man to blackmail over this any day. In the span of a few moments, I'm two steps away from her table. Once she looks up from her book at me, any semblance of something to say disintegrates.

She grins and says, "Hello there."

"Would you like to be left alone?"

"I'm sorry?"

"I wanted to introduce myself, but if you'd like me to leave you be, I can."

She chuckles. "No, that's quite alright. I'm Elizabeth Drummen. What's your name?"

"I'm Arthur. Arthur Fey."

"Pleased to meet you, Mr. Fey." She puts forth her hand to shake. I oblige.

Once our hands lock, the warmth her being radiates fills something inside of me. Something that's been left empty since I don't even know when. Keeper above, so many expectations that I'm lofting onto this poor stranger.

"What do you have in that notebook there, Ms. Drummen?"

"Elizabeth is fine, and I'm writing about the riots. I work for the *Ophidian Gazette.*"

"A journalist. That must be an exciting life."

"It has its moments. I care more for my side projects, however. What do you do?"

"I'm a business negotiator."

"You must be taken care of. What business do you work for?"

I hesitate. "A security firm. I go to businesses for contracts and the like."

"That sounds exciting. Or rote, depending on your outlook."

"It can be both, to be sure."

"Are you less nervous now, Arthur?"

I scoff, "Rather direct, aren't you, Elizabeth?"

"I just like to ask questions, that's all."

"Well," I scratch my neck and awkwardly chuckle a bit. "Yes, I suppose I am. You know how the mind boggles when you're meeting someone new."

"Indeed I do."

"Well, I'll let you get back to your writing."

I turn and start to walk away. Wait! I forgot.

"Say, Elizabeth, do you have a telephone?"

"Yes, I do."

"Would you like to exchange numbers?"

"I'd like that very much."

She offers her pen, and I write down my number on an open space in her journal. She rips a portion from the same page, writes hers down, and hands it to me. I return to my seat and eat my meal absolutely glowing. The civilized world has missed me and rewards me as such to keep me here. Message received loud and clear, Ophidia.

CHAPTER 23

I didn't give the ink enough time to dry. Astraea's directions from our phone call this morning are smudged and blotted on the one cocktail napkin I could find. I stand like some dumbfounded tourist on a street corner in the Row, decrypting my rushed scrawlings.

It reads: *Shortly after the… bell, get to B…ea… Brewery at 32nd L… Avenue. Will appear abandoned, but isn't. Ask for Mr. Cl… Report back at public booth.*

I rub my eyes and take a look around me once more. I've tried the door on a few abandoned, signless buildings that were once perhaps breweries already, on Lagangre and Lyaron Avenue. Perhaps Labafel Avenue is the one. The building I'm across from has a sign on it; the word *Brewery* is there. Promising. The name is decayed and scratched off, though, with only the letters B, E, and A.

"I believe my detective work ceases here," I mutter.

A nearby old woman catches me talking to myself, and I wave at her. Her weak smile does little to hide her judgment.

The cold air has stabilized since my return home, probably due to the number of buildings to stand in its way. The coat I was given during the last job works wonders to keep me warm.

The smell of coal and chalk is thick in this part of the district. When a lapse in street traffic occurs, I rush to cross the street in front of the building. The door opens and stops itself, stuck on something inside. I shove it with my shoulder once, twice, thrice, and on the fourth shove, something cracks and gives behind the door, and I stumble inside.

An empty bar awaits me inside. Beams of sunlight shine through in between the boards on the windows, leaving bright shafts and lines on the tables and stools in the room. Dust from my disturbance twirls and rushes away from the door in plumes. At the opposite end of the room is a boarded pair of wooden doors. Off in the right corner, a skinny stairway leads upwards into some unknown place. Any metal that was on the taps and countertops has been scavenged or stolen a long time ago. There are still unlit lanterns and sconces set on beams and walls throughout the room. There's no hint of this place ever knowing what electricity is. Whatever brewery this was, it was from far before my time. It's also the wrong one, too, evidently. There's no sign of anyone ever being here.

As I turn to leave, a gun's bolt-action is pulled and pushed back into place.

"Stop right there," a male voice flatly says. "Stay facing that way, and take three steps back in here."

I comply.

"Who sent you?" he asks. "And who are you looking for?"

Void below, I don't know the man's name! Mr. Cl, what're the next letters? Clemens? Cloyams?

"Astraea sent me," I say, hoping for divine inspiration on the man's name. As usual, nothing comes. If this is it, so be it. "I'm looking for Mr. Cl."

"Cl? That's it? Nothing else?"

"That's all I was told to say," I lie.

A few moments pass. He's likely sizing me up, deciding if I'm worth shooting.

"Alright. Come in, then."

I turn back around, and a middle-aged man with a flat cap is standing on the stairs. He's slinging his rifle and going up them, and I hasten to catch up with him.

"Dwarves made this place, so watch your head."

At the top of the stairs is a narrow hallway with a shortened roof. Two pairs of doors are on either side, and a doorway awaits on the opposite end. The man goes past the pairs of doors and opens the door at the far end, with me right behind him.

Inside is a well-kept office. The large window behind the desk is still boarded shut, but everything else, from the wooden filing cabinets to the typewriter, is devoid of any grime or dust. An electric lamp sits on the desk, filling the room with a bright orange glow. Next to that lamp is a telephone and a stack of papers. A man in a pressed three-piece suit rises from his seat behind the desk. Like the gunman, he has a few lines and wrinkles from age. His balding hair is slicked close to his scalp. A thick mustache hangs over his upper lips. His nose is crooked to the left and holds a pair of brass spectacles over his eyes.

He looks just like that man that Bjorni met in the alleyway. So much so that he has to be that same man. The ideologue we apparently want nothing to do with. Desperate times, it seems. I should have expected this turn of events. The dots between that meeting and working with Cillian and James were so obvious, begging to be connected.

"This our man, Rennir?" he asks. His voice is dry and a little shrill, yet somehow soothing to the ears.

"Believe so, sir," the man with the rifle says.

"Good. Then you must be Mr. Fey. I'm Mr. Clarke."

He holds out his hand to shake. I still stand in the hallway just before the doorway. Something about this still feels off.

"Come on in, sir," Mr. Clarke says. "We won't harm you. You'd be dead by now if that was the case."

"How… reassuring."

"Come, now." He does his best to disarm me with a smile. "We won't even frisk you and take away that fine pistol holstered in your jacket."

"You won't be offended if I leave the safety off then, I take it."

Mr. Clarke laughs, and Rennir cracks a smile.

"If that will permit you to come inside, then no."

I step inside and slowly reach out to shake his hand. When I release his grip, he sits back down.

"I'd offer you a seat, but we're still getting moved in. I do apologize for having to make you walk into this decrepit state of affairs."

This man talks like my professors did. So polite and excessive.

"That's quite alright."

"I'm also glad you were able to find us, despite our... ambiguity on the directions. One in our business can never be too careful."

Wait, that's how the directions were told to me? Keeper above, I need to wake up more before answering the phone.

"No need. For both my time and yours, I'd like to be frank. I'm simply here to hear what you need from our business, so please."

"No trouble, no trouble at all. I believe it's no secret that your enterprise has worked for us already. You've already met some of my comrades, Cillian and the late James, Keeper preserve his legacy."

"Oh. Yes, we have. Poor James. Nasty way to go. How's Cillian getting on?"

"Taking some time to be with his family. He took the loss poorly, I'm afraid. He looked up to James quite a bit."

"Cillian wasn't very affable on the ride home. He directed a lot of that pain at me."

"Yes, I heard. Don't worry, you won't be seeing much of him anymore. So, tell me, Mr. Fey, how involved with politics are you?"

"Not any more than your average man."

His smile wanes a bit.

"That's unfortunate. But an apolitical perspective is not without worth."

He opens a drawer and pulls out a tobac-stub box from it.

"Would you care for one?"

"No, thank you."

He draws one from the box and lights it, taking a deep inhale.

"Officially speaking," he begins, "your business has no direct association with my party. Are we clear on that?"

"Of course. I wouldn't want to be associated with me either."

An exhale rushes from his nostrils. "Yes. My group represents the interests and livelihoods of every working individual in Ophidia. Every steel-mill worker, assembly-line worker, dry-dock assembly-man, and nullification powder dispenser looks to us to protect their wages and families."

Something about all this gives me a flash of remembrance. In that small hotel room, Cillian tossed me a lighter, and it had letters and a symbol on it. I've read about them in the papers, too, once in a while. What were they again?

"I'm sure you noticed that the bills passed and representatives voted into our Statehouse have stopped representing these people's interests for some time."

It was a fist with four letters. I think. What were they?

"Am I accurate in saying this, Mr. Fey?"

"Indeed you are, sir."

"Since that's the case, it is only natural for a party to bring about its own existence and remedy the political disease that is the business-backed Statehouse!"

He slams his fist down on the desk. The explosion of anger takes me back for a second.

His face softens, and he lets out a diffusive laugh.

That's right! That's what the letters were.

"I apologize. I get so fired up about the state of affairs that I can work myself into a frenzy. The rallies I hold every week don't do much to help my disposition, either. What I'm trying to say is, your business and its leanings, its methods, align with ours, and we'd be honored to have you here at the—"

"NCLP," I finish.

"That's correct, Mr. Fey," he says, smiling again. "You do pay attention to the *Gazette* then, don't you? Tell me this then: What do our letters stand for?"

"Well, you have me there, sir."

"No problem, you don't need to know those sorts of details, anyway. We're the New Colonian Liberation Party."

"Quite the name."

"We plan on delivering on that name. Journalists can write about us being 'tree vipers' or 'tunnel wolves' as much as they'd like. We're here to help the toiling masses. But that's too far from now. You can tell your employer that I'm glad to have you as our go-between. You have a good head on your shoulders, Arthur. I can tell."

"You're too kind, Mr. Clark."

"Well," he says, rising from his seat. "Safe to say this first meeting is a success. You can expect a call from us very soon."

I can't help but get the feeling that I missed something during this meeting. These two had some hidden purpose to bring me in for this little contrivance. Perhaps it's some test of loyalty. Maybe they wanted to see if I'm squeamish about statecraft, and become a whistleblower of some sort. I can't tell for sure.

"I'm pleased to hear that, sir."

"Good, good. Rennir will show you the way out."

The rifled man opens the door behind me and walks out into the hallway. I start to walk as well, but then an impulse stops me in my tracks.

This man has to know at least a little bit about Astraea. Who she is and what she's working toward. At least enough to give me some more hints as to what I'm risking my neck for. But can he be trusted? Will he lie? Can I even afford to poke my nose further into the hornet's nest like this?

"Something wrong?" Rennir asks.

"Not particularly," I say. "I simply forgot, I do have a few questions to ask you, Mr. Clarke."

"Oh?" Mr. Clarke says. "Well, I'd be happy to answer."

I turn back around to face him.

"What exactly do you know about my employer?"

Mr. Clarke scrunches his eyebrows and looks at his desk.

"Hmm. Well, that's a pointed question, Mr. Fey. I'm not sure how to answer it."

A delicate touch is all that's needed to pry him open. As far as he's concerned, I'm a cautious man, testing his consummate professionalism.

"Allow me to try again. I want to make sure you're aware of the type of venture you're about to embark on. So there are no surprises or resentments, you see. In the spirit of this, I think it's only fair to make sure you know the type of partner you're about to have."

"I see, so you wish for me to tell you what I know, so you can fill in the blanks, is that it?"

I nod and smile.

He leans into his chair and taps ashes off of the tip of his cigar.

"Makes sense, I suppose. Hmm. Well, the main thing I know is how effective her teams are at resource acquisition. Silvum and 'tools' and all that."

He raises his eyebrows when he says tools. An indicator of sarcasm. He means guns and bombs, most likely.

"We also have the same enemies, too, you see."

"Who would that be? The Statehouse?"

"Oh please, the Statehouse is just full of paid lackeys. It'd be as sensible to be incensed with them as it would be to shake your fist at the ox instead of the farmer. I mean the ones who *own* the Statehouse."

"And who would that be, exactly?"

He scoffs. I've pried too much.

"If you're asking that, then you haven't been paying attention. The ones at the head of Wayward Industries, cutting wages and privatizing successes, keeping the winnings and paying to make sure it stays that way. The mighty 'Robber Barons' that have everything in this country on a silver platter. At the expense of everyone else's sanity. Such success that it will eventually spell our collective doom."

"How so?"

"The same way a balloon at the captured-beastkin circus pops once filled with too much air. One balloon filled with too much at the expense of the other balloons means the other balloons get desperate. Start to think of ways to kill one another for the paltry air they can find. The balloon society becomes the same sort of void-cursed jungle as the shifting one past the Ophidian gates. And the full balloon just gets to float above the chaos and laugh with a martini glass."

He finishes his tobac stub and puts it out.

"The analogy started to shift at the end, but you see what I'm getting at. It's high time we all had a little more financial security. That's how we prevent our collective doom."

The breadth of what he's getting at makes a little sense. Not all of us at the conceptual top of the food chain are sitting around sipping martinis. It's just as easy to fall from the top of a mansion as it is from the top of a tenement building, in my experience. But all this is an interesting move from Astraea. As far as I can tell, there's not a political bone in her body. Strange, for someone constantly playing the power game of the underground. It should be just another lever to pull for the eternal power grab.

"I see, I see," I say. "That all lines up with what she told me."

"So, have I passed, then?" he asks. "Do I have your trust?"

"That's a cynical thing to say, Mr. Clarke. I'm just doing my due diligence after all. Of course, you have my trust."

"Good, good. Then don't patronize me."

Void, the facade wasn't so ironclad, after all.

"Right," I say, "I always was bad at faking a smile. My sincere apologies. Nothing but transparency from now on, yes?"

"Yes. But before you go, I have a final question myself. Is it true what they say about your employer? About how she got into this line of work?"

"That depends. What do they say?"

"Well…" He leans in. "Just between the three of us, I heard she's an exile from the Post-Monarchic Union. A survivor of the Royal Purges. That true?"

Now, that's something I never thought would factor into her reasoning. But it makes sense. The majority of royalty in our sister country were elfbloods.

"I cannot confirm nor deny these statements," I say. "I'll just leave it at that."

He chuckles a bit.

"Yes," he says, "I would assume so. Just can't avoid a little gossip here and there. You're free to go."

I return to the hallway, and Rennir hasn't moved from his spot. He is just as silent on the way back to the front door. So, we're not working with politicians but revolutionaries. Them needing help from the likes of Astraea and Bjorni is alarming. The typical sort of political rally doesn't need a conniving half-elf and dwarf berserker. And why am I the go-between? That's always been Bjorni's job. And no matter how small our operations will be, we could eventually get the attention of Security Affairs officers. That's a fate I'd like to leave for once I'm dead.

But this insight into Astraea's past is enlightening. Her reasons for all this are similar to mine. Cast out from her family, forced into loneliness by the cruelty of fate. There's more in common in between us than I would've assumed. Perhaps that's why she was so eager to pounce on Gren and me—looking for a comrade, a fellow refugee. The old blood is dying, and we should stick together as much as we can.

There's no way I'm going to tell her I learned all this, however. She'll tell me the truth in her own time.

Rennir motions for me to stop where I am and takes a few minutes to peer through the boards on the front windows. When he's assured that whatever out there isn't dangerous, he opens the front door and waves me through. I nod to him as I leave and pull out a pipe to light once I'm on the sidewalk. This unease is something I haven't felt in some time. Fear is always there, in the back screaming its lungs out. But this foreboding, like something painful awaits way out on the horizon, that's an old ache, something that's been quiet for a while.

Oh, right, speaking of, I'm supposed to call Astraea and let her know what he said.

I cross the street to a nearby telephone booth and ruffle through my pockets for change.

CHAPTER 24

A singer on stage is wailing her heart out, singing one of the many songs about fate stealing away a lover; her gentle crooning giving way to rising soprano notes. Sifting veils of pipe smoke transform the deep purple lights of the cabaret, adding a soft glow. I take a sip from my virgin cocktail. Turns out giving up spirits is a little easier than I expected. Urges crop up every so often, but as long as I smoke a pipe or do something with my hands, it goes away in time. Maybe you and mother should've tried it.

"It's not often," Elizabeth says, "That a man I just met takes me to a place like Curtain Call."

"I have my ways," I say.

I take another sip and look back toward Elizabeth. Something about her is still intimidating, so eye contact is difficult.

"So, how was work, dear?" she asks, with a smirk on her face.

"It was wonderful, darling. Met a new client today, and he only ranted and raved a little bit. A noteworthy improvement, if you ask me. Yours?"

"Interviewed some dastardly criminals. I'm sure *you* know the sort."

She points a finger at me, and a moment of nervousness passes over me. Until she defuses it with a laugh.

"Don't be so grim, Arthur, I'm only kidding."

"Kid or not," I say, lifting my glass, "you may know more about me than you realize."

"Oh? And how's that?"

Void, a slip of the tongue. Too much for a first date.

"I just deal with some… Unpleasant people. That's all."

"Ah, I see."

Another moment passes as we look back to the singer wailing about her woes. Just how many songs about heartbreak exist?

"I should admit I was partially lying, for humor's sake," Elizabeth says. "I interviewed a gentleman who fled a Wayward-Industries-owned company town up north. The disappearances of their surveyors are increasing, and shockingly, Wayward's doing nothing to combat it."

"How unfortunate. Is it beastkin that's kidnapping them?"

"Most likely."

"Dreadful, absolutely dreadful. Keeper forbid a company like Wayward protects its workers."

"Of course. In a way, I really feel for them. So angry and powerless against their employers. Little wonder that the protests in the city are getting worse."

Her eyebrows scrunched, and she bites on the inside of her lower lip before taking a sip from her drink.

"You really care for those people, don't you?" I ask.

"I suppose a little. It just depresses me to see them suffer so, whenever I speak to them. I can't help wanting to change things. All those laborers are being crushed at their mills and steel plants, and I'm unable to do anything about it."

"Writing an article is doing something about it, isn't it?"

"Perhaps. If my lunk of an editor decides to run some of the stories I write. He's not partial to 'incendiary' articles."

I chuckle a bit. "'Lunk.' That's a new one. Is it an evolution of 'oaf?'"

"I think so," she smiles. "That's what people in the Culvert use to describe idiots and such."

"I'll have to remember that."

The waiter comes back with our meals, and we eat most of them in silence. The sounds of gentle piano playing and the crooning of the singer give a comforting sensation.

"The way you hold your utensils," Elizabeth begins.

I look up to see her eyes fixated on my hands.

"What about them?"

"I can't remember where I've seen that before."

"It's how I was taught to eat. I come from aristocratic stock. A silver spoon and all that."

"Ah, the Arthur thickens. What's your surname?"

"Uhh," I hesitate, "Fey."

"Fey, Fey… It sounds familiar. One of the old bloodlines from Veneria, maybe?"

"Right on target, Ms. Elizabeth. You're talking with the kin of Vizegard the Wise. Last of his name."

"My, my, I'm so honored."

"Don't have much to show for it, though."

"Still, that would explain why you're always so composed."

"The nervousness of a first date helps."

"Oh? This is a date?"

My eyes shoot up to her face, and her quizzical look turns into a sarcastic grin.

"My, my. The wit on this woman."

"So, what do you mean when you say you don't have much to show for it?"

I mean all of the woes and joys in the final branch of the Fey line. I mean you and mother. I mean the strict schooling when you weren't around. Our leaving behind Veneria for this cursed place, trading a grand estate for some small manor in Founder's Square. The zeppelin crash. Your corpse. Mother's hospital tubes and machines. The grand machinations of modernity leaving us pompous, weaker bluebloods behind, another vestige of a dead age. I mean how the unceasing misery came all at once in the last five years, upending and destroying any semblance of inner peace or happiness I could have found. All before I was even fully grown.

Far too much to talk about on the first date.

"There's too much there for polite company."

"Some pain in your history?"

"That's a safe way to put it, sure."

"I'm sorry to hear that."

"Don't worry about it. You might hear of it sometime and maybe find something interesting enough to write about. *If* you play your cards right."

"Ooooh, some mystery. May the Keeper guide me."

We stop talking and listen to the singer once more. The narrative of the song is now about the singer's husband dying to a beastkin that reminded her of her brother.

That word, that dreaded word. 'Beastkin.' Flashbacks of the night in the barn stain my eyes. They stalked around that decrepit barn, waiting to kill us all. I didn't even get to see any. Just heard their vile brays and screams. What evil creatures. They almost killed me. Keeper above, *they almost killed me*. I was shot and should be dead. Should be dead, just like James. Those visions of Ophidia, walking through those empty and decrepit streets. What happened that night? *What happened?* Why am I not dead? I don't even deserve to truly be here, do I?

My heartbeat launches upwards. Suddenly the somber atmosphere is threatening. Sweat appears on my forehead. I can't help but breathe faster.

"Arthur. Arthur, are you alright?"

"Yes, I— I just…" I stutter. "Just need a moment."

"Arthur? What's wrong?"

"I need to go to the water closet. That's all."

I rise from my seat as calmly as I can and turn for the restroom. My hands are squeezing themselves until I can feel nothing but cramping muscles. Shadows turn into looming threats in my periphery. There's some sort of presence here. Something that's been hiding. Hiding and waiting. It's here, in this cabaret, this darkened club. And it's going to kill me. Tonight. Now. Keeper above, I must look like a madman. I pick up the pace until I shove open the door to the men's room. The attendant near the door is startled by the intrusion.

"My word," he says, reaching over to me, "Sir, are you alright?"

"No," I shout, shoving him back. "No, I'm not."

I reach into the pocket where my flask usually is but find it empty. That's right. I've gotten rid of it. Void.

"Do you need me to fetch someone?" he asks.

"No, that I won't," I say, putting my back against a wall, so I can watch the door. "That won't be necessary. Does your establishment have something for nerves?"

"We may. Let me check the counter. Stay here a moment, please."

The attendant rushes back out into the cabaret. Once the door closes, every acute sound becomes deafening. The dripping of the water droplets in the sink. The wind outside the upper window on the far wall. Someone flushing a toilet in the other restroom. The presence is all around me. I can't tell which way my death will come. If only I brought my pistol tonight. Stupid. Stupid stupid stupid. What's taking that attendant so long? How long have I been in here?!

The door opens back up, and I spin over, ready to fight whoever came in. It's the attendant again.

"You're in luck, s——. Please, sir. Calm down. You're safe here. You're perfectly safe."

I look down at my clenched fists and relax them.

"Were you followed? Was there anything behind you?"

"What?" he asks, confused. "No, I wasn't. Here, sir. Here, take these pills to calm your nerves."

I snap them from his grasp and swallow them immediately.

"We see this sort of thing pretty often. I'm sorry for the sorts of things you must have seen on the frontier."

He comes a little closer and clasps his hand on my back. The contact is a little comforting, even though it's from a complete stranger.

"Yes, it's freakish out there. Good thing I'll never have to go back out there. Thank you for the tablets. Now, excuse me."

He nods and steps back to his post, and I step back out of the restroom and take a few deep breaths. Even the loss of you and mother wasn't that… Dangerous. I take one more look around and see that there isn't anything waiting to kill me. My heart rate is returning to normal. The feeling of a presence is gone too. It felt so real. Like there was a visceral connection between some mystifying being and me. Could that be a leftover from the poison? Or have I finally cracked from too much of this life?

I wipe my forehead with my coat sleeve and slowly walk to return to my seat. Elizabeth is waiting and has a look of worry.

"You rushed away from here so fast. What happened, Arthur?"

"Some bad memories just came back, and I wasn't prepared for them, that's all."

"Oh no," she says, eyebrows scrunched in pity. "I'm terribly sorry to hear that."

"No need for sorries. They're gone. Everything's alright now. Let's enjoy the evening, shall we?"

The singer continues on her emotional journey of lost love, but something about the enjoyment of her performance feels more distant now.

"Sorry that I've been so reticent tonight," I say. "You've just found me at an odd point in my life. I'm not sure what to talk about."

"Oh, that's quite alright," Elizabeth says. "A lot of people are like that. At least the ones I interview. They either don't know or don't want to say much about problems that befall them."

"I must be quite the poor interviewee."

"I'd say you're a fairly normal interviewee."

I smile and chuckle a bit at that.

"That's a humbling thing to say. It's pretty dreary, isn't it? How little people often want to say to one another?"

"Sometimes. It's the dreariest when such a lack turns things into violence. People beating or killing one another when a few sentences could prevent it."

"Indeed, sometimes. But other times, words just aren't enough."

"Too right, Arthur. Too right."

The shadow from my flashbacks still hangs over the two of us as we sit and listen once again. I just can't help myself from some melodrama. I pull a pipe from its pack and light it. Still, she doesn't seem too phased.

"I hope you enjoyed yourself tonight, and my neuroses didn't put you off too much."

"Please, not at all."

She leans toward me a little, with the softest, most loving eyes I've ever seen.

"You're as neurotic as everyone else in Ophidia." She reaches over and holds her hand over mine. "But you're able to keep it interesting."

I smile and grip her hand in turn.

"You're the most caring person I've ever met," I say. "I'm so glad I panicked and approached you."

She grins and takes up her glass.

"To first encounters," she says.

"To first encounters," I repeat, clinking my glass with hers.

After all of this time, I've come across someone who has struck me. Every time she talks, I can't help but listen and want to know more—finally, a benign channel for my curiosity. The loneliness was starting to become a comfort, albeit a painful one. During my whole time at Oxlen, only a few of the women I've met enticed me. Not to say I'm an exceptional person, you know that, Caddock. It's just that I was too busy chasing the drink even to consider them. Too busy following those hollow "friends" that have probably already forgotten about me. More time spent wasting youth, I suppose. All the more reason why this timing with Elizabeth is perfect.

Still, there's a distance between us that's unavoidable. Not the usual distance of meeting someone for the first time, but something deeper. She still has the innocence of a life without violence. She may talk with those who have and write about it, sure. She has an idea of it but not an experience of it. The gnashing teeth and smoking barrel that death comes along with has yet to touch her. A happy woman living a normal life. She drinks and smiles, taking in the ambiance of this cabaret with gentle bliss. I have to be greedy to want to be a part of that. Is it fair, me being near her and risking exposing her to all this?

"Something on your mind, Fey?"

"What? Oh. Nothing. Just enjoying the evening, that's all."

"If you need to talk with me and unload something, I'm here. Understand?"

She puts her hand on mine again. Hers is so comfortably warm.

"Thank you, I really appreciate that. Another time, I promise. You'll get your interview yet."

She smiles and retreats her hand, lifting her glass to take a drink.

CHAPTER 25

Stillborn vines and branches crawl up the faded brickwork of the building opposite of me. "Go to Upper West Grove, and you'll be contacted," Mr. Clarke's people said. Well, technically, it was a phone call from my 'grandmother' asking if I could 'go to the Grove and fetch her medication,' but this phrase is merely a code. 'Grandmother's house' means this specific street intersection, and 'medication' means a written message to be destroyed after reading. I'm already lamenting not having Bjorni as a handler anymore. Oh, how Gren and I would magically appear wherever we were called to. Simpler times. Speaking of those two, I haven't talked to them in a few days. I wonder what illegal acrobatics Astraea has them performing.

"Please don't smoke near the vegetation, sir," a server shouts at me from a café across the street. "The powder makes them highly flammable."

I nod and stamp out my pipe, and take a step out from the alleyway back onto the street.

Upper West Grove is the home of the elfbloods, the humans who have an elf's genes somewhere in their bloodline. The gardens that used to be raised alongside the housing and businesses must have been a great wonder when they were constructed. But ages of nullification powder have petrified the wood and calcified the vines and flowers. Trees three stories high are lifeless and bereft of any leaves or buds. Flowerbeds between tenement buildings are as hard as bone and stay upright in the breeze. The feeling of going through the 47th

Street Garden is one of macabre beauty. Like going through a wondrous mausoleum.

This thought has run through multiple times, but I can't really get over how much better I'm feeling. Ever since leaving Fallund, I haven't touched a drop of alcohol, and only now am I seeing the havoc it wreaks on the human body. Fewer headaches, less fatigue. Just less pain in general.

"Noonday publication," a boy across the street shouts into the crowd of bypassers. "Today's story: Five men shot dead in bank robbery!"

"Are you looking for ya grandma?" another young voice asks behind me.

I look down to see a young girl, knotted pigtails sticking down from behind her ears.

"Yes, I am," I say.

She hands me a piece of paper and runs away. I'm not that scary of an adult, am I?

I unfold the paper and squint to read the cursive scribbles.

Mr. F,

You're to meet with one Jarimetti Phrancsi, a prominent political writer and journalist that writes speeches for legislature as well as pieces in the Gazette. His prose will prove invaluable to our cause. Do not try to persuade him with appeals to our politics and the working class. Mr. C has already tried and failed to do so. Simply approach with that affable nature you're so adept at being, and convince him to join you at our protest this evening at South Gaman's Bridge. Do your best to appear as a mildly interested third party that's willing to pay before showing him the passion our party inspires in the masses.

He will likely be at the "Concrete Syntique" Café at 34th Street in the Grove. Look for a bent left ear and square-shaped spectacles.

Destroy this after reading.

I rip it up until it's confetti in my hand and stoop down to drop it into a sewer grate. 34th is a good ways away, so a taxicab would be the most sensible option. Elfblood men with suitcases are already lined up, waving for taxicabs to stop. I take my place near them and join in on the ritual. Since I'm human, I'm passed over a few times as the ones driven by elfbloods prefer to ride with their own. This is why I never go to the Grove. Even the working stiffs are uppity about their pedigree.

Finally, a carriage stops, and I push forward to get into it first.

"In a rush today, are we?" the driver says through the open window between his seat and the carriage.

"Just don't like crowds, is all. 34th Street, please. The Concrete Syntique Café."

"Yeah, you look like the artsy type," he says and whips the horses into motion.

Sinking back into the frayed leather seats, I let my mind wander. Having at least some sort of negotiation tactic would be a decent idea. Since this Jarimetti is a political writer, he's likely opinionated and stubborn. The name implies elfblood, as does the district. That also suggests opinionation and obstinance. I suppose Astraea is busy; otherwise, she's the obviously better option as a negotiator. Why isn't she doing this sort of handshaking, anyway? Entrusting such an apparently vital task to me is a strange choice. The first job for our new employers, and one that could guarantee an uptick in membership. Is that all political movements care about? Membership and ideals? And how can working for a populist movement be a good idea for someone who's escaped the Royal Purges? If they had their way, she'd be done for here, too.

You're getting distracted, Fey. Cool it. Anyway, appeals to ego usually work for this sort of thing, especially to artists and writers. Hold on. The name's familiar. What piece did he write in the *Gazette* recently? Something to do with riots, right? That could work, then. I could frame it in a way to say that if he writes for the ones doing the protesting, he could stop innocent lives from being lost or somesuch. It'll have to do.

The passing scene outside of the foggy window shows more still-life trees and flower bushes, turned cracked and light-brown from age and powder, in front of tall brick buildings. Most trees have torn and hanging branches near human height, likely ripped by passing schoolchildren. The way they're dead and left alone outside of closed cafés and business buildings is strange, for some reason. How many years did those flora wither and die right in front of hundreds of bystanders, and no one did anything to help them?

"We've arrived, buddy. That'll be eight silvum."

I hand the bills through the window and step out of the carriage. As he clops away, some of my confidence leaves with him. Things are more complicated when coercion isn't involved.

The café is far grander than I'm used to. There's a certain degree of rich darkness to the interior, largely due to the type of wood used for the pillars, chairs and walls. It has two floors, with the second having a balcony facing over the first floor. A mural the first of sentient-kind's ships emerging from the portal from the World Before adorns the western wall where the staircase is inset. Every other wall consists of tall windows facing decrepit gardens. To the right is a vacant stage with a piano. Rows and rows of tables are filled with denizens. Some are writing or typing on typewriters. Others are showing sketches and crafted masks to one another. The atmosphere is still reserved, however. Everyone's presenting as relaxed of a disposition as they can.

Finding someone in this makeshift opera house will take far too long. I flag down a passing waitress.

"Excuse me, miss. Could you lead me to Mr. Phrancsi?"

"Mr. Phrancsi," she says, enunciating the "a" with a hard instead of soft sound. "He doesn't like to be disturbed at this hour."

"That's alright, he's expecting me."

She ponders for a moment.

"Very well, but expect him to be frank. What's your name?"

"A—" I stutter, stopping myself before giving my actual name, like an amateur. "Adam Pilus."

"There's an old name for you."

She leads me between the booths and tables up the nearby stairwell onto the second floor. Snippets of conversations pass by, using new terms I've never heard before. Various artistic and philosophical movements ending in -isms, with people calling themselves an assortment of -ists. Some I've heard about back in Oxlen: "Anti-Arcanism," "Revival-Arcanism," "Anti-Unionists," "Yovalists." Some I've never heard of: "Yayanism," "Ophidian Revivalists." "Post-Monarchic Retirists." The raw exchange of concepts makes me want to sit and eavesdrop all day.

The waitress slows for a bit, and we eventually reach a booth next to the handrail of the balcony, where an elfblood with a bent left ear and glasses sits and writes into a leatherbound book.

"Excuse me, Mr. Phrancsi," the waitress says. "Mr. Pilus is here for you and says you've been expecting him."

"He's lying. Get him away from me."

She turns to me, about to say something.

"Thank you, that'll be all," I say, handing her a few bills of silvum.

She looks down, shrugs, and walks away.

His gaze stays focused on his writings as I take a seat opposite him in the booth. The view of all the little worker artists is nice. It's almost possible to see the rhythm of inspiration. Some struggle to get across what their pieces are trying to say, and the strain is visible on their faces. Others are smug with whatever they've created and don't care what others have to say about it. Others still are invigorated and possessed with whatever their mind's eye has devised for them. The rise and fall of dozens of conversations. The initial impression of everyone trying to stay reserved dissipates from this view.

"You're still here," Jarimetti says.

"Indeed I am, Mr. Phrancsi."

"Don't Mr. Phrancsi me. I'm not my father."

"Is Jarimetti preferable?"

"That would— that would be implied, wouldn't it?" he says, with a slight stammer.

"My apologies. I'll try to be less obtuse."

"Obtuse, he says." Jarimetti takes a sip from a nearby cup of blackbrew. "What do you want?"

"I have a job for you."

"I don't need a job."

"How about one that pays better than the *Gazette*?"

He stops writing and looks at me for the first time.

"Have you— have you been spying on me?"

"Not really. Your name's next to the articles you write."

Mentioning the legislature speeches probably isn't a good call. Noted.

"A fan of my work then," he returns to his writings.

As expected, ego appeals it is.

"Of course, your prose is excellent. The way you succinctly report on events like the riots. It makes the rest of the paper look bad if I'm being honest."

"Alright, alright. Settle down. I'm glad you like my work. I wish— wish my other writings would have as much impact."

"Oh? What other work?"

He goes into a satchel seated next to him and grabs some papers from it. He sets them down in front of me, folded paper with type-written sentences.

One look about the streets east of the Grengara shows the ineffectiveness of our current system. Modernity has brought many technological wonders. We've finally wrested control back from the New World, subdued its wicked magic, and peace has settled between the countries. But why must suffering still accompany us so?

Progress has left many archaic notions behind, but still, too many vestiges of the Old Age remain. Prayers given to a deity left behind in the World Before. Institutions still giving superstitions as solutions to the working masses.

I think I've got the gist.

"A lot of strong statements here."

"Do you agree with what I'm saying?"

"With parts. We are in the growing pains of a new age."

"Grow— growing pains?"

He laughs.

"You call unparalleled poverty and crime 'growing pains?' Orc gangs are slaughtering each other at rates higher than ever before recorded! I don't think I'll get along with your employers if you're what they've sent."

"Hold on a moment, don't get too incensed. Fortunately for you, I'm not like my employers at all."

I shift in my seat to lean forward more in the booth.

"Look," I begin, "I'm not supposed to get you to say 'yes' right here and how. I'm just supposed to take you to a protest they're leading tonight, and you'll be able to make up your own mind then. I'll even pay you 400 silvum for giving me the privilege. They just want you to help them fire up the masses' want for change, just like you're writing about here. You want this sort of manifesto to get published? Then this is your best bet."

He looks at the table for a moment. Fidgets and adjusts his glasses. Then he pulls a pack of pipes from his pocket and lights one and takes a few inhales.

"Is this protest going to get violent?"

Probably.

"Probably not. If it does, I'll be able to make sure you don't get harmed."

"How do you expect to do that?"

I press my jacket close so that the shape of my pistol's grip is visible in the fabric.

"Keeper above. You've brought *that*? In *here*?"

"Keeps me safe, doesn't it?"

His eyes wiggle back and forth nervously. The notion of attending is both exciting and frightening to him.

"Here," I say, pushing over a table napkin. "Write your address on here, and I'll come around later tonight and take you over there. You can make up your mind either way then. It'll make no difference to me. My job will be done."

He flattens the napkin against the table and brings the fountain pen over to write.

"Swear to me that you know how to use that thing."

I make direct eye contact with him.

"I know *exactly* what I'm doing."

He's convinced and writes his address down quickly.

"Protest starts after the early-eve bell. Expect me shortly before then."

I take the napkin and rise from the table, buttoning my coat closed. As I walk toward the stairwell, I feel the judging glares of elfbloods and humans from the nearby tables. Somehow, they know I'm some outsider, a foreigner to the Grove. I look back at a few with disdain. Go back to drawing portraits, you ineffectual nobodies.

Once back outside, I go further down the street for the midday meal. The call back to my "grandmother" can wait.

Part of me hopes tonight takes a turn for the grim to shock Jarimetti's system. If my naivete was violently ripped from me, then it's only fair.

May the "working masses" revolt.

CHAPTER 26

"What stop are we getting off at again?" Jarimetti asks.

"Williman Street, and we're walking the rest."

I check my wristwatch again.

"We're already late."

A nearby clocktower gongs, signaling the early-eve period.

"You're— you're sure we'll be alright? That— that nothing will go wrong tonight?"

It's like he's an automobile with a faulty engine that needs a few tries to kick itself awake.

"You know I can't promise that. What I can be sure of is that you'll get plenty of insight into how the impoverished and over-worked are feeling this evening. Consider it inspiration."

Our tram hitches downward, landing on the tram bridge that takes us over the Grengara and into the Culvert. This protest is sup-posed to be one the largest ones yet, bleeding from one of the main streets in the Acre out onto North Gaman's Bridge. Clarke said he was initially supposed to be the one giving the speech, but was called elsewhere, so one of his underlings will be doing the riling for him.

"Ey, would you look at that?" one of the men in the car says, pointing out the window off to my left.

On the roof of a tenement building, two children are running toward the edge with a big bucket. Once they reach the edge, they dump it, and a puff of glittering specks spill out from it into the air.

The setting sun catches the specks and illuminates them against the slumbering building. Then they smile and wave at the tram car.

"Oh, how precious," an elderly woman crones.

"Better hope it don't get in anyone's home," the first man says. "Nully powder tears through the lungs over time."

"There he is, ruining pretty little moments again," the woman sitting next to him says.

The puff and building rush past the moving tram. Once a little past, the puff catches the flow of air behind the tram and follows with it. If I was in a better mood, I'd call the moment enchanting. But the weight of the future hangs too heavy. I catch myself reaching for my flask again and just press into the empty breast pocket. You're trying to be a better man, remember Arthur? The better man who's always depriving himself. I reach for my pack of pipes and light one instead.

The tram descends back down to street level and slows to a stop in the station.

"Come on," I rise from my seat, "Time to go."

"Wait, wait, I—" he says, patting himself down. "Oh, never mind. Notebook's right here." He taps his breast pocket.

Jarimetti checks his pockets over once more, puts his bowler hat on his head, and follows me out of the tram car into the station. The wind is picking up slightly with the setting of the sun and the occasional howl beats against the buildings. Mill and dock workers are returning home from their shifts, tin lunchboxes in hand. A handful sit on the concrete benches in the station, smoking and drinking from glass bottles. The sight of the green blown glass and long necks triggers something inside of me. An itch to find a spirits store too. I mustn't. Stop it.

We exit and hustle through the busy sidewalk. I keep looking back to find Jarimetti falling behind, too polite to shove through folk as I am doing. Finally, I go back and grab his wrist, forcing him to keep up.

Blue-collar changes to retail as we cross from the Culvert to the Acre. Women with shin-length skirts and bleached-white coats. Men with slacks and wool jackets. The occasional suited dwarf sticking to the building walls to not get trampled. All going to or from the amalgam of department stores near Parkland Avenue.

"Shouldn't we have caught a cab?" Jarimetti shouts over the noise of the crowd.

"Do you see the cars moving on the street?" I shout back.

Carriages and cars are almost touching end-to-end for as far as the avenue can stretch, moving along at a snail's pace.

A few blocks later, we start seeing criers for the protest, shouting over the collective noise and handing fliers.

"Come to Westland near the northern bridge," a woman shouts. "Join us in protesting the Business-Market Proposals and others!"

"We hear your grievances," a man beside her shouts. "The NCLP is here to help! Join us on Westland Street nearest North Gaman's Bridge!"

As soon as we get near one, they lock eyes with us and try to force a pamphlet into my hands.

"That's alright," I say. "I'm going there now."

"Oh, good, grand," the woman smiles. "It's already started. You better hurry."

We continue going and start to hear the incensed mob even from a few blocks away. The bob-and-weave of the crowds is getting worse the closer we get. People are either being pulled ever closer to the eye of the storm or trying to rush away to somewhere quieter. Once we round a building and see it for the first time, I start to finally get nervous.

A ramshackle stage has been made out of scaffolding, and the mob surrounding it bleeds out past the sidewalk into the street itself. A few cars are unfortunate enough to be in the middle and are blaring their horns to no avail. Every race is in attendance. Humans pumping their fists. Orcs lifting up the humans pumping their fists. Dwarves stand atop telephone booths to avoid stomping feet. Elfbloods holding up signs with the slogans of the movement on them: "Corrupt Statehouse No More," "BMTP Will Drown Us," "NCLP Will Set You Free." Keeper above, they've won over more than I thought. Jarimetti is shouting something, but I can't make sense of it. I tighten the grip on his wrist and go a bit farther into the avenue. We get close to the riverside, where a building's entrance is up a small set of concrete stairs, giving us an impromptu balcony. Once we get to the top of it, Jarimetti gets close to me and shouts again.

"Did you know it would be this big?" he asks.

I shake my head.

The noise starts to turn into a chant as one of the people on stage, a tall half-orc woman, goes to the forefront of it.

"Fraud no more. Fraud no more," they chant.

Jarimetti pulls out his notebook and turns his body toward the street lamp on the right, squinting as he writes.

"Ladies and gentlemen," the half-orc woman booms, forcing the crowd to simmer and hush. "My fellow Ophidians. My fellow countrymen. I'm so glad that so many of you share our ideals and took the time to be here. To those that are seeing this for the first time: Sorry if this looks insane."

The crowd laughs.

"Good introduction," Jarimetti says right into my ear. "If a little rote."

"I am known as Yveg," she continues. "And I'm here because of what my inaction has caused me. I sat by as Wayward Industries and its ilk began their State Cooperation Program and whispered into the Statehouse's ear. I sat by as the labor unions were declawed and gagged, smothered in the crib before they even had a chance to assemble. I sat by as workhours got longer, and wages were cut week by week and month by month. Now, my family can barely afford rent and groceries, and my race slaughters each other for what little scraps they can find. Despite all this, those rich folk in power are still not appeased. Now, they want to enact the Business-Market Trade Proposal and be able to use their power and influence to trade out their failed investments to the unwary public. Wayward will masquerade their botched business investments as innovative assets that will make you rich. Then once you invest, you'll find that the worth of these assets is bunk, and they can take your money and run. Now tell me, common folk, does that sound fair?"

A resounding "No!" comes from the crowd.

"Then the New Colonian Liberation Party is here to make your voice heard. We will strive day and night to make sure that democracy is restored in New Colonia! We will strive for no more special interest deals done behind closed doors! And bring back labor unions that fight for our needs! And one day, your children will grow into this restored nation and be happy to—"

A blaring siren resounds from across the bridge, getting closer. Flashing lights from multiple police vehicles approach from the same direction. A mass of walking officers accompanies the lights and noise.

"This demonstration is over," a voice blasts from a blow horn. "Everyone disperse now or face judicial punishment!"

"Oh, here come the watchdogs now," Yveg yells. "Just in time to grind us under their heels. Will we run with our tails between our legs?"

The crowd screams "No!" again, but already a few weave out of the crowd and down the street as subtly as they can. The ones that try to leave find the mass of police officers coming down the other street as well, and they're grabbed and arrested. The noise of blaring sirens and enmassed screaming is almost nauseating to listen to.

"Void," I spit.

"Uhh…" Jarimetti says, visibly scared. "What's happening?"

I try to open the door behind us, and it's locked tight.

"You can see it as well as I can," I say.

"They think they can trap us," Yveg yells. "But we are not afraid of such impish tactics. Form a line, my countrymen. Don't let them get in!"

Several of the protestors start brandishing makeshift melee weapons. Pipes, large wrenches, wooden planks. Most of the crowd is willing to make this stand.

The police on the bridge keep marching toward the crowd. The police in the Acre are standing still, performing their role as the anvil.

Rocks and bottles start flinging out from the protestors, hitting police on both sides. Yveg and the others have gotten off the stage and into the crowd.

I press as far into the door's alcove as I can and press Jarimetti into the door to do the same. So far, no one notices us. The police on the bridge have stopped about ten or so paces away from the crowd, unphased by the mass of projectiles being flung at them.

"This is your final warning," the blow horn barks. "Disperse and submit, or you're all subject to judicial punishment!"

The protestors are filled with a berserker's zeal, eyes wide open and teeth gnashing. One can almost see into the near future. It's so inevitable. Soon enough, the piles of bodies will be beating each other senseless, and many will get trampled in the heave and ho of the sweating, living piles.

Just then, I catch a flurry of movement near the bridge-side of the mass of protestors. A figure moving their hands in strange patterns parses out from the crowd toward the police. Bits of dark matter fall out of their palms as they continue their strange movements. Finally, they look up and shove their palms outward, and chutes of flame blast out in all directions. A stray fireball comes straight for my face before puffing into smoke.

Like a rodent, I fall to the ground in fear. The noise of the crowd goes from screams of anger to screams of panic. Time distorts to a crawl as my pulse rushes behind my ears. A stray shaman has brought sheer horror with a simple spell. I look back up and see that neither Jarimetti nor I were in flames, so I get back on my feet. The police on the bridge, however, are not so fortunate.

Several comets fire into them, jumping from uniform to uniform and setting them ablaze. Slowly and gently, their faces contort and scream, and they fall to the cold ground for sanctuary. The way the bodies move before they fall is almost like a dance. Like a cabaret jig without any music. Torsos twist back and forth. Hands flare out and about, dropping all blackjacks and handcuffs they have inside of them. Legs thrust in front of and behind the body before giving way to the ground itself. The melting faces, however, that's unlike any jig I've ever seen. A line of officers a few ranks behind the burning bodies pull out pistols and shotguns, and the ringing shots snap me back into the present. We need to get out of here, or we're dead.

Jarimetti is huddled behind me, whimpering and crying. I grab him by the collar and pull him to his feet.

"We need to leave," I scream.

I look back to the crowd rushing the officers with their makeshift weapons. A great deal are also dropping to their knees with their hands raised. But the police don't care about arresting any more.

My eyes dart back and forth, looking for an exit. There aren't any nearby alleyways. We could break a window and jump in, but we'd get lacerated to the void and back. Wait a second, the river!

"We're going for a swim," I say to Jarimetti.

"But it— it— it'll be frigid at this hour."

"You want to be cold or dead?"

I yank on his suit before he can answer and rush us to the guardrail. A shot whizzes by my head, and I duck to a crouch. I look over the rail, and the fall is dizzying. What was that lesson about diving safely? Getting real straight, right?

"When we jump," I shout, "get as straight as you can. Like a pen."

"Like a what?" Jarimetti shouts back.

"Watch me," I yell.

As much as I want to hesitate, I jump straight over the rail and straighten my limbs as much as possible. The fall is a few moments before crashing cold and muffled gunshots. My head lunges back above water, and the current pulls me fast northward. Something splashes near me a few moments later, and I look over to see Jarimetti.

"I—" he says, interrupted by the bobbing current. "I think I lost my glasses!"

I focus on keeping my head above water and breathing. My body's shivers are already nearly convulsive from the cold. Keeper above, don't let me die like this. We're helpless and thrashing amidst the mighty pull of the Grengara. I keep hoping in vain for ground to be felt beneath my feet, but there's nothing every time. Nothing but undertow, wanting to suck me under.

A light appears in front of us, and a horn honks. The light gives way to the form of a small fishing boat underneath it. Someone on the boat shouts and throws a lifesaver near me. I grab onto it, and it pulls me back toward the ship. A strong grip reaches down into the water and pulls me up onto the ship. A short bit later, the same is done for Jarimetti.

"Follow me into the cabin," a gruff dwarf longshoreman says. "I have a fire in there to dry ya."

Shivering, I get up and follow. Once he opens the door, and I crouch in, the warmth that washes over me is almost embryonic. Like I'm a newborn babe. I never want to leave.

"Get those coats off," the dwarf says.

I strip off as many layers as I can until I'm down to my sleeveless undershirt, my holster, and my pants. I drop to my knees and get as close to the furnace as I can.

"You boys mind telling me what you're doing in the drink, besides freezing to death?" the dwarf asks.

I wipe the saltwater off of my eyelids and look up at him. "A protest at the Acre went bad. Police started shooting."

"A protest," the dwarf says. "Were you aiming to shoot back?"

He points at my holstered pistol.

"No," I say. "Dear Keeper, no. It's just for self-defense."

"Fey," Jarimetti squeals. "Could you tell me why you refrained from saying—saying your bosses used shamans?"

"Void below," the dwarf says, "A shaman?"

"I didn't know that either," I yell back.

"Boys, boys," the dwarf says. "Shut up a second. From the beginning, tell me what happened."

"I was hired," I say, "to bring this fellow to a protest by the NCLP. The police showed up and started cracking skulls. Then a shaman appeared and lit some officers on fire. After that, gunfire started, and I took us into the river because it was the only escape route."

The dwarf sits on a nearby chair and leans into it, dumbfounded.

"You short-lived ones really know how to jutter everything up," he says.

"Oh, Keeper," Jarimetti says, "I lost my notebook too."

"Buy a new one once I pay you," I say.

"No," he says. "Keep your filthy money! You and your accursed ilk stay far away from me. I'm getting out of this madhouse town as soon as I can. I'm catching the first boat east I can find."

I search my discarded coat for my pack of pipes and find them waterlogged and useless. The dwarf offers me a tobac stub, and I take it.

"And how could you have knowingly brought me to a massacre?" he screams. "Did someone hire you to kill me? Is that it?"

"I didn't know," I scream. "You think I would've risked my neck like that if I did? You think I *like* freezing to death in the Grengara? I don't even fully work for these people, for the Keeper's sake."

"What? What do you mean you don't work for these people?"

Void, I've said too much again. I look back and see both Jarimetti and the dwarf longshoreman looking at me in disbelief.

"I'm," I stutter, "I'm just a contractor is all. I'm not political enough to bother with these things."

"Then who *do* you work for?"

I stand back up and try to be as intimidating as I can.

"People who would kill the both of us if I even mentioned them. Let's leave it at that, shall we?"

Jarimetti's eyes go wide, and he tries to swallow his fear.

"Besides, it's all over now," I say, sitting back down in front of the furnace. "All I had to do was bring you there. You can make up your own mind. Get as far away from all this as your silvum can take you. I don't care."

He stutters and tries to come up with a retort but fails to do so. He swings the door into the cabin open and stomps out of the room.

"Say," the dwarf mutters, "I'm not factored into the whole 'kill us if you mention them' bit, am I?"

"No," I say, "I won't even mention that we escaped by boat. You'll be safe."

"Good, good. Well, I'm going to the docks now. It's going to be a short while, so you'll have time to dry off. You can find a telephone booth and get this all sorted once we dock."

He gets back off of his chair and goes for the door.

"Wait until I tell the boys about this," he says to himself.

I light the stub and take a deep inhale. My mind wants to race and worry about what happens next, but the shock of the ice-cold water seems to slow it down for a spell. The primal terror of death and its aftermath are starting to find themselves comfortable in my mind. Part of me wants to be consumed by panic. To retreat to memories of fear and terror, matted fur, and the stench of blood. But it's all too much to feel and think about. I just can't care.

I fall onto my back and lie sprawled out in front of the furnace. The rocking of the boat is comforting. I can hear Jarimetti talking to himself, muffled through the cabin door. Trying desperately to soothe himself, I assume.

The rest of the night is going to consist of a half-hearted phone call and a stay in the nearest hotel.

Speaking of which, I better dry off my wallet.

CHAPTER 27

WANTED:
  Any and all pertinent information regarding the sha-man at the Chimeg Acre protests and their co-conspirators. 5000 silvum reward for anything that results in the arrest of this dangerous criminal.

Wanted posters line the walls of Upper West Grove's 32nd Street tram station. The police sketch of the shaman is about as vague as possible. A hooded face with a narrow chin. I'm sure someone saw this very person just last night, at one of several alleyways throughout Ophidia.

The authorities are so desperate to catch them, all other bulletins are covered up by these notices. It's no surprise either. I can't remember the last time a shaman tried anything inside the city walls. I can still feel the naked heat of that stray fireball. I could have been seared alive, just like all those officers. The mere thought sends a shiver down my spine. Death comes along and laughs in my face, once again, always reminding me of its proximity. Always one bad move away from complete annihilation.

Mr. Clarke's reception to last night's news was tepid. He thanked me for a job well done and said that he'd be in touch in a few days. Astraea has also been equally reticent.

With that being the case, on today of all days, I called and set up a date with—

"Bah," Elizabeth jeers, creeping behind me. "Did I get you?"

"As if I would give you the satisfaction."

She laughs and motions for me to lead the way back onto the street.

"So no fancy dinners this eve, I take it?"

"Perhaps. It depends on if you behave. Come on, let's go to Sir Gellan's Park, shall we?"

"Sounds grand."

She locks her arm with mine, and we amble down the busy Cross boulevard. People go past in a hurry, but for once, I get to take my time.

"So," I begin, "what have you been up to these past few weeks?"

"More interviews with protestors and foremen, about the riot that happened in the Acre. The editors won't leave that story alone because it writes itself. I got some good work done on my side project, however."

"Side project?"

"Did I not talk about that yet? I'm sorry. I'm writing a book about an assortment of people around the country, with interesting stories to tell. A few days ago, I talked with a man who served at Fort Eri'dahn."

"My, my, I didn't know soldiers from back then were still alive. That's quite something. Did he say anything about the genocides the mountain clans went on before the fort's founding?"

"You'll have to read it to find out. I will say that his vocabulary regarding indigenous populations was fairly colorful."

"Sounds like this story is writing itself, as well."

"In some ways. How about you? What exploits have you been 'negotiating?'"

"Well, my firm partnered up with an up-and-comer, and I was tasked with overseeing the partnership. The first contract, uh, didn't go so well, so I'm sort of sitting on my hands and hoping things smooth themselves out."

"Oh no. That's dreadful. You can't get fired for this sort of thing, can you?"

"I don't think so. I've proven my value a handful of times before. I'll just be walking on eggshells for the next one."

"For what it's worth, I think you're quite charismatic, and they'd be a fool to be rid of you."

"I appreciate that, Elizabeth. Let's pray my employers feel the same."

We pass under the stone arches of the park's entrance, and the scents of subdued flowers and pollen start to wash away the smell of car oil and horse manure. The cold snap of the last few weeks is starting to go away, and the vegetation is already coming back to life in parts. Seeing the small bushes and flowers keeping their form and being static is so strange now. The foliage in every part of Ophidia was brought over during the Exodus, so their makeup is quite different from what's growing out on the frontier. I suppose they don't dump nully powder in places like this, so the leaves and buds can actually breathe.

Most of the foliage is a dull green, but the different colors of yellows and reds are starting to bud out from the closed flower petals that adorn the bushes and flower stalks. Statues of knights and warriors of the founding council of civilized kind are equally spaced out along the cobblestone walkway. There are little-to-no bird droppings or moss growing along the carved stone of the faces and plaques of the statues. The first we go by is of the Elven Council. They were the only dozen or so elves that decided to stay with civilized kind after the Exodus. The rest of elvenkind deemed us all cursed to die and went to live with the beastkin and their morphing forests. Sounds like a horrid trade-off if you ask me.

To the Elven Council, helping lead the Civilized Empire until their collective doom in 265 AE, the plaque on the statue reads.

The second statue is of Sigesar the Bold. The figure that history can't get enough of. According to intellectuals, both alive and dead, he was the reason that the Civilized Empire spread as far as it did. I'm sure his council of wizards and generals helped as well. Speaking of wizards, his spymaster is opposite of him, Edelbrand Gremliche. Apparently, he was of a line of mages that were able to control the arcanosphere of the New World, but that's apparently no longer the case with today's magically-enabled. That shaman that almost singed my eyebrows seemed to know what she was doing.

"I always loved reading about him," Elizabeth says.

"About who?" I say, pulling my mind back to the present.

"Vizegard. The way he could intuitively understand anyone he came into physical contact with would be so helpful nowadays."

"What'd be even more helpful is a nice cabin in the middle of nowhere, so I could be left alone."

"Oh come now, Arthur. Don't be so misanthropic."

"I'm joking, I'm joking."

I emit a mild chuckle.

"Mostly?"

"Mostly."

"Not everyone's all bad. Maybe you're just around the wrong people."

"Yes, it's likely that. Care to have a seat at that bench? I could use a break from all this walking."

The two of us sit down underneath a broad-branched tree bereft of leaves, and I reach into my pocket for my pack of pipes. As I go to light it, I see Elizabeth looking at me.

"What?"

"Can you promise you won't get mad at me?"

Oh no.

"What for?"

"Promise first."

"Okay, I promise."

"So, a few days ago, I wanted to learn more about your family after learning your last name. I hope you forgive me for this, but I did a little bit of snooping and found a bunch of stories regarding your family a few years ago. Your father, Caddock Fey, specifically."

Pangs of nostalgia and shame fly through at the mention of your name.

"What I'm getting at is I want to do an interview for my book, on you, your family, whatever comes up. If you don't mind, of course."

Why? Why can't I ever escape my accursed parents? Everywhere I go, there you two are! Refusing to be left in the past, refusing to give in to obscurity. You're dead and gone, and that's still all I'm good for. All the dinners and 'negotiations' that Astraea dragged me to, just to use my accursed family name. It's probably the only reason she hired me. A brief, intense flare of wrath flows through me, and for a moment I want to direct it at Elizabeth. Then the anger turns towards that statue of my ancestor. Maybe smashing him to pieces will finally help me move on.

"Arthur? Are you alright? You look a little perturbed."

For a brief instant, I consider laying into her, just to let it out more than anything. But I decide against being a child in this moment. Grow up, Arthur. You taught me better than that. I feel the hot wash of shame and anger roll up and down my back.

"Sorry," I finally say, "This whole area. My lineage, my parents. It's just a touchy subject, that's all. I thought I'd moved on, but that doesn't seem to be the case. You have a right to be curious."

I take a deep inhale.

"We don't have to do it if you're uncomfortable."

Her soft eyes disarm me once again.

"No, that's quite alright. I'll do your interview. What do you want to know?"

"Grand!" She takes a notepad and a pen from her purse. "Now, take a deep breath and relax for a moment before we start, okay?"

She rubs my shoulder, and the contact is heartwarming.

"I'm calm, I'm calm. Apologies once again. Go ahead."

"It'll be a real easy start. Just introduce yourself and tell me how you got to where you are today."

"How I got here?" I mumble.

She sits patiently as I try and piece together the thesis of my lifetime. Any and all witty remarks and amusing anecdotes fall flat in my mind. No comedies to devise this time. Finally, I take a deep breath and let the words come out on their own.

"Alright, my name is Arthur Fey. Latest in the line of Vizegard the Wise, council to Sigesar the Bold. My father, Caddock Fey, was an ambassador that was a great and strict man, and... As much as he tried to raise me right, I never truly caught onto what is required of us old bloods. And my mother, Amelia Fey, was loving but didn't know how to raise a son. They both died in a zeppelin accident three years ago, and I haven't wanted to mourn them since. If the Legacian exists, then their memory is doing just fine without me."

My throat tightens up and chokes the words back.

"I have failed out of Oxlen University," I spit. "And currently have no idea what I'm doing with my life. All I know is that... That everything feels wrong, and I don't know what to do about it."

That last sentence has stayed inside for years and years. Letting it out hurts.

Elizabeth stops writing and reaches her hand out to touch me.

"Don't. Not right now. Sorry."

"No, I'm sorry. You've been in a lot of pain for a long time, haven't you, Arthur?"

"Not any more than anyone else, I imagine." I wipe a tear from my face.

"Well, I think it's only fair for me to share my story."

"Please," I say.

"My name is Elizabeth Drummen. Daughter to an amazing mother and father that have since passed away. I hope they are enjoying being in the stories of the afterlife and can look at mine from time to time. They both fell victim to the wasting sickness, and I miss them every day. I'm a journalist at the *Ophidian Gazette* and am on track to become Editor. If I do, I will be the youngest one in the company. I am also adrift in the continuum that is life and am unsure of my place in it. All I know is that I love to write stories and will continue to do so until I die."

I lean back into the bench, breathe in again.

"I envy your assuredness of purpose," I say.

"I'm not sure if that's what I'd call it," she says. "I'm just doing my best to be satisfied with my life."

"I don't know if I can strive to be satisfied right now. Not while I'm embroiled in this madness."

"What kind of madness? Do you want to talk about it?"

"No. No, not at the moment. There's too much going on that would get you in trouble if I told you."

"What kind of trouble?"

"Elizabeth…" I say, looking into her eyes.

"Sorry," she says, looking down and smiling. "I can't help it sometimes. Asking questions is my job, you know?"

I laugh a little and smoke my pipe once again.

"But, either way," she says, "the madness makes living so exciting, doesn't it?"

Her innocent smile. Oh, if she only knew.

"Maybe. Maybe."

The puffs of my pipe pass between the two of us.

"Thank you. I'm really glad I overstepped my fear and walked up to you the first time we met."

She giggles a bit. "You were afraid? Of me?"

"You don't know the half of it."

The setting sun lowers in front of us. The great ball of orange painting a mélange of red and pink around and above it, in the deepening blue sky.

"How beautiful," she says.

Despite everything, I can't help but smile.

CHAPTER 28

❝ …And this prescription is of particular importance, so don't be late," a tinny voice rings into my left ear.

Hold on a moment, am I on the phone?

"Yes, yes, and that's at the usual place? The brewery?"

"Um," the voice says, "I'm not sure about that, dearie. I don't know about any brewery."

Oh, the code. Right.

"Sorry, grandmother. I don't know what I was saying. I'll drop by once I get your prescription from the doctor's office."

"Very good, dear. I will see you then." Then they hang up.

The morn sun-rays shoot through the gaps in the balcony blinds, and I get up from the floor. A bottle falls off of my chest and clatters along the tiles. Keeper, did I drink this much? No, Gren was over last night. We were celebrating… Something. Was it me moving into a new apartment? Again?

Ah, that's right. We both moved into nicer apartments in the Acre, and he convinced me to make an exception and just drink for that night. I had no idea I could get drunk again so easily. I just assumed that once one built up a resistance to the drink, that's just how it'd always be. Like some sort of immunity.

Either way, the pounding headache and nausea are things I loathe to experience again. If anything, this is all the more convincing to keep away from the stuff. Oh, how times have changed.

Wait, they didn't say when I'm to go to the brewery. My closet door lies open, and I rush in to cobble together a suit for the day. Gray slacks, slightly wrinkled. Suspenders, slightly stained. Jacket and shirt, a darker shade than the rest, but they'll do. The holster and piece lie on the coffee table, along with a piece of paper with scrawled lettering on it.

Fey I hed 2 go 4 work. Meet at Tilted Hilt latr?

Gren's getting better. I can make out what he tried to say this time.

Crumpling the paper up and tossing it in the bin, I struggle to remember when they said I needed to go meet. The phone call was a few seconds ago. The code for time is the type of prescription. Eye medication for evening the same day. Pain medication was for as soon as possible. But which was it?

To the void with it, I'll just show up now. Have them kick me out if they need to. As I lock the front door and go down the hall, sounds of the world waking seep through the doors and walls. Couples squabbling over this and that. Children fumbling on shoes and not wanting to go to school. Pets mewling and barking. On the stairwell, the superintendent struggles with some bags of trash, and I step past as politely as I can.

The city noise makes its way into the building as I open the front door. Men and women are already in a rush to get to work. I stay on the final step of the stoop and bask in the glory of not needing to clock in. One lit pipe, and a few breaths later, I step off and meld into the moving mass.

The general buzz of the crowd starts to concentrate and get more aggressive, off to the right. A large group is forcing their way through and past. A man screams something at me and pulls on my arm. I try to push back and out, but they pull me deep into the moving cell until I'm squarely in the middle. The powerlessness brings panic, but I'm unable to do anything but follow. The sidewalk is turned into a streetway as folk get out of the way of the pack as fast as they can. The journey blows through intersections and avenues until we're at the entrance to a block of low-cost tenements. Another group is there already, with picket signs and upshot fists. *Eviction is Invasion* they read. This must be a round of evictions striking mill families are facing. Large bull-necked men and orcs are shoving smaller men, women, and children down the stoops, having the hastily packed suitcases fly open. A father goes back up the steps to fight back but is socked in the stomach for his defiance.

Something inside of me is truly disgusted by this display. I thought I'd stopped caring about all this nonsense long ago. Being a do-gooder only gets people killed these days. But still, I could do something, just this once, right? Make a small bit of difference and help another soul for once. Would that even count for something, in the grand scheme of things? Does it even matter?

Even so, what could I do? I'm armed; I could stop things right here and now that way. But an escalation that rapid would just trigger a riot—this time with a gunshot instead of a fireball. The memory sends shivers down my spine again.

The crowd is waiting for an excuse to unleash themselves upon the company's bullies. It's as if they're on a leash, barely being held back. There's no way shooting or threatening is a good idea here. Another genius notion, Fey.

The father gets up with the help of some protestors, and a crying girl's things are getting gathered back into her suitcase.

What am I thinking, having such flights of nobility? An extortionist turned hero. What a joke.

Beside my pistol is my wallet. Money seems to be the only answer, at least the one I'm familiar with. The father and his family start to set off away from the situation, and I weave through to intercept them. Once he sees me approaching, he puts himself between him and his family.

"Whatever you're about to do," he says, "don't. Leave my family be."

"Ah," I say, "I— I don't work for them. I just. Here."

I hold out a folded bill of silvum. Close to a thousand, it must be.

"Just take this, please."

His face fluctuates between shame and relief.

"No, I can't take that."

"Please do. I beg of you. Your family needs some help. Until you can get past all this."

He looks between me and his wife, then solemnly nods and takes the money.

"What's your name, mister?"

"Oh, no need for that. I'm just some nobody."

"Nonsense. What is your name, sir? I need to know it when I write of you in my prayers."

"It's Arthur."

"Thank you, Arthur. You don't know how much this helps. You're a good man."

I nod and make way for the trio to leave. Guilt sets in, even though I've done nothing to start all this.

"Hey, mister," one of the woman protestors says, "my family got kicked out too. Could I get some silvum?"

A few more heads turn at the mention of money.

"Go get it from your unions," I say, hurrying away from the mob before they catch on too.

It's a short walk from there to the tram station, and the ride starts without event. The brightening sun starts to give me a headache, so I close my eyes and try to get a few more winks of sleep.

The tram car judders and screeches to a stop for the fifth time. My eyes peel open as I arrive at my stop. The pulsing headache subsides for a moment, but as soon as I stand back up too quickly, it returns with vigor. I'm never drinking again. I wince as I step out of the station into the bright morning sun, and a taxicab whisks me away in short order. The drive is thankfully silent as he takes me to the brewery.

Once he drops me off and putters away, the street is overcome with a strange stillness. There are only a few people walking on either side and no cars to speak of at all. The Row seems to come alive after the noon bell. I go to the brewery door and open it slowly, hoping someone is there to await me. No such thing occurs.

The creaking door is the only upset to the oppressive silence of the barroom. I quietly lean back into the door and close it shut. Wires haphazardly run across tables and floors up the stairs, with a few plugged into unlit lamps. The windows are still boarded, so the room is barely lit by peeking sunbeams. Guess I am too early after all.

"Anyone there?" someone shouts down the stairs.

Footsteps pound down the stairs, and instinctive fear overtakes me. I tiptoe over to a corner table to hide under. It's a man I've never seen before, shouldering a rifle as Rennir did. He lazily sweeps his gaze over the room, tries the door to see if it was unlatched, and returns up the stairwell and back to where he came.

Some unnumbered moments pass, and I have no idea what to do. They despise unnecessary phone calls, so popping back across the street to check in on granny would risk the relationship. But wouldn't already being here be worse? They might think I'm spying on them or something. Decisions, decisions. And all while I'm cowering under a shortened table.

A shrill scream reverberates from the back of the building, giving me a start. It comes from behind the second set of double doors across the bar. I step out from under the table and slowly and gently, step by step, creep toward the second set of doors. Whenever the floor creaks, I stop and wait to see if the man upstairs heard it. Once I reach the door, I crack it open a little, and another yelp of pain comes from the back out when I do. The second room is a large, tall distillery. A vaulted ceiling and decrepit wooden vats line the room. The floor is some sort of stone. The room itself was pungent with the smell of mold. Some twenty paces ahead, two figures are moving about by a dim electric light. The one on the right fidgets his arms, and another cry of pain echoes forth. What in the void is going on here? I crouch low and weave between the vats until I get behind some boxes and can see what's happening. Mr. Clarke and Rennir are standing with stained hands in front of a bleeding elfblood man tied to a chair. His nose is broken and already swelling.

"You best be thankful for your seat in the Statehouse," Mr. Clarke says. "Or you'd be a corpse by now. But such privileges have their limits."

He winds his arm and swings at the man's face, landing square on the jaw. The man cries out again.

"You idiots," the bleeding elfblood says. "You blithering idiots."

"Now," Mr. Clarke says, "the rest of the fine gentlemen in your party have agreed to vote against the approval of military action against the riots. You're the last holdout. All alone. Surely this beating and worse can't be worth all that. If you join the rest of your ilk, you'll have both your life and some fine healing thanks to the folk underground. Now, please be reasonable, statesman. I'm getting sick of asking."

"After that riot with the shaman," says the statesman, "good luck not stopping boots from Fort Schid descending upon your riots."

"That shaman wasn't ours, and you know it!"

"You think that this little charade is worse than what the Family will do? Humans and their impudence, I swear. Tell me, have you ever lived three lives as a rat on fire? You'll get to once they find out about your actions here today."

Mr. Clarke turns away and comes back with a lit stick and puts the smoldering end in between the statesman's eyes. The smell of burning flesh and more screams follow.

"What family? Who are you talking about? You mean the Obermans? The ones that own Wayward Industries?"

The bleeding man lets out a raspy laugh.

"You fool. You simpletons. Not some rich family of business owners. *The* Family. They know of your cooperation with the Betrayer, too. That elfblood witch has doomed you all."

Clarke and Rennir look at each other.

"Seems we beat him too hard," Rennir says.

"I would have to agree," Mr. Clarke says.

Mr. Clarke takes off his glasses and begins wiping them with a handkerchief.

"I hate to resort to such extremes, statesman," Mr. Clarke says. "Keeper's honest truth. How about I sweeten the deal? Once you agree, we'll shake a few hands and bribe a few others, ensure you get another term in office. Would that be satisfactory?"

"Your violent, painful death," the elfblood says. "That would be satisfactory."

Clarke looks at Rennir, pondering something. Finally, he nods, and Rennir pulls out a pistol.

"No, no, no, n—" the elfblood says before a bullet goes through his brain and lodges into a nearby vat.

"Rennir," Mr. Clarke says, "take this body and call for Hennan from upstairs. The two of you can dispose of it. Then find someone to get a picture of this man from his home. We'll have to hire a mage. Play imposter until voting day."

Rennir nods and hoists the body over his shoulder, grunting as he does so. He lumbers out and leaves the room, leaving Mr. Clarke to stare at the blood-spattered chair.

"Such vile things we must do to free our nation from tyrants."

When he turns and leaves the room, I sink to my knees and fall into despair. I have fallen so far. Each and every day, I push away doubts and regrets, hoping that in the end, it'd all work out. Stealing, shooting, blackmailing, and all it's gotten me is a life with villains. I should have seen it by now. Keeper damn me, I should have seen it by now. I keep back up on my feet and begin to sneak out of the distillery as quickly as I can. Footsteps slowly stomp down the stairs from the office, and I'm forced to hide under the table again. Rennir and Hennan both carry the corpse, which is now wrapped in a tablecloth.

"Void, he's heavy for an elfblood," Hennan says.

"Got a truck parked outside," Rennir says. "We'll drive him out to the Yard. Dump him in some alley. No one should care."

"Sounds about right," Hennan says.

Eventually, the two wrestle the front door open and leave. I wait for a few moments before going out as well.

Then something hits me. I should get answers. This sort of evil was never in the cards. Or at least it never should have. Enough of this blind leash-pulling. I need to know why we're *really* doing all this.

I turn from the door once I hear the truck engine start up and roll down the street. Once I draw my pistol, I creep up the stairs and down the hallway, stopping at the door at the end of the hallway.

"Rennir?" Mr. Clarke's muffled voice calls from the other side. "Something the matter?"

I ready my pistol and kick the door open. Clarke jumps, and his eyes go wide from the loud noise.

"I'd say so, Mr. Clarke. It's about time you tell me what *exactly* is going on around here."

"Ah, Mr. Fey, I didn't expect to see you so soon."

"Hands up. Now!"

His arms shoot above his head. He surely has a pistol hidden somewhere convenient on that desk.

"Some answers, Mr. Clarke. That's all I want. Then you'll never see me again."

"That's unfortunate. I was beginning to enjoy our relationship."

"Stop being cute. Why did you kill that statesman? Who was he?"

"You saw that? I'm sorry for that. May I stand up?"

After a few moments pass, I nod.

"But keep your hands up. Any fast movements, and you're dropped before you can even blink."

"Of course, of course."

He rises from his leather chair and paces a little behind it, back and forth.

"That," he begins, "was New Colonian Representative Gillian Bhankis. Elected from… Some backwater up north. His party is some remnant of old reactionaries that used to have a majority hold in the Statehouse. His little band of commercial bootlickers were the last few obstructionists holding our movement back. They've always been voting to keep the officers' hands tight around our necks. You have *no* idea how much bribing and extorting I've had to do to get them and a few other parties to finally toe the line and stay out of our way."

"So, this sort of casual murder is normal for you, I take it?"

"Drop the righteousness, Fey. You know better than to be so naive. Besides, you don't even have the high ground, to begin with, considering who you work for."

"Yeah? And who would that be, exactly?"

He stops pacing and looks at me.

"You mean you don't know?"

"Just answer the question, Clarke."

He smiles and laughs a little.

"She really keeps her muscle in the dark, doesn't she?"

"Answer me," I shout.

I thumb back the hammer on my pistol.

"Alright, alright, easy, son. Shortly after our first meeting, your calculated, and frankly hogwash, answers didn't leave me convinced, so I did some digging of my own. She never came from Volhansk. She never survived the Royal Purges. She's New Colonial, born and raised. However, she is making moves to consolidate wealth and political power. To what end, I have no idea. Whatever nonsense that politician was spewing, I also have no idea. She could be from any one of the families that either run the biggest businesses in the country or the ones that have had multiple family members in the Statehouse for generations. Now, that's the Keeper's honest truth, Arthur. Trust me, that is all I know."

I believe him. That's a truth that's more bitter and sensical. She never felt like royalty. She wouldn't have needed me if she was. It was just another lie. I doubt she even wanted to use it; otherwise, she would've told me herself. The thin amount of camaraderie that was starting to form between her and me crumbles into nothing. She never was or will be my ally.

"So, is that satisfactory?" he asks. "Can I put my arms down now?"

I think about it, then lower my pistol.

"Sure, sure."

"Thank you."

He lowers his arms and leans against his desk.

"I'm terribly sorry things had to end like this. You had a rocky first job, but it's to be expected. With the shaman and everything. But you had real potential."

"Well, it's about time I stopped working for murderers and villains. Don't you think?"

He laughs dryly.

"If only you knew what we were working toward."

Then he twists his body and reaches down into his desk. Clarke, you fool.

He starts to bring up a pistol, but I aim and fire into his right shoulder before he even lifts it past his thigh.

Clarke cries out in pain and drops it immediately. Blood sluggishly soaks his suit around the wound.

"I told you, I was going to leave," I shout.

He brings out his handkerchief and presses it into the wound. His right arm is completely limp. I must've hit some sort of nerve.

"Idiots, you're all violent idiots."

I close the door and walk back down the hallway.

"Only idiots know the stakes and choose to do nothing. You're just as evil as the ones keeping us all in chains!"

Once I exit the building, I walk a few blocks before getting a ride home.

With yet another shock to the system comes clarity. Clarity toward my mindless criminality. I fell into this crowd so easily, without even a word of protest. I always hoped it would turn out for the best. That I would secretly be working for those, who were actually shooting and stealing for the right reasons. Void, Clarke and his party might even be some sort of twisted version of that if I stayed in the dark and started paying attention to what's happening in Ophidia; if I pretended to understand what the working stiffs are being subjected to. If I was even half as good as Elizabeth is.

But all that aside, nothing can justify torture and murder. Keeper knows what other things I don't know about.

All that aside, the reasons for why I fell into this life so easily make sense now. The days of extortion and gunshots were freely given out of an inner well of nihilism. Senseless rebellion against a system that didn't want me. I think now that I was rebelling against myself all this time, too. A swashbuckling persona versus the vision you and mother had for me as the last of a long and noble line. This feeling of treachery now feels self-imposed. Like both identities aren't what I should be. Or maybe the opposite—both have a place.

Whatever the case, I need to vomit and then call Bjorni to hand in my resignation.

CHAPTER 29

My shaking hand holds the telephone receiver of the public booth across from my apartment building. Doing this surrounded by strangers feels safer. Forcing myself to stand near the transmitter is a test of will. My primal brain fears Bjorni reaching out from it and wringing my neck.

"Yes, operator," I say. "Get me the line of The Delirious Dogs tavern, in Xaggik West, occupant of room 15b."

"Please hold," the woman's voice says.

The gentle buzzing of the line accompanies me to my doom. Why am I even being so formal? I could just run away, just like that. Get all my belongings and go to ground. But I couldn't even run anywhere. My passport's expired, and I don't know any smugglers. Scurrying like a rat into the sewers wouldn't even last that long. No. No, this needs to be done. I owe Bjorni this much, a goodbye between compatriots. Maybe he'll sympathize. Find me a way out of this den of violence.

Eventually, the buzzing stops, replaced by slight breathing and someone bringing the transmitter to their mouth.

"Who is this?" Bjorni asks.

"Arthur."

"You know better than to call me like this. What is it?"

"I— I," I stammer, "I— I'm calling to—"

Bjorni lets out a deep sigh.

"Don't. You know what happens if you say it."

"Say what?"

"That you're leaving. Or running away. Or had enough. Any variation of these. You know what I'll have to do if you say it."

"I think I owe you this much. A goodbye between friends."

"You don't owe me anything, and I'd rather you didn't. Give yourself some time before I have to hunt you down."

"Hu-hunt me down?"

"Yes, you fool," he shouts. "What do you think happens when folk like us try to walk away? We just get to hand in a letter and wash our hands of it? Don't be daft!"

I lean against the glass of the booth, unable to say anything.

"I should have known. I just... I just assumed I was special or something. That there was a special path out if I just... I don't know."

"They always think that."

"I just have one question. Am I granted that, at least?"

His heavy breathing fills the line.

"I suppose."

"Why is Astraea known as the Betrayer?"

"Who told you that?" he shouts.

"I overheard it," I say. "What does it mean?"

"Don't you *ever* say those words over the phone again. No way in the void am I answering that."

"That's to be expected. Just thought I'd try."

"Great shame, it ends like this for you, Fey. You showed promise if you would've gotten past your fears. Better shot than most men I've trained."

"Don't worry, Bjorni. I'll miss you too."

I chuckle awkwardly to try and defuse the tension, but he doesn't do the same. Just more breathing into the receiver.

"Pack your things. And get as far away from your home as you can. Because if you don't, I'll shoot you like a dog in the street."

He hangs up the phone, and the buzzing comes back to my ear. I hang up the phone as well, intent on calling Gren immediately, before numbly remembering his note. I know where to find him soon enough. I go up the stairs into the apartment building, eventually getting to my home. I limply pull the steamer trunk out from beneath the bed and fill it with clothes and silvum I have hidden around the apartment. My time is limited, and yet I'm still filled with terminal apathy. It almost all feels pointless running from such skilled killers. I find the revolver from Gren and I's very first job, still loaded. I aim it at the wall, memories of the poor dock guard I held up coming back. Is that me now? Broken and helpless against a force far stronger than me?

"Tossed around all my life," I mutter, "just to end up here, stuffing rags into a suitcase."

Memories of Caddock come back to me. "Would you look at yourself?" my father would always shout. "So pitiful and morose, all the bloody time!"

Every time as a child, I'd resent the statement. But as it stands, he's right. That version of myself is pitiful. Too pitiful to be worth living.

This limp sadness is disgusting. I'm so sick and tired of this feeling, this inner resignation. What nonsense! I refuse such circumstances and how it makes me. I look about the room. I went from college dropout to this! Extorting little men with glasses and having more silvum than I know what to do with. Stop being so pathetic, Arthur. It all ends dock guard ends now.

I finish packing my trunk, filling it with tied stacks of silvum and the pistol and holster. Holding the revolver in my hand, I decide to stuff it into my pants and leave the apartment. Gren and I will turn this around. We always have and always will.

CHAPTER 30

Gren agreed to meet me in due haste after my call with Bjorni. I assume my panicking voice probably did most of the convincing. The two of us are sat at some dive bar close to my apartment. His lumbering foot kicks the suitcase leaning against the bar counter underneath us.

"Careful," I hiss in a whisper, "there's a loaded gun in there."

He chuckles, holding a jeweled pipe holder. "That going off would be a good laugh."

"What's the deal with that? You getting in touch with your feminine side?"

"Is it feminine? I was just, I dunno, findin' things to spend silvum on."

"I always knew you'd make a terrible affluent," I say, waving my hand at the barkeep to get his attention.

"What piece is in there, anyways?" he asks, pointing down at the trunk. "The dock job one?"

"Yes. The usual one's on me, just in case."

The barkeep eventually finds his way beside me. His gaze asks the usual question.

"I'll have a—," I say, stopping myself from ordering a stein. "A virgin hayberry daiquiri. And whatever he wants."

"Mix of Slanthen's Ether and tonic water," Gren says.

The barkeep nods and walks away. The ambient sound of the bar is pretty muted. The eve is young, so many conversations are still reserved. Hushed. Billiard balls clacking on a nearby table is the loudest sound there is. Our backs being to the majority of the bar is nerve-wracking. Any moment now, some agent of that witch will come and finish me off for good, and likely Gren for being next to me. What an idiot I am for hoping to get away from all this. But I can't be complicit anymore. Now that willful ignorance is an impossibility. All these crimes against civilized kind being committed, for some madman's goal, and I was just another cog inside of the machine. Stupid, Fey. Stupid, stupid, stupid.

"Virgin daiquiri, eh? You were serious, then. You gave up drinkin' for good this time?"

"Cillian's words after our job out by Fallund stuck out to me. Got me thinking about how much of a crutch the drink is to me."

"Cillian? You cared about what that weaklin' was sayin' to you?"

"Just this one part. About the drinking."

"Fey, that kid was frozen solid the entire time we were fightin' those beastkin on that farm. He never moved even when I wanted him to start helpin' me fight them off."

"What if I'm a coward, too? That's why I'm running from all this?"

"You, a coward? No, no. Your thing is all different. You're still able to get past it, shoot if you need to. That's about as close to bravery as you can get. You're a fighter, Fey. Always have been."

I look over at him and smile.

"Thanks, Gren. I appreciate that."

"No worries, chum."

He throws his massive arm over my head and tussles my hair.

"Alright, alright," I say a little too loudly. "I get it. Thank you, this is very touching."

"Yeah, you get it," he chuckles. "Man, it's always such a laugh messin' with you."

He releases me, and I look around to the rest of the bar. See if anyone's taken an interest in us. The few people at the counter and nearby tables looked up at the commotion but quickly went back to talking to whoever is next to them or enjoying their drink. I still can't feel safe. So exposed and in public like this. A woman called the Betrayer must have all sorts of spies.

"Man, the dock job," Gren says, "was only a few seasons ago, wasn't it?"

"Sure was."

"Lookin' back, I can't believe how sloppy we were. We should've been shot down for sure."

"Just a couple of stupid kids."

"Not as stupid as what you're doin' now. Who calls someone like Bjorni and just quits like that?"

"I know. I know."

The barkeep comes back with our drinks and sets them in front of us. Someone yelps behind us, and I spin to look around, revolver gripped tightly. It's just some friends bellowing each other's names in greeting.

"Easy, Fey," Gren whispers, patting my shoulder. "They don't know about this place. You're safe here."

"You have no idea what they know."

I turn back around to see the barkeep confusedly holding my drink.

"Thank you," I say, taking the drink from him.

I take a sip and turn back to Gren.

"All of this has felt like a mistake for a long time. But what I saw in the brewery, what I heard. That was the final nail in the coffin. And I don't know, I felt like I owed Bjorni a goodbye at least, for all the trouble he's gone through for me."

"Heh, that old curmudgeon probably hated you callin' him. Dwarves are all like that. Hate bein' all mushy and sayin' goodbye. What'd you see in the brewery?"

A mutilated face, skin torn and bleeding. Broken nose. Screaming pain. Point-blank execution.

"Uh…" I say, voice wavering. "So, you know that guy that Astraea set me on? Mr.—"

"Easy," Gren whispers. "Stay vague. Never know who's listenin'."

"Oh, right. So, that guy I was working with. Turns out he— He, umm…" I get real close to Gren's ear and whisper, "He likes to torture and kill politicians. Enjoyed it too."

"Pff, torture. Coward's play."

I look at Gren and can't help but laugh. What horrors he must have seen to have built up such an immunity. He looks back and smiles, not knowing what the joke is.

"Still, though, gettin' away ain't gonna be easy."

"You got away once, didn't you? When you left that one orc gang. How'd you do that?"

"Killed the head orc. Those meatheads got some old customs. Golkatha? Golketha? Something like that. You beat the toughest, you get to leave, take over, whatever you want. But only if you's in a certain spot in the food chain. I was his second-in-command. Plus, all his kin was dead by then, so there wasn't anyone that wanted revenge or whatever."

Keeper above, how depressing.

"So, what're the options for people like me who aren't apt for single combat?"

"Going to ground. Scurryin' off and bidin' your time."

"Sewer life it is then."

"No, not exactly. I got some friends you can stay with. They'll make sure you stay alright, long as you pay 'em."

"That's one of the few things I can still do well. Where are they at?"

Gren mouths "The Yard" but doesn't vocalize it.

"Isn't that place full of riots and killings now? Because of the protests?"

"That doesn't mean much there. Just ruin a suit and wear it, don't look anyone in the eye, and keep your gun around, and you'll be fine."

"I'll take it over sleeping next to runoff sewage. Thank you, Gren. You've always been the best man I've known."

"Must have some sorry competition, then," he says, glibly smiling.

The spinning from the brew is starting to set in. Oh, small comforts.

"You know, all this reminds me of one a' them radio plays you got me listenin' to," he says.

"Which one?"

"The one with the detective and the woman. One a' them cases was a guy who used to be a gangster and now wanted to stop his boss."

"How is this like that?"

"Because, first he was doin' jobs, killin', and whatnot, then he wanted to stop whatever evil his boss was doin'. So, he became an informant, gave the detective tidbits about drop-offs and stuff like that."

"I'm already on the run, though. How can I be an informant?"

"No, no. Keeper, for a smart guy, you can be real dense sometimes. You'd be the detective." He leans in close and whispers, "I'll be the inside guy."

What an insanely careless plan. I look intensely into his eyes. He can't be serious.

"Don't look at me like that. I'm serious."

"So, what? You just ring me up, and we go play heroes and stop the nefarious deeds and save the day?"

"Oh well, sure, you talk all down on any plan like that, and it'll sound stupid. Look, Fey, I've seen so many men and orcs become like you. They take on this life because it's exciting and fast silvum, and then they start to get filled with regret or shame or whatever.

Then, because they didn't make things right with themselves, they become more and more depressed. Before they get so filled with it, they finally kill themselves. Is that what you want? To wait a few years and then just hang yourself somewhere?"

I go from looking at him to the bar counter. Take another deep drink and lean back into my chair, lifting the front two legs off of the ground. For all his obtuseness, Gren's right. I can already feel the deep shame of my actions settling in. One can't commit all this evil and violence and then just leave and ignore it. So much inner peace was shot and punched away. Some greater calling to stop whatever games these monsters are playing is in there too, but it's so far off, I can't attribute my want to help to nobility.

My chair's legs clack back onto the ground, and I rub my eyes.

"You're right. So, what do we do?"

"Right now, you go to this address," he says, pulling out a pen and writing something down on a napkin. "And tell them the Halfborn sent you. They'll know."

"You carry a pen now?"

"Like I said, runnin' out of things to spend on."

He hands me the napkin, and I pocket it.

"There's also a phone in their building. A public one. They live near it. I'll call you on that."

"Got it."

A loud bang comes from the front of the bar. A woman stands at the opening of the swung-open front door.

"Everyone, come outside," she shouts. "A tenement building on Fallen Star Road is burning down!"

That is, or was, my home. Everyone rushes from their seats to get a look. I look to Gren and place some silvum on the table for the tab.

"I got it. You need to get goin' anyways. We can't be seen together any more than we already have."

"Thank you, Gren. Stay safe."

"Always do," he smiles.

I pick up my trunk and rush out of the door. The barkeep is shouting something about people leaving without paying. I finally break out of the doorway, squeezing between the leaving bodies. A torrent of people are going to see the great blaze, and I struggle to weave between them. A couple of long blocks later, I turn the corner and see the massive inferno that billows forth from my old home. People are pouring out of the building, screaming and clutching children of all sizes. Fire engines roar ever closer, ringing the bells atop their chassis.

For a moment, I'm frozen, getting shoved around by passing bodies. Then comes the realization: Whoever did that is still nearby.

I immediately turn and run down an alley, then another, and another. Until I come out on a street that's relatively calm and whistle for the passing taxicabs to pick me up. The one that finally gets me is hesitant to take me to Plimred Yard, but after paying extra, he agrees to drop me off at the bridge. So much is happening so fast, the spinning from the spirits isn't helping. Fear also sets in from going to the Yard at night. For once, when I emit this prayer, I mean it.

Keeper above, if you're still around, please don't let it end here.

CHAPTER 31

"This is as far as I'm taking ya, buddy," the driver says.

His cab is pulled over to the curb on the edge of the Acre.

"Thank you, I appreciate it."

I hand over the fare and step out of the vehicle.

"It ain't my business or nothin'," he shouts through the window, "but you might wanna dress down. Be less of a target."

He backs up the car to turn it around on the street. Traffic is nonexistent in this area, with only a few people walking on the sidewalks. The border between the Acre and the Yard is almost a physical anomaly, with tenements and business buildings rapidly deteriorating and becoming more abandoned the further down the street I look. No single building is taller than four or five stories, at least not in the original construction. A few ramshackle additions come out the side of or on top of the tenement buildings. Rusty tumors growing forth from decaying brickwork. A few of the additions are so much as to make the smaller buildings buckle under their weight, with cracks spider-webbing up the sides of the buildings. Shattered windows, kicked-in doors, slumbering homeless, planks of wood holding up corrugated awnings. All as far as the walled-in eye can see.

Looking down at my gray double-breasted smoking jacket, tie, and slacks, I can see the taxi driver is right. I would appear to be a "mark," to use Gren's words. I take off my smoking jacket and tie and throw it into a nearby abandoned carriage. I grab some dirt and rub it into my slacks and shirt, and put on my greatcoat, and do the same. Tearing some holes is a good idea too. Fray the edges of the sleeves too. I try the holster on and see if the revolver can fit, and since it won't, the pistol goes in there, and the revolver is tucked in the back of my pants.

"There we go," I mumble to myself. "Look like a proper lunatic now. Armed like one too."

With my outfit in place, I pick back up the trunk and begin my pilgrimage.

Wind whistles through the barricaded windows of nearby buildings. The scene of this desolate place reminds me of that one dream I had, given by that beastkin's arrow. The homeless stay inert and barely move, resembling corpses more than anything. Quick movements of figures in windows dot my periphery but are gone as soon as I look at them. For a district full of orcs, there is a distinct lack of them.

"Stop right there, manlin'," a husky voice calls from the alleyway I'm passing.

A shiver shoots up my spine as I immediately heed the command. I start to turn my neck and see who's talking. I catch a glint of a long metallic barrel.

"Ah, ah. None of that. Stay nice and still. Set down the suitcase, slowly."

I gently place the trunk on the ground. My mind races looking for a way out. Gren used to be a big name around here, right?

"Would you happen to know of Gren Halfborn?"

"I've never heard of him. I don't run with no mixed-bloods."

"He used to be a big ganger around here. And he wouldn't li—"

A loud shotgun blast blows apart a segment of bricks two steps in front of me.

"Shut it," he screams. "One more word, and you'll get buried in a closed casket."

Involuntary shudders run through my body.

"Aww, is the little human gettin' afraid? That's too bad. Don't worry. This will be over before you know it."

He takes a few lumbering steps toward me, grabs the trunk, and brings it back to where he originally stood. Sounds of the trunk locks clicking open and fumbling through clothes soon follow. Once he finds the stacks of silvum, he whistles, and chuckles to himself.

"This is a bad day for you, manlin'. I saw that piece you got holstered too. I'll be taking that. Place it on the ground, and slide it to me."

My pistol skitters on loose pebbles along the broken sidewalk.

"Pleasure doin' business with you, and welcome to the Yard."

A deep rumble of a laugh recedes back down the alleyway. Soon, I'm by myself once more. I've been here only a few moments, and I'm already robbed of pretty much everything. Delightful.

I look around once to see if anyone's watching me. A few pitiful glances from windowsills saw the exchange and walk away after seeing it through. I'm still shaking like a coward. After taking a few deep breaths, it doesn't stop, either.

Something comes over me, and I start sprinting toward the address I was given. It was a few blocks away, but if I get there as fast as I can, then I should be fine, hopefully. Heckling comes from stoops and open window sills the further I get into the Yard. As I turn at avenues and keep going, people start to appear more and more, sitting on stair steps, talking to one another, washing clothes.

"Go, little man, go," an aged, deep voice calls, laughing as he says so.

Other people clap and laugh at the pathetic display of a man in a dirty coat wheezing and coughing as he runs for fear of his life. If I had any shame left, I'd care at all about how disgraceful I am.

Once I get near the address, I stop for a breather and lean against an electrical pole. My revolver almost fell out of the back of my pants a few times, so I adjust it once more and straighten out my jacket before setting off once again, walking this time. So many of the tenements here are picture-perfect examples of how to have a plague. Litter and decaying food-waste lie scattered all around the lawns in front of the buildings, frequently spilling into the streets. Gren's friend's place was no exception. Decomposing food with flies hovering over them. Rotting wooden beams hastily covering holes in the timbering or windows.

I top the steps into the building, and slowly open the entrance, deciding not to draw my revolver for safety. It'd probably trigger a response from these orcs more than prevent them from doing anything. If one of these mountains of meat wants me dead, I don't think a gunshot would stop them in time.

Conversations, shouts, and songs from radios spill out from both sides of the hallways as I amble through them and up the stairwells, walking as quickly and quietly as I can.

"Alright," I mumble, unfolding the napkin again. "Room number 404."

The door is a few steps away from the stairwell, and once I get there, my limbs turn to stone before I get the chance to knock. The shaking intensifies, and I wonder just how different orcs really are. The first one I encounter holds me at gunpoint, and the others did little to help me. Although, what were they supposed to do? Talk to him? Surely someone knew him and could've convinced him to stop.

"Gah," I grunt. "Can I go one day without arguing with myself?!"

I have no choice. I knock on the door before I can third and fourth guess myself.

The laughter that was coming from the other side abruptly stops, quickly replaced by whispers. Soon, someone walks to the door, pulls back a deadbolt, and cracks open the door. Gray skin and an eye that's a full head taller than I am peers through the crack.

"Leave, manlin', we don't want what you're selling."

I sigh. "I'm not selling anything. Gren sent me."

"Gren?" he asks with a rising tone. "Gren Halfborn?"

"The very same."

The door flings open. "I haven't heard from that idiot in months," the mound of muscle that is this orc says. "Get in here!"

He's wearing a sleeveless undershirt and has a scar under his chin, with a thin crop of hair on top of his head. He throws his arm around my shoulder and brings me into the apartment. A short hallway breaks off and reveals a packed living room that has two more orcs seated on a couch. One is bald, and the other has greasy pomaded hair. This whole room is thick with the smell of sweat.

"Gentlemen," the orc that brought me in says. "This is…"

"Arthur."

"Arthur. Gren sent him."

The two on the couch come alive at the mention of Gren, asking how he is and what he's been up to.

"Boys, boys, settle down," the door orc says. "We'll get to that. Let's be polite. Introduce ourselves first. Arthur"—he takes his arm off of my shoulder and stands near his friends on the couch—"I'm Olur."

"Grogne," the pomaded one says.

"Rinly," the bald one says.

"Pleasure to meet you all."

"Here, have a seat over here," Olur says, motioning to a short wooden bench that was probably at a park some time ago.

"Thank you," I say, sinking into the stiff wooden planks. A newfound exhaustion awakens once I'm comfortable.

"You want some swill?" Rinly asks. "We was just about to break it out."

"Um, not right now, thank you."

"Well, Arthur," Olur says, "Gren doesn't send friends over often. Or even once, I'm pretty sure. So, why are you here?"

Somewhere inside, I hear paranoia telling me to lie. Just go ahead and lie, Fey. If they know too much, they could snitch and kill me. Surely some sort of bounty is out on me by now.

"I just—" I stutter. "I just needed some time away, is all."

"Time away?" Olur says. "From what?"

"I've uh, I've incensed, or angered, sorry, the girl I'm seeing, that's all. And I need some time away until she cools off."

"The void does incensed mean?" Grogne asks.

"Wait, wait, wait," Olur says. "You've come all the way to the Yard to hide from your missus? Why not just go stay at a hotel?"

"She's in control of the expenses. For the family. This is all pretty last moment."

They exchange glances between each other. They're not buying it.

"Look, gentlemen, I won't stay here too long. Just a few work-weeks, until things calm down, and I'll be out of your hair."

"Arthur," Olur says, "are you in trouble? Are you puttin' us in trouble?"

"No, no, no, of course not, it's just... I..."

Something inside of me shatters. To the void with all the lies.

"I'll be completely honest. Some very capable people want me dead, and Gren said this was the safest place to be."

Grogne looks a bit surprised, but Olur and Rinly nod with sage comprehension.

"Now that," Olur says, "makes a lot more sense."

"You all are safe, though. I don't have any friends in the Yard, so they won't think to look here. I'll just be here until Gren and I are able to take her down and settle things."

"How do you know we's all safe?" Grogne asks. "Who is you working for exactly?"

"She had me doing extortion and blackmail, mainly."

Olur nods sagely.

"That's pretty standard these days," Olur says. "Was she SA at all?"

"Was she what?"

"Security Affairs," Rinly says. "She a statie?"

"Oh, no, no, nothing like that. We were just racketeers. Pretty small time, I think."

The three orcs relax a little at that small revelation. Tension starts to be exhaled from the room.

"You should be squared away soon then," Olur says. "With Gren helpin' you, you'll be fine. Besides, the first few days after goin' on the lam will buy you time. It's not like you called and told 'em you quit, right?"

The three smile and laugh a little at each other.

"Yes," I chuckle. "Right."

Rinly stops laughing and looks at me.

"You didn't do that, right?"

I feel the judgment oncoming and dive wholeheartedly into it.

"Yes, yes, I did. I called them up and notified them. I just wanted to be polite, that's all!"

The three look at one another before erupting in laughter, Olur and Rinly grabbing each other.

"This guy," Rinly says, pointing to me.

Grogne straightens his back, mimics holding a telephone in front of him.

"Why yes, my sir," Grogne says, putting on a posh voice. "It was a riotous time killin' and robbin' for you, but I do say I must hand in my two weeks and leave abroad. It's been a right popping time with you."

His impression of a radio drama star makes the other two laugh twice as hard.

"Why didn't we think of that?" Olur says. "We wouldn't have had to kill our head orc or anythin'!"

If I wasn't so sapped of energy, I'd have a right to be upset, but laughing at my expense isn't anything new.

Eventually, the three tire of the notion and start to settle down.

"Well," Olur says, wiping a tear from his eye, "there's no better place to hide than the Yard. We've a spare mattress, so you'll have a place to sleep. But it won't come for free. We got to pay rent and all, you understand."

I nod and pull a hundred silvum from a coat pocket and slap it onto the blackbrew table.

"Will this suffice?"

The three are taken aback a bit. Olur takes the silvum and pockets it.

"That'll suffice just fine, Arthur," Olur says. "Welcome to Room 404."

CHAPTER 32

An old orc, probably forty or fifty years of age, hobbles with a cane, made of tied-together wood-planks, back up on his stoop. He returns from his fevered pilgrimage that is taking a walk around the block. He only bothers to wear a stained sleeveless white undershirt and hole-filled brown pants. Moth-eaten suspenders barely hold up the pants themselves. In a turn of events that borders on sadistic, I'm envious of an old, beaten-down orc because he's able to leave his home and walk about as much as he wants. Meanwhile, I'm stuck up on the fourth floor of a dingy tenement building, fearing for my life and dying of boredom. I run my hand over my hairless scalp once again. Olur demanded that I cut my hair off, so I'm less recognizable to my peers. But it only adds to the feeling of imprisonment.

"And he's going to tap his cane twice on the top step," I whisper to myself. "Riiiight now."

The old orc stops atop the stairs, taps his cane twice, and continues into the tenement building he calls home.

"Keeper above, I've memorized this decrepit orc's routine. I must've been locked in this apartment for a lifetime."

"It's been three fortnights," Olur says. "And stop complaining about our home. It's better to be bored and alive than the other way around."

Man, that old orc needs some sort of actual walker. His ramshackle cane looks like it'll cave under his weight any moment. Wait a moment.

"What did you say?"

"Tch," Olur says. "You know what I meant."

Wry wit would have escaped me now if this were another time. But such things are dead and gone. Good riddance.

"When will Grogne get back?" I say. "This hangover is killing me."

"The market's a good bit away," Olur says. "He'll be gone for a while longer. You can live a few ticks without some drink, can't ya, Arthur?"

"I have lived a few ticks. It's been who-knows-how long since we ran out of that gutter brew Rinly concocted."

"Hey, don't knock Rinly's craft. Stop with all the bellyachin'."

Olur's right and the fact that he's right makes me even angrier.

"I know. I'm irritable! I know! I've been stuck in a broom closet that stinks like feet and sweat, and the radio doesn't work half the time, and we can't even get the blasted paper here, and I had to get my head shaved clean to 'not stick out so much,' and Gren hasn't even called yet, so who knows if he's even still alive anymo—"

The final words catch in my throat.

"Who even knows if he's alive anymore?" I say, falling back into the sagging couch cushions.

Olur's face looks confused. By now, he'd shut me down for comparing my "rich boy" airs to the apartment he's worked hard to get, but bringing up Gren seems to have struck a chord in him too.

"Gren's fine. You know it. I know it. That fool could get himself stuck underneath a burnin' buildin' and find a way out. Just bide your time and wait. It's all you can do."

"But if I do that then I'm stuck with myself. And I'm finding it's something I could do without."

"No choice, though, is there?" Olur says. He looks at me with upturned eyebrows, like the face of a schoolteacher who's got his student logically cornered.

A droll moan is my response.

"That's what I thought," Olur says.

Olur gets up and starts to tinker with the beat-up radio once more. Snippets of different music stations come in and out. Dissonant rhythms and instruments combine together and make some odd new type of sound. They're followed by a bit from a news broadcast.

"…Reactions… fuel… a decision in the Statehouse today," a dulcet female voice begins.

Olur goes to turn the dial once again, but I motion for him to hold for a moment.

"Business-Market… A proposal long hated by many… Seen as…" she continues, interrupted by waves of static.

Olur gives the radio another hearty bang, and the station comes in crystal clear.

"Many upstart movements have taken to the streets in light of the proposal passing through the Statehouse earlier this morning," the newswoman says. "Many reporters with connections to said movements say that protests will likely last until the non-workdays. Our City-Officer will be giving a speech on the current state of affairs in a few days. Now a report of the weather."

Well then. That thing that's sparked dozens of violent protests has been brazenly passed anyway—some more model leadership from our elected officials.

"What's all that mean?" Olur asks.

"That more people will be angry. And even more will be arrested or killed."

"Another day in the Legacian, right?"

The return of static in the radio causes me to sink back into the couch and want to thumb out my eyes. This complete lack of anything in my day-to-day fuels a new insight. I never knew how much I thrive on chaos and action in my life. As much as I was afraid and petrified when I was on-the-job, I was also exuberant. It's as if I was hoping both for and against a violent climax. Would that be sadism? Evil? Simply the body's reaction to constant threats? Oh, if only I had a miniature psychoanalyst in my breast pocket to tell me what my mind is doing.

"Hmph," I mumble, "maybe the men underground have an artifact for that."

"An artifact for what?" Olur says.

"Nothing."

The sound of a door being swung on its hinges comes from further back in the apartment, followed by Rinly storming into the room.

"Fellas, fellas," he says, with a small keg under his arm, "have I got the day for you. I went to the market and was able to land us some of this." He motions to the keg under his arm. "Thanks to Arthur's goodwill. Got a few nasty looks for it, but no one dared to come at ol' Rinly and Grogne."

"Great," I say. "Olur, do you have a tap we can use anywhere in here?"

"Wait, wait, I'm not finished," Rinly says. "And just as I was comin' into the tenement, Mrs. Durz was at the phone and asked if I knew who A. was and that someone who simply went as G. said that A. was staying in a room on the fourth floor."

Gren!

"He called just now?" I ask, rising from my seat.

"And I was thinking," Rinly goes on, "'A? That's kinda vague, but it's gotta stand for Arthur. Then that only means that G. stands for—"

"Rinly," I say louder. "Focus. Is he still on the phone now?"

"Oh, yeah, stayin' on the line. I said I'd get you down there in a jiffy."

I start to run out of the apartment, but a pulsing migraine stops me only to walk as fast as I can. I catch Grogne on the flight down.

"Hey Arthur, Gren's waitin' for you on the phone."

"Yes, I know Grogne. Thank you."

Once I'm on the ground floor, I find the phone's receiver resting face down on the table. I scoop both the receiver and transmitter up in one movement.

"Hello?" I say.

"Fe—" Gren begins. "F? Is that you?"

"Yes, it is my friend. How are you?"

"I'm fine, fine. I'm sure you've been worried sick about me. Don't worry. I haven't made any fuss."

"Me? Worried about you? Don't be ridiculous."

"Uh huh, sure pal."

"So, how are things? Any developments? Please tell me I get to leave here."

"Maybe. A start to you bein' able to leave. And before you ask: No. As— I mean A. A2. and B. haven't said anythin'. I've been doin' the same amount of work. Haven't asked any questions. But we've got somethin' you could be brought in on. Maybe get enough money to skip town. A2 has me poolin' together with them types you were rollin' with. The NCLB or whatever. We're hittin' a truck that has some sort of government bond or somethin', headin' for the docks. I was thinkin', you come in and help me deal with the truck and the NCL whatevers, and that should be enough for you to get a ticket out of this dump. Void, maybe even whatever you have already is close to enough to get a you-know-what passport and a ride outta here."

"I was robbed of all that, Gren. An orc with a shotgun took most of my silvum."

"Oh. Bastard. You get his name?"

"No."

"Ah. Well, such goes in the Yard. Anyway, meet me at our old dive in the docks, and we'll figure out a plan, yeah?"

"Yeah."

"Alright. I'll be there after the mideve bell."

"Sounds good. I'll see you then."

I hang up the phone and set it down. Finally, something that feels like hope. I can't help but smile. I even have a keg of something that may be drinkable waiting for me upstairs. This might start to become more of a vacation than I thought.

CHAPTER 33

No matter how many times I rub my bare scalp, it still feels alien. I doubt it will do much to keep Astraea and company from finding me, but when a three-hundred-pound orc tells you to sit down and get your hair cut, there's not much room for argument.

"Turn right up here, sir?" the cab driver asks.

"Yes, right here's fine. Thank you."

His carriage stops on the street corner, and I get out and pay him. The revolver still feels loose tucked into the back of my pants, and I resituate it as subtly as I can.

Ah, the docks. A place I was burrowed in only a few short seasons ago. The smell of burning fuel and seawater gives me nostalgic pangs. To think I was probably happier back then, too, although a little more bored. My little rebellions were toward simpler things. Staying out past curfew, deliberate negligence toward my studies, bringing along a half-orc when it wasn't in proper etiquette. Events that were as far from life-threatening as possible. I had a better idea of who I was, too. Another aristocrat that begrudgingly enjoys himself. Nowadays, I'm not sure exactly what I am or if I even care.

The bar Gren suggested is a short walk away, and once I get inside, I continue the healthy buzz I have going and order a drink. The barkeep pours from the wooden tap in short order.

"Thank you. By the way, has a certain half-orc been around yet? Baldhead with tusks that are smaller than usual?"

"I have no idea, buddy. You just described most of the dock-workers that come around here."

I nod and take a sip from my drink before looking around the room. Mainshift isn't over yet, so there aren't many folk in the room. Plenty of half-orcs to be seen, but no Gren. It's completely unlike him to wait so long for us to meet up. He could be still working, maintaining his cover, and waiting for an opening to skulk away. Even though he's the worst skulker I know, maybe so much is going on that his schemes are being overlooked. Hopefully, Astraea thinks too little of him to suspect such a thing. Elfbloods' opinions of half-orcs tend to run about the same as with full-blooded ones.

No. No, I'm lying to myself. There's no way he isn't suspected. Tonight is wrong. I need to find out where he is.

"Do you have a telephone?" I ask a little too loudly.

"There's a booth outside, a few doors down," the barkeep says back.

I check my watch while making my way to the door. I am late. Something doesn't feel right. Dread and paranoia have set in in equal measure. It could be all that time spent in hiding, making me jump at shadows and worries. But that has to be a good thing. Paranoia is the most sensible worry for a hunted man to have.

The sooner I set my eyes on him, the better. I slide into the glass booth and put some coins into the box.

"Operator, get me Ophidia, 35-113-39."

"Please hold," she says.

The line clicks and clicks. An old woman at the nearby inter-section starts to cross the street. She leans on a brass walker with wheels that squeak so loudly, even I can hear them past the closed booth. The line keeps clicking. She finishes her measurely walk and steps back up on the sidewalk. One of the wheels hitch and catch on the edge of the sidewalk. "Oh, bother," she's probably mouthing to herself. The line isn't done clicking. Why do telephone lines have to *click*? Just stay silent until it's connected, for Keeper's sake.

"Come on, come on," I whisper.

The old lady is still stuck at the edge of the sidewalk. She turns her head up and looks around her, head slowly turning before spotting me in the phone booth. She raises a hand to wave at me.

"Excuse me," she calls out, "I appear to be stuck, young man. Would you mind?"

I slam the sliding door open. The filthy line *still* isn't done clicking.

"Not now," I shout.

"I'm sorry, sir," the operator says. "But the recipient isn't picking up th—"

I slam the receiver back into its slot. Not tonight, not tonight. Please not tonight.

Off in the distance, a block away and to the left, a large half-orc exits an alleyway and starts to walk in this direction. I recognize the silhouette immediately. At least I think I do. The familiarity releases the pit that was building in my stomach. And then tires screech from a car rounding the street corner behind him. He turns and sees it before spinning and sprinting back into the alley from where he came.

I leap out of the telephone booth, pulling out my revolver in the process. It will *not* end like this. No way in the void will it end like this.

The half-orc gets to the entrance of the alley and makes it three steps before the car screeches to a stop. The windows roll down on the side facing the alleyway.

"You knew this was coming, Gren," a voice in the backseat shouts.

Gren's voice echoes something back at them. A shout of anger and defiance.

A barrage of machine-gun fire erupts from the side facing him. I sprint to get closer but am still thirty steps away. I stop and lean against a parked vehicle, bracing my shooting arm and aiming at the driver's seat. They unleash a few more volleys, and the car starts to peel away. The time is now. I take the shot. The trigger stops, and the hammer jams.

"No!" I shout. "You void-blasted thing! Not now!"

But it's already too late. In the same time it takes for a deep breath, the car tore back down the street, disappearing completely. With my heart in my stomach, I sprint across the street and stop at the alleyway opening. A body leans up against a mess of trash cans, face down in the garbage.

It can't be him, right? It's just another half-orc that got into this gang business.

I try to open my mouth, but I can't do it. I can't say his name.

The body doesn't move. As its muscles release, it sags deeper into the refuse bags. I don't want to get closer to it. My legs may as well be fixed in cement.

If I stay right like this, then I'm still where I was earlier today, talking to him on the phone. Still in a more naive time. The two of us came so far, robbing a dock and two guards to all this. So far, that we thought nothing could stop us. We were going to be heroes, weren't we, Gren? The gallant rogues that radio stations and playwrights can't stop writing about. Finally surmounting our greatest quest, vanquishing our evil employer. After killing her off and doing away with her, what, were we going to just ride off into the sunset? Keeper, Fey, you blasted *idiot*.

I doubt you even cared about such idiotic notions, Gren. You just wanted me to be safe, didn't you? You were doing so well at keeping your head above water, in the cruel and violent game your kind must play, until I came along. Your *stupid* damsel in distress.

The body's wearing his favorite tweed suit. The head's bald. These damnable facts. The things I can't change. I could tear the sky down and rain fire upon the entirety of civilization, and these things would stay the same.

My legs give out, and I fall to all fours. The world spins more and more, faster and faster, until I vomit. After that come tears. He's gone. He finally got in over his head, and now he's left. You bastard. You miserable, stupid bastard. All the ideas and brawn in the world and death tears you away just the same.

Finally, come the moans and cries of a wounded animal that I think are coming from me. I crawl up into a ball, unable to even get back up. This could be my new eternity. Sitting and spinning in this landscape of loss.

I grab the breast part of my coat to dry my tears before burying my face into it to scream some more. Something inside the pocket presses into my cheek. It's circular, some kind of coin. I stop for a moment and pull it out.

Oh yes, the trinket from that frontier witch. My ticket to salvation. Did she even say how to use it? What, do I rub it between my fingers and say some chant? The metal feels soft, bending, and almost giving with even the slightest pressure. Some woman's profile is on one side of the coin, eroded down to its basest features. Some inscrutable runes are on the other side. How ridiculous. How ridiculous!

"What utter and disgusting nonsense," I shout, throwing the coin at the wall.

It clinks against the brick wall, the light catching the pieces as it chips off from the impact. A puff of sparkling smoke hangs from where it hit the wall. I stand back up and wait, praying and hoping, and lo and behold, nothing happens.

"I really appreciate it, my magical friends," I call out in the air. "Your arcane wonders know no bounds!"

I fall to the ground and sit looking at the corpse, bereft of anything to do. Oh please, Gren, please come back. I want it to happen so bad that I'm starting to imagine him twitching back to life. He could come back and say he was just faking it so that they'd think he was dead. Then he twitches again. Oh, Keeper, don't let me be imagining this.

The body twitches once more and starts to wheeze. The wheeze turns into a cough, filled with phlegm. Just moving his muscles seems to be taking all the energy he has.

"Gren," I shout, rushing to his side. "Gren, Gren, come back to me! You're not out of this yet, you bastard."

"Mmmn aaa," Gren moans, eyes barely opening. Blood oozes out of several wounds on his chest, caking his entire shirt and tie in it.

The pact long forgotten is finally seeking fulfillment, some withering voice in my head says. Wait, it sounds familiar. The underground place, that's right!

"Wait, is this about the coin? Who's talking to me? What's happening?"

The pact of Rivenfell demands fulfillment. What do you require, executor?

Unholy void, that old witch was right.

"My friend Gren, I require him to live. Keep him alive now. I demand it!"

A breeze starts to pick up with rapid gusto, whooshing down the alleyway. The tangy taste of iron forms in the back of my throat. Then the shadows start to grow in darkness until it's impossible to see four steps away from me. Keeper above, what have I done?

Step away from the half-orc.

My body heeds the command before I can even think about it. Gren's coughing, aching form gets enveloped in the darkness.

"No, no, I take it back," I shout. "Leave him alone!"

Have no fear. His soul will stay on this plane...

My body refuses to heed my command, and I stay still until the darkness and wind fade away. Gren has disappeared, and I can't help but feel like I've made a morbid mistake.

After a few moments, the aftershock of the night starts to set in. My hands start shaking, I want to vomit again, and my brain isn't sure what to feel. Besides something hot. Something full of hate. Whoever did this will die, and I know who did it.

I stumble out of the alley and reach for my flask that I've forgotten I've gotten rid of for the fiftieth time. My shoe crinkles against a bit of paper on the ground. I stoop and pick it up. A fresh bit of paper has rough Highrock lettering written on it.

Come and find me, boy.

CHAPTER 34

There's the engraving of the Delirious Dogs tavern. A dog's head gulping down a dwarven beer stein. It still sits beside the shortened door that I passed through just a season back and so long ago. Bjorni's second home, a den of snakes, as well as a pub.

Drawing the revolver from the back of my pants, I flip out the cylinder and try the hammer again to see if it's still jammed. As soon as it doesn't move, I pull on it as hard as I can before it finally gives way and some flecks of rust flutter out. The hammer then swings and stops with a resounding click once the trigger's pulled.

"Alright, you bastard. Here I am. May the trap be sprung."

I tuck the revolver back into my pants but keep my hand on it as I duck down a little and open the bar door. I crack it open a little at first, glimpsing around to see if I can see that bald tattooed scalp. All there is instead are eyefuls of long hair and beards caked in ale. The uncertainty makes my heart race faster, and I pull back the hammer on the revolver and push the door open fully.

When an unseen gun doesn't fire and kill me, I take a few short breaths and try to calm down.

"Hva Gaehelim," the barkeep says with an upward lilt, her hands polishing the metal tap on a keg.

She turns and looks at me fully.

"Oh, I remember you. You're the long-legs that came with Bjorni. How is he these days?"

Her ignorance seems genuine. So, he hasn't come through here then.

"He's rather busy."

"I'm sure he is. What can I do for ya?"

"I'm actually looking for him too. I don't suppose you know where I can find him."

"Are you going to stay standing in the doorway, dear?" she asks.

I close the door and take one more step into the bar, my head still brushing against the roof.

"And take your hand away from whatever it's holding onto, please."0

"Oh. It's—. It's nothing, I assure you."

"If it's nothing, then you'll have no issue having your hands where I can see them."

Void, the she-dwarf's got me. I take my hand off of the revolver and leave it cocked and tucked into my pants. I get near her on the other side of the bar counter and lean on it, getting close enough to whisper.

"I'm in a hurry myself, you see, and really need to know where he is. Do you have any idea?"

She takes a long look at me and puts down the rag she was polishing with.

"What did he do, long-legs?"

"I can't say that. I just need to find him."

The silence and lack of an answer add to my profound frustration.

"You know, there's a word for what you're about to do, in Highrock. It's Vaegolun. 'Blood Quest.'"

"Keeper above, I don't care. Do you know where to find him? Yes or no?"

"That depends. Does he know you're coming?"

This conversation is too blunt yet friendly to make sense. Does she plan on phoning him once I leave? Is she actually aware of what's happening? Did he tell her what to say?

"What difference does that make?"

"A great deal. If not, who knows where he is. If so, he's probably at a Temple to the Unforgotten, maybe the one a few blocks away."

Of course! It's so obvious. What more melodramatic of a place for a showdown than some stupid temple?

"I see. Thank you for your candor."

As I turn for the door, she reaches out and grabs my forearm.

"A word of advice, though. If you go through with it, don't let the guilt kill ya. Take it from a veteran."

"There's no guilt involved. None whatsoever."

"Heh, right. If you say so."

She lets go, and I rush out the door, asking some nearby dwarf for directions and going as fast as I can toward the temple without breaking into a sprint. Once I pass deeper into the district, typical brick-laid buildings are replaced with stone-cut citadels. Frequently I'm bumping into the little folk as they're perpetually in no rush whatsoever. What a *boon* it must be to live so long. Centuries more than us stupid humans, eh?

Rough-hewn faces of male and female dwarves affixed to the tops of walls look down on me with a silent glare as I pass underneath them. It's impossible not to get a sense of judgment from their chiseled eyes.

"Ah, to the void with you," I say to them. "What do you know?"

What am I doing, talking to statues? This paranoia is gnawing away at my mind.

Soon enough, the wide and tall double doors of the temple emerge in front of me. It's twice as long as the smithy and grocers' buildings next to it. Six thick, slate gray columns hold up the outstretched roof and facade. The facade has the words *Temple of the Unforgotten, Lost to the Great Undeath but Always Remembered* written in a thick and crude font. Smaller scripts in Highrock surround them. Aside from the doors, not a plank of wood is in sight. The columns have a similar esthetic to them. Dwarven script and little archaic renderings of small folk. All one grand love affair to times gone by. Times that will never come back. As much as Bjorni and his kind wish for them to.

I push on the heavy doors, and they give a little. Unlocked. I draw my revolver and lean onto the left door until it's open enough for me to slip in.

The inner halls and sanctum of the temple are thick with shadows. Archaic sconces lining the walls hold lit torches, and the light they give is dim and orange. The hall is short and has an opening at the other end of it. Past the opening is the sanctum, with more pillars and pews and an altar at the opposite side of the room. The pillars are covered in deep etchings, telling the fabled tale of the short-folk and a great many clan's martyrdom against the Great Undeath. Entire generations and clans were lost to that undead-raising evil, and for a moment, the artistry of the etchings distracts me. Then I turn to the great altar, where a statue of a faceless dwarf clad in armor holds an axe in its hands and looks downward. Downward at a small, bald dwarf. Once I'm ten steps away, I pull back the hammer on the revolver, and the mechanical click causes him to turn his head.

"Is that you, Bjorni?" I shout.

"Sure is, boy."

"Are you alone?"

"Of course. You?"

"Yes."

"Good. This wouldn't end right otherwise."

The pounding of my heart fills my ears. He turns around to face me, with his hands raised up beside his head.

"You see that over there?" he asks.

He nods his head somewhere off and behind me.

"I'm not looking. You're just going to draw and kill me."

"Just look, will you?"

I tighten the grip on my revolver and steal a glance back where he indicated. All I catch is a small wooden box with a green glow. It's all I need. I recognize it instantly.

"The box we got from the frontier," I say.

"Promise me that when this is over, you throw that into the expanse and never look back."

"What?"

"Promise me!"

"Alright, alright. I promise, Bjorni."

"Good. You look terrible. Your hair gone like that."

I nod in agreement. He looks around the temple, eyes landing on different sagas engraved into the stonework.

"About time to join my lost brothers and sisters."

"What're you talking about?"

"Where we are," he swings his arms, motioning to the Temple. "What this will be. I'm tired, Fey. I've had enough. I've seen enough. This is to seal my fate."

"'Seal your fate?' What are you saying?"

Bjorni looks into my eyes and sighs in that tired knowing way I've come to know. With his right hand, he unlatches the catch of his holster, freeing up his hand cannon.

"Fey, I say this only once: If you don't shoot me before I draw, you're a corpse."

As my hands start to shake, the anger returns. How *dare* he stay so calm at a time like this.

"Come on now," he shouts. "Don't make m—"

I shoot once. Then once again. Both landing in his chest. He stumbles back and drops to one knee. When I realize what I've done, I drop the revolver.

"Don't get to flinch away from this one, do ya boy?"

He wheezes and enters a series of soaking-wet coughs before spitting out bloody phlegm. I hit one of his lungs.

He dips two of his left fingers into his own blood and dots it along his cheekbones, humming some sort of hymn. By now, all righteous fury has flown from my body, replaced by pitiful and incomprehensible remorse.

"Did you do it, Bjorni? Did you shoot Gren?"

"What difference does it make?"

He continues his humming. Sometimes he stops humming and says the words out loud. Words like "Ghaelimna" or "Healonin." I never got to ask him what that greeting meant.

"Bjorni," I say, starting to sniffle. "Bjorni, I'm sorry."

He continues to hum.

"I said I'm sorry."

"Don't interrupt me!"

The humming continues for a few moments more before stopping completely. He makes a few more hand motions and coughs up more blood.

"Is that it then?"

"Not quite. One more thing. Come over here."

"What?"

"Come here! Now!"

Even in his final moments, I'm compelled to obey. An unruly child before his master.

"Got one final gift for you. You'll need it more than I do."

I look back at the revolver. Void, he had one last trick after all.

"I'm not gonna hurt you, boy," he mutters. "Least not too much. Hold out your hand."

I hesitate for a moment before complying, reaching out my left hand.

He reaches back behind himself and draws his axe. He whispers some more Dwarven and then grips the axe head. After steadying his hand as much as he can, he slices the inside of my palm open.

"Ow," I cry out.

I try to pull my hand back, but he has it in an iron grip.

"Don't move. Just trust me, boy."

His humming and whispering slowly and surely rise in tempo. He closes his eyes and grips my hand tightly. Then he forces my cut palm onto one of his gunshot wounds. As soon as our blood makes contact, his body convulses in response. He grunts and continues. The tattoos on his head begin to glow a dull amber color.

"Bjorni. What's going on? What are you doing?"

The tattoos glow brighter and brighter before they fill the entire antechamber with that sickly amber. Once they can't get any brighter, and I have trouble even looking at them, I can swear they're moving. Moving down the side of his scalp, then his neck, before disappearing beneath his shirt. Amber light spills through the threading and holes in his vest.

"No. There's no way."

A moment later, a searing pain shoots up my arm. I can't help but scream in response. My arm is frozen in place, rendered immutable by his void-cursed spell.

"Let go. Let go!"

For an instant, the pain spreads throughout my entire body. Every nerve being personally set on fire with a match. Then the pain retreats, pulsing further and further back down my arm before staying on my forearm, just above my elbow.

Just as soon as the room was blindingly bright, it all blinks back into darkness. Bjorni's chanting stops, and he falls to one knee, letting go of my arm.

"What in the cursedness of the void was all *that*, Bjorni?"

"A gift. Like I told ya. It'll help if it needs to."

I jerk up my sleeve, and the tattoo that surrounded Bjorni's skull is snaking up my left arm. A serpent surrounded by runes, with its mouth open below my palm.

"Served me well, she did. Just as she did my father. Get it back to the Blackblood clan if you get the chance."

He wants to keep talking but is interrupted by another wet coughing spell. Once he hacks up more blood, he falls backward, sitting on the floor. His wheezing gets louder.

"If it means anything to you, you and that half-breed are the closest thing to kin I've had… in a long time."

How perfectly depressing.

"Say, what does that greeting of yours mean? 'Hva Ghealum,' or however it's said?"

"Hva Gaehelim," he corrects. "'Welcome back from the void.'"

Instead of a wisecrack, I start to sob a little too loudly.

He continues wheezing before moaning and falling forward into his own pool of blood. His whole body tenses, then completely relaxes. What can stoicism do in the face of such uncaring destruction? My whole world, one that was doomed to fail anyway, still collapses in such a hopeless fashion. My best friend stolen by warlocks. My evil bastard of a mentor branding me before being murdered by my own hand. Who can even care about such things anymore?

Once I realize I'm crumpled into a ball, I slowly rise, pick back up my revolver, and amble back to the exit. It's not worth thinking about. Not worth thinking about at all.

But before I leave, my promise to that decaying old dwarf returns to my mind. I turn and look at that wretched little box. Its sickly green glow emanates from the cracks in the wood, fading in and out like a heartbeat. Is such a vile little device the reason Bjorni's will to live gave out? Is that the source of my nightmare, back out in the frontier? What disastrous piece of the wild has Astraea tricked us into bringing back here to Ophidia?

I get a few steps closer to it and immediately feel a sense of dread. The glowing green brightens a little as well. At least I think it does. There's no way I'm carrying that despicable thing anywhere.

I look back at Bjorni, and that anger returns once more.

"So, forcing me to kill you isn't enough, is it? You entrust this… This *thing* to me too? One last test, is that what this is? You stupid, decomposing fool! Always pushing me toward these desperate, insane acts! Damn you, Keeper damn you and your legacy!"

As much as I hate him for doing this, the crate must be destroyed all the same. Before letting that sense of dread overtake me, I rush the box and bring my heel down upon it as hard as I can. It gives a little, and a sharp hissing sound seeps out. The greenness brightens and dulls more rapidly. I stomp again, and again, and again. With each strike, the box makes the sound of a dying wolfviper.

"Rot in the void, you and the monsters who made you," I scream.

Just then, a sharp wind knocks me from my feet. It bursts out from the box, and a shrill cry comes from it as well. The green illumination is almost blindingly bright. For a few moments, a primitive fear crawls up my spine. What have I done?

Finally, one more gust flows from the box, and the sound and brightness die as soon as they appear. The antechamber returns to its dim state.

For a time, I still don't know if what I did was the right thing or not. I don't think I'll ever know. But at least I did something, I suppose. I brush the dust from my pants and get back onto my feet, and take one last look at Bjorni.

I need to say something, anything.

I can't. I turn around and slowly walk back to the entrance.

I pass back out through the heavy doors, and the cool night air caresses my face. With him dead, I lose one more tether keeping me here, in this place.

The cool air rushes forth faster than I'd like, and then a hemp bag is forced over my head. Two more sets of hands subdue me and force me along as if I'm even going to put up a fight. Then I'm shoved into the back of some vehicle, and off it putters to what I can only assume to be my execution.

CHAPTER 35

W e speed and turn along crinkling streets, and rain patters slowly against the roof. I'm unable to tell how many people are back here in the car with me. Kidnapping in the dead of night has granted them that advantage. The bag on my head is impossible to see out of. I can barely infer shapes from the dim lighting of the streetlights. No one says anything. They just adjust their suits or rustle for their pack of pipes. Something deep inside tells me to be scared. Be terrified of my final moments. But that same part of me knew this was coming. This was always coming, as naive as I wanted to be. Bizarrely enough, I'm able to sleep for a moment or two before an abrupt stop wakes me back up.

At one point, the driver's window rolls down, and he says something to someone on the street. The man on the outside says to "Go on through." We're either going into some private compound, or we're going into Founder's Square.

So, this isn't Astraea finally sending to finish me off. She wouldn't bother with bringing me in, anyway. I think. She also would've stopped whatever Bjorni tricked me into doing. This must mean the Security Affairs suits have finally found me. I suppose it's obvious, but it still registers as genuine insight. Knowing how people they catch disappear, there's no real difference between them and Astraea. No difference besides timing.

The car slows and drives more respectfully of its surroundings, taking turns without any lurching or squealing tires. Eventually, it reaches another stop, and some grand mechanical gate shudders along its track. The sound isn't grating or whiny, implying regular maintenance. A manor then, more than likely. I can't help but scoff at myself. As if analyzing all these minutiae will change anything.

"No noise, you," one of the men says.

I clear my throat in protest, and a hand slaps me across the face. Bastards.

The car goes along into some sort of driveway before stopping completely. The men open the doors and file out, and two pairs of hands grip me and shove me out onto the lawn.

"Get up," one of them barks.

"My hands are tied, officer," I say.

Another kicks me in the ribs with such force that I'm lifted off of the ground for a brief moment. I try to breathe but can't. My diaphragm won't move, making me gasp like a dying fish. Some of the rain is starting to soak through the bag over my head.

"What was that?" the first man says. "Care to repeat it?"

I try to say some sort of curse but can only continue gasping. I can't breathe. The bastards hit me once, and I can't breathe.

"Enough toying," a third man says. "He's waiting."

They yank me onto my knees and cup their hands under my armpits, lifting me up with no trouble at all, dragging me along to wherever their grand overseer deigned to have me. A large door is opened, and I'm taken out from the drizzling rain into some sort of mansion. Every footstep echoes down the corridors. Reminds me of the grander estates you and mother would take me to. This must be terrible for you, your son getting tortured while you only sit back and do nothing. Void, I'm imagining you alive again. So weak, Fey.

"Stop dragging him, for Keeper's sake," a man says. "Let him walk."

The two vice-like grips under my armpits let go of me, and I fall to the floor. I get up as quickly as I can before they can harass me more.

We go down a set of stairs and then down another set of stairs. The further down we go, the hotter it gets. It's a weird heat, not too humid and not too dry. Like a well-maintained radiator.

Eventually, a door opens, and I'm led into a room that's almost boiling hot. A nearby furnace must be on at full blast. I can already feel sweat forming on my forehead as soon as I'm shoved inside.

"That is enough," a man says, somewhere nearby and in front of us. His voice is strained and hoarse but somehow strident. Like a far-off foghorn. "Remove his hood, and unbind him."

Someone cuts the rope bound around my wrists, grips the bag, and tears it off. The sight of a dark atelier appears around me. The room is large, with the ceiling barely visible beyond the dim. Half of the room is up on a stone stage, with three wide steps leading up to it. On the stage sits a small hooded lamp beside an easel. The easel holds a canvas with the painting of some landscape half-finished. The lamp barely lights the tall man standing in front of it. He's almost twice my height. In front of the easel is a mirror. Or at least what looks like a mirror. It doesn't reflect the dim atelier, though. It shows some patch of moonlit forest, acting like a window into the frontier. He's setting down a paintbrush, still looking at the mirror. Lightning within strikes above the treeline, lighting his haunting frame. No thunder follows the flash.

The more I look at him, the more it doesn't feel right to call him a man. His ears are longer, and his hair is long and silver, more like silk than hair. He looks like an elfblood, but not quite that either. Their ears aren't that long, and their hair isn't silver.

He turns his head back to look at me. As soon as our eyes meet, I buckle a little and look away. His being emanates something truly intimidating. Like he's some sort of alien deity that manifests authority merely by existing. It reminds me of my first meeting with Astraea. She made me feel small and insignificant too, but not like this. It's as if I'm a speck of dust before a giant. My fear is kept in check by the fact that they never frisked me, and my revolver stays tucked in the back of my pants.

"Before me lies the little worker ant," he says, "that has done so much in such a short amount of time."

Keeper above, this isn't a man or elfblood. It's an elf. The kind that's been dead longer than this country's existed.

"What's an ant?" I ask.

I'm the only person I know that's seen a living elf.

"Ah, I forgot. They must not teach your kind about such things. Too much time has passed. An ant is a good little insect, from a better place and a simpler time."

He takes a few steps away from the easel toward me, and I get a better look at his face. At least as much as I can see in the glimpse I take. The creases and wrinkles on his face are limitless. The skin is still soft and supple, but time has still done its part in ravaging him. As soon as our eyes meet again, I look back at the floor.

The door I was brought through opens again, and a short man in a black suit enters. He crosses the room to the elf in short order and whispers something to him. The suited man takes a disdainful look at me and goes to leave once more.

"Ahh, excellent news," the elf says. "The Tal'harren has been recovered, and its seal has been weakened. This will make my efforts take place even more expeditiously. Was that your doing?"

"What are you saying?"

"The Tal'harren, the spatial ingress, the miniaturized portal, whichever term you like. Someone damaged its framework and made it more volatile. For your sake, I will assign the credit to you. You have my thanks."

He turns his back to me and cups his hands behind his back, facing the easel once more.

"Now tell me, little ant, what name does the traitor go by now? The elfblood woman that employs you?"

I keep my gaze focused on the ground.

"Who would that be?"

"The Betrayer!" he shouts. "What name does she give you?"

I wince when he shouts. What sort of evil spell is he compelling upon me?

He turns his head back toward me. He could sense the flinch.

"Do I frighten you? Has your kind learned to fear me and my feral brethren, out and about in the shifting forests?"

"Most do, sure."

"But you are above such things. Yes?"

"I'd hope so."

"You act as if you are above superstition, yet you still look at the floor. That is unfortunate. You are as contradictory as the rest of them."

He turns back around, gazing down at me past his nose.

"Look at me," he commands. "Eyes upward, now!"

With great effort, I pull my eyes up to look at his ancient face.

"Answer my question. What name does she currently go by?"

This must be it. The one last tidbit of information they need before they can dispose of me.

"I won't ask again, ant."

All those times Gren talked about snitches floods my mind. Is that what I am now? Some failure of a criminal that has no choice but to flip and spill his secrets? Or is this how it always ends? Is "snitch" the final title for people in the business who want to get out alive?

I'd tear out my hair if any of it was still left.

"Astraea," I finally blurt out. "She goes by Astraea now, at least to me."

His gaze lingers on me for a few more moments, but mine returns to the safety of the darkened tiles on the floor.

"Very well. A quaint title. She must be proud of that cute little reference."

He snaps his fingers, and sound instantly emanates from the mirror. Distant thunder and rain hitting changing leaves.

"So peaceful, the frontier. One day, we shall control it."

He turns back toward the mirror, gazing into it.

"I must say that you are not what I expected. When I envisioned the agent responsible for the grand affair that is about to occur, the man using or used by destiny. I expected you to be... taller or broader. Something more grandiose."

I want to speak out-of-turn so badly, to say "I'm sorry to be such a disappointment," but some pre-rational terror holds me back. When I look at the tall freakish thing before me, I just want to turn around and run. And beneath the fear is something else: resentment.

He turns back around, and his stare feels like the one of a disappointed parent.

"Only a child, and yet you have changed so much. Or perhaps, only enabled others to do so. All will be clear in due time."

He picks back up his paintbrush and continues painting the scene in the mirror.

Then something starts to bud within me. That nascent curiosity, always wanting answers.

"So, are you the, uh... The puppet master, then? Orchestrating all this?"

"All of what?"

"Nothing, never mind."

"Finish your thought, ant. You'll never get to again after this."

"Are you the one behind all this? Behind all of the things I had to do for her?"

"Hmm. In a way, I suppose I am. All of these little plans of hers are to try and stop me. She thinks since she's the first to buck against our vision, the first to leave our family behind, that she can undo *centuries* of progress. But none of her plotting matters. We have you to thank for that."

"What?"

"We've been watching you since you returned from the frontier. Us and Security Affairs. Once we heard of the death of two different beastkin clans near Fallund. Dead from starvation of all things, we became curious. Then we learned of that little box you stumbled upon. Our magisters sensed it immediately."

He turns his head again to look at me.

"You have no idea what that little box is, do you?"

"Should I?"

"With your family background, I assumed so. Your father failed to pass some things down to you, it seems."

How *dare* he invoke your memory. If I wasn't such a coward, I'd command him to leave you out of this.

"No matter." He turns his head back to the easel. "You shall see soon, just what machinations you've helped set in motion. It's the reason you get to live, you see. You're as pivotal to history as Vizegard was to Sigesar during the expansion of our civilization. But while Sigesar gave us an empire, I shall give us the world."

The way he says such things, so flippantly, is so confusing. Like all of this is assured, and no passion is required.

"Do you know how old I was when we fled from the World Before?"

The more this thing condescendingly speaks, the more my resentment grows. He talks too much to be some mysterious malefactor.

"A young child, perhaps a few years old."

"Very close. I still remember the terror. The overwhelming terror of seeing death itself destroy everything. People jumped off the ships in droves, their little minds too full of horror to think of anything else. The worst part is it could have all been avoided."

Impossible, at least going from the scribe's accounts. The Great Undeath was a sorcerer that reincarnated every time he was killed and could raise fields of corpses with a wave of his staff.

"How?"

"If the Baranian Empire came to the aid of the Eastern Fiefdoms when they were summoned. If the orc warbands were unleashed instead of imprisoned. If the Dvargnen Clans came out of their Keeper-damned mountains for once in their miserable lives. It is a pattern as old as sentience, really. Those in power believe the terrible things will leave them alone. Overlook them. And by the time they realize it's coming, it is far too late. It was what happened in the World Before. It was what happened when the Mad King was betrayed by his daughter in Xeveria. It will happen a million more times after we're all dead and gone, I imagine. Your kind is blinded by just how important and few their choices really are."

The easel is starting to reflect the scene in the mirror with perfect precision. Centuries of practice will do that.

"Why did you stay then? If we're all so intolerable?"

"Oh, come now, you are not intolerable, just frustrating. I cannot speak for the other elves, but I stayed because covering myself in hides and living in the woods with beastkin sounds like a fate worse than death. Also, someone has to keep things in order."

He sets the brush back down.

"I'm not quite the villainous puppet master you imagined, am I, ant?"

"No, no, I guess not. You're too..."

Void, I've said too much.

"Too what?"

"Wispy, I guess."

He stops painting, and I fear that I've offended this ancient being. But then he just laughs.

"Wispy. That is novel."

He starts painting again. The anticipation and dread are eating me alive at this point.

"So, can we get on with this? Can you just kill me or let me go already?"

He stops admiring his painting and turns to me with a gaze as hard as stone.

"So impatient, aren't you, short-lived one? Is that what you wish? For me to murder you?"

In one question, the conversation turns from meandering to malignant.

"N-no, I just assumed that's how your organization operates. You talk to me for a while, give me a false sense of security. Then someone comes in and shoots me or stabs me or something."

"Firearms, blades," he says. "How barbaric. No, that is not your fate. This time is one of change. For me and, hopefully, for you. If we wanted you dead, you would be rotting beside your short friend in the Temple of the Unforgotten. This time we wish to try something new. Call it a whim if you like. We wish to leave a loose end fettering this time and see how the outcome plays out. Besides, you're not much of a threat anymore, are you?"

I have to bite my tongue to hide my indignation at those last few words. The absolute nerve of this old elf. This decadent thing thinks it can tell me if I'm not a threat? For the first time since coming into the room, I take a look around to see if there's anything to defend the elf. Any weapons, guards, arcane sigils. When nothing comes to my eye, I smile a bit to myself. If I can outdraw and kill Bjorni, then I doubt some decrepit, unarmed painter stands a chance.

"Tell me, elf, do you feel safe in this room? So deep inside your mansion?"

He smiles again and whispers a few quiet words. The heat of the room doubles in the space of a second, and chains shutter forth from invisible holes and wrap around me before pulling and drawing taut. They pull and pull downward until they drop me to my knees. The chains themselves are hot, too hot to make sense. I can feel parts of my skin burning. He takes his time walking the two steps of distance between us and gets down on one knee with no issues.

"Indeed, I would say I feel quite safe, human," he spits. "You thought I was negligent in leaving you armed? Like I could not smell the gunpowder from where I stood?"

He steps down the few steps of the atelier before he's a few paces away from me, his tall form looming over my head.

"Arrogance, oh arrogance, thy face appears on Arthur Fey. Do you want to know why I think you are harmless? Because the stench of utter, total defeat wafts from your skin. You would fail to uproot or conspire against your prison cellmate if your life depended on it. I have murdered and outmaneuvered usurpers, divine charlatans, people with *ambition*. The kind that have risen and toppled countries. Not some pathetic nobleman's son who failed even to get educated properly. Your worth is that of a parlor trick. Something novel to entertain myself with. Guards!"

The wide double doors fling open, and a pair of men in suits appear from the hallway.

"Get this worm out of Founder's Square."

The chains loosen and slither off of me, with holes burned into the sections of my suit where they were drawn the tightest. The two brawny men scoop me up under my armpits and start to drag me out of the atelier.

"Go ahead and tell people what you've seen tonight. The stink of alcohol will defy anything you say."

As the guards haul me away and the door closes, the elf shoots me one last condescending glare.

"Go forth and live with your choices, Arthur Fey," the elf calls out. "And their children!"

The guards get me halfway down the dark hallway before they put the bag back over my head. Once I'm back out in the rain, they rebind my hands behind my back, and a car motor comes back around in front of us, and I get shoved inside of the cabin.

The haze, the familiar haze, settles back in. The feeling that protects me from the unalienable facts. Gren is likely dead. Bjorni dead by my own hand. Elizabeth, a name as distant as the sunrise, is the last possible person I wish to see right now. And then, when it has no right to, this elf in the basement of some grand manor looks into the core of my soul and lays it bare before me. As if I needed such things dragged out into the light, where I'm forced to do nothing but think about it.

We cross back through some checkpoint and the car wheels to a stop. The men in the car rip the bag off of my head and shove me out on some street in the Snap before speeding off into the night. I take a few steps into a nearby alley, get underneath a fire-escape for some cover from the rain, and curl into a ball.

Oh, how utterly useless I have become.

CHAPTER 36

A pregnant tension hangs over the inside of the vehicle. It's possible to hear every shift of their bodies and brushing of their suit fabrics. Every single bump of the vehicle and creak of its axle. Someone pulls out a pack of pipes and lights it. I can even tell that he's offering it to his friends wordlessly, with the extra crinkles coming from the pack.

I'm filled with things I want to scream at these captors. All the things that I should do and try to get out of this. They retied my hands behind my back, but that's still workable. I could probably hatch some ingenious escape plan right about now. They didn't bother to fasten my seatbelt. I could headbutt a window and wriggle out, like a dressed-up worm. Kick over a few gentlemen as well. But to be honest, there's no real reason to. I'm a miserable mistake, and whatever happens next is incredibly deserved.

That elf probably wasn't even telling the truth in letting me live. They could be driving me to the docks right now. To chain me to anchors and drown me in the expanse. Maybe it could be something more mundane, something more fitting. Like what happened to Gren. An alleyway and twenty-six rounds to the chest. That was before I condemned him to an unnatural fate. Oh Gren, what in the unholy void did I do to you? What unspeakable acts are being done to keep you alive?

Finally, the car's brakes screech, bringing us all to a halt. The passenger door across from me opens, and whoever's next to it steps out of the vehicle. The few others are shifting, and tension gives birth to expectations. Expectations of death and its final, welcoming embrace. After a lifetime of failure, I may finally be free.

The door I'm next to opens, and someone pulls me out of the car, jerking me to my feet. While they're still behind me, they pull something out of leather. A knife, probably. I don't even get the luxury of a bullet, I guess.

"Now, hold still," he spits, squeezing my right forearm tight.

Once I show no signs of fighting back, he finally pierces the knife into the ropes tying my hands together and saws them free. After they fall onto the sidewalk, he shoves me to the ground.

I reach up and rip the bag from my face. The man climbs back into the car.

"Wait!" I scream, pushing myself up from my back. "That's it?"

The door slams shut, and the car starts to pull away. The men inside don't even look back at me as the vehicle rejoins the main avenue on the street and disappears back into the nighttime traffic.

That is it, then. No beatings. No "we're watching you." Just a shove to the pavement.

Strength leaves my arms, and I fall back onto the sidewalk.

This is it. This is complete defeat. The powers-that-be continue to politick and play their games, and their hundredth, thousandth, or millionth pawn is left behind like all the others. I am granted the gift of life, at least. I probably have that on all the others. But I failed to get to the bottom of things in time, all the same.

Sobriety is a fool's chore. I was stupid to take Cillian's words to heart. Four weeks of chasing it was a waste. I need a drink.

I climb back up onto my feet and slowly make my way off into the night. Somewhere along the passing avenues, a liquor store sign appears in front of me. Its neon letters blink on and off. I turn and pass into the store. It's a small establishment, with a young woman manning the till; a wall of bottles lie in wait behind her. She's looking down, reading some novel.

"Good evening, mister," she says, not looking up. "What can I get for you?"

"Whatever's strongest and cheapest, miss."

"You're going to have to be more specific."

She looks up at me, and her eyes flutter a bit in bewilderment. "Are you okay, sir?"

"No."

I get a little closer to the register and point at a random bottle on the bottom shelf.

"I'll take that one. Actually, make it two."

She is about to say something but stops and turns back to pick up the bottles and taps some keys on the register.

"That'll be fifteen silvum."

I reach into my coat pocket and pull out the silvum notes.

"Would you like me to bag these?"

I shake my head and take the bottles.

Returning outside, I immediately stick one of the bottles in my coat pockets and rip the cap from the other.

"Here's to you, the world of nightmares," I toast to Ophidia.

The bite of the spirits is lukewarm and welcome. I swallow and swallow until it burns too much to continue.

Looking around the street, I don't even have much of a clue where I am. Somewhere middle-class. The Cross or the nicer part of the Acre, perhaps. The apartments have large brown brickwork. The ground floor of the buildings has an array of shops, bars, and restaurants. It's all so wholesome and naive.

Soft winds of night air pass along as I find a welcome drinking spot. I lean against the wall and take another drink. Smells of smoked meat and car oil.

But I can't focus on it or enjoy the feeling of the night. Not with the thoughts of what has happened just looming behind me. Thoughts of a dead friend, a murdered man. How could I have murdered someone? He probably isn't even my only murder, for all I know. Thoughts of you and mother. How I keep hoping that talking to you will bring you both back. Keeper above, it's all too much.

Sometime before finishing the first bottle, the spins and a drunken oblivion start to set in. Welcome whispers of sweet release.

But then someone bumps into me and I almost fall over.

"Hey," the man cries out, with a hoarse voice. "Watch where you're going, will you?"

I turn over to see him and his friend. They already look like they were waiting for someone to talk to them the wrong way. Bullies that never grew out of being bullies.

"Maybe I will. Thanks for letting me know."

"What'd you say?" his friend asks. "You trying to be smart, kid?"

Their eyes widen at the notion.

"Not so much trying, as doing an alright job. Unlike some poor saps in front of me."

The one I affronted immediately shoves me to the ground.

"That right, boy? 'Cus, as far as I know, smart kids tend to not talk back and get their hides beaten!"

He swiftly kicks my chest with the bottom of his boot, knocking the wind out of me. I turn and ball up as hard as I can. They start to vent their frustrations and impotence into my back, kicking and kicking and kicking. Immediately, I'm afraid of it. The idea of getting beaten within an inch of my life. But soon enough, the pain and bruising feel good. Something far easier to focus on.

Eventually, they laugh and stop kicking.

"Had enough, you little baby?" the other man heckles.

I get up from the ground and wince from the sprained ribs.

"Why did you stop?"

The two stop and look at each other.

"What did you say?" the first man asks.

"Why did you stop?" I rise and shove one of them. "We're not done here!"

The shift in dynamic leaves them mystified. These idiots can't even beat a man properly.

"Whoa, whoa," the second man says. "What's wrong with you, kid?"

"Just," I say, fighting back tears, "Just beat the life out of me, will you? Can't you stupid bastards at least do that right?"

They start to back away from me.

"This is too much, Marvin," the first guy says. "Let's get out of here."

Once they leave, I fall back to my knees and finally give in to the tears.

Then I pick up and finish the first bottle.

Some time has passed. The sun has gone up and down a number of times. I've gotten something to eat once or twice, always returning to this alleyway, this fetid dumpster. It's starting to become a comfort. I don't even really mind the smell. So many things just don't matter anymore. My being is just rolling along the continuum of time, and whatever happens to me just doesn't confound me. When the cool night air sets a chill in my bones, I simply wrap my ruined coat closer to me and curl up into a ball. Some drunkards even walked up and tried to bully me out of some silvum, some time ago. But once they found me too limp to be entertaining, they walked away, staggering out into the night.

A bright gray hangs low from the clouds as the sun lies somewhere above in the afternoon. Part of me wants to take another trip to the spirits shop, but I'm already too buzzed and malaised to want to move.

"You've seen better days, haven't you?" an old female voice says to me.

I look up to see an aged woman, clad in mostly black, save a white headdress, a square atop her head with white fabric flowing from it. She's an abbess, a holy woman devoted to the Keeper.

I don't have any retort to say, so I return my gaze to the floor.

"How long have you been here, sir? Have you lost your voice? Or worse, have you lost your will to live?"

"Go away, please," I mutter, the first words I've said all day.

"No, I don't think I will. Not unless you've come with me. My Keeper's Study is just down the road. We'll get you cleaned up and fed."

She stoops down and offers her hand.

"Come now," she says, so softly it's almost crooning. "Please."

For a second, I feel a maternal wanting that wishes to be fulfilled by the abbess. But it's too fleeting to be felt entirely. I stumble up onto my feet, stomach awakened and burning from the lack of food. She puts her arm around mine and leads me to the nearby Study. Stolen glances from incredulous strangers come at us from all sides, but she is probably used to this sort of thing.

"Can you tell me your name?" she asks.

I can feel her stare on me. Like she wants me to look at her and give her something, but I'm not ready for that yet. Our dynamic feels like a reversion to childhood.

"Do you know where you are?" she says, slow and plodding like I've been struck dumb.

"Of course I do. Some street in the Snap. Stop treating me like a child."

"I'm sorry, dear. I'm just making sure you're cognizant. So many homeless like you don't really know what's going on around them."

"I—" I begin, wanting to correct her and say that I'm not homeless.

But that's just it. My home is nothing but ashes.

"What's that?" she says.

"Nothing."

We finally reach the Study. It's three times the size of the neighboring buildings around it. Old brickwork and a pair of large steeples are typical of the holy buildings' archaic architecture. Six narrow stained-glass windows sit above the entrance, holding iconography of the Keeper's religion. Opened books, a pair of eyes overseeing everything, and simplified human, dwarven, and elven forms marching beside each other in harmony. Orcs and half-breeds need not apply.

Something about this place rings a bell of familiarity in my mind, but I can't put my finger on it. Have I been here before?

The abbess leans on the large wooden door and guides me into the building. A packed, quiet library awaits inside. There are only a few people around milling between the cramped bookshelves and reading at the long tables in the middle of the room. The change in atmosphere makes me acutely aware of just how horrid I smell.

"Right this way," the abbess whispers.

She takes me past a pair of counters where librarians are writing down and tracking books being lent from the Study and through a set of doors leading into the sept proper. Pews stretch all the way back toward the chancel, where a cleric would give his sermon. I can't help but marvel at how large the building is. Another large stained-glass window rests on the wall above the chancel. A knight of old is depicted on it, holding a sword facing up toward a pair of eyes, always watching.

Passing through another door is a small courtyard behind the building, nestled tight between a pair of brick buildings. A smaller building is on the other side of the Study, and that's where both the abbesses and clerics live, as well as where they help the needy.

I've always heard stories and hoped I wouldn't wind up here. All throughout the years, so many jokes were made by your friends about becoming a Legaciary charity case. Now here I am. Hope you're proud, Caddock.

The first floor of the building is a large sort of barracks. Cots line the floors with chamber pots near each of them. Some cots have men and women moaning in pain, while others have people that can somehow sleep through all the noise.

"The baths are just through there," the abbess says to me, pointing to a nearby door. "Just strip down and have a wash, and we'll give you a clean pair of clothes."

"What happens to my old ones?"

"Well," she says, "I don't mean to offend, but do you really want to keep what you're wearing?"

I look down at my suit. My dress shirt and longcoat are filled with holes, and my pants are layered in dirt and other odd stains. There's also the gun bumping into my back. As tattered as I look to be, I still feel an attachment to these rags. Like they're the last remains of another time.

"Yes."

The wrinkles on her forehead crinkle as she lifts her eyebrows in worry.

"How about this: you can keep the coat and shoes, but we replace the rest. Is that fair?"

"Hmm," I cast another look down. "Alright. These terms are agreeable."

She laughs a little.

"I'm glad to do business with you. And what was your name, again?"

"Arthur."

The abbess goes to a nearby row of wooden cupboards and pulls out a folded shirt, pair of pants, and socks.

She returns to me and hands the clothes over. "Nice to meet you, Arthur. Now take a bath, please."

Nodding and taking the pair of clothes, I pass through the door and enter the bathroom. A tin tub is in the center of the small room, already filled with soapy water. A narrow shuttered window is set into a corner of the wall to the left, facing back out onto the courtyard. The water is warmer than I expected, and the soap cleans a layer of grit and dried sweat from my body almost as soon as I submerge in it. The thick smell of lye and dried flowers soaks into my wet hair and skin, and with the soaking comes a revitalizing feeling. The temperature forces my muscles to relax and slacken, and the soul follows behind them.

This small kindness, this bath, also brings a pain along behind it. Squalor and nothingness were starting to get comfortable. Losing everything isn't as horrid as everyone makes it out to be. I suppose I could go back to that fetid apartment in the Yard with Gren's pals. Carouse and drink with the derelicts that a man like me belongs with. Finally try that one orc's swill.

But then I'd have to tell them what happened to Gren and the horrible mistake I made to try and keep him alive. There are so many stories of the Arcane Society's "healing." Insanity, mutation, and so many other horrors accompany their medical failures. And I just handed over my best friend to them. *Keeper,* how could I do that to him?

It's enough to make a man sick of living.

A rough knocking pounds on the door.

"Hurry it up, please," a man's voice calls. "Others need to have a bath, as well."

"Alright."

Steam and droplets peel away from my skin when I get up from the moist haven. After drying off and putting on the scratchy new woolen garments, I return to the barracks room and see that abbess's smiling face.

"Did you enjoy yourself? We have warming pipes that stay underneath the tub."

"How extravagant. Yes, it was what I needed."

A moment passes. She's waiting for something, and I finally figure out what heinous thing she wants from me.

"Thank you," I finally force out.

"You're very welcome, dear. Now, tell me, when was the last time you've undergone your Observance?"

Void, I should have expected this. The holy types always have a way to rope someone into rituals like this.

"Quite some time, abbess."

"Well," she turns her hands outward in a semi-grand gesture, "No time like the present, as they say. Which hand do you turn the page with?"

I have to stop myself from scoffing. Answering which denomination of the Legaciary I belong to always feels like pulling teeth.

"I don't really practice it anymore if I'm being honest."

"What branch were you raised under?"

"Obstinates."

"Very good," she says. "We cater to both branches here. The Keeper doesn't discriminate, and neither do we."

The abbess opens her mouth as if to say something but decides against it and takes my hand instead, leading me back out to the courtyard.

"I really don't think it's a good notion for me to conduct Observance, abbess. It would be disrespectful to the Keeper."

"Nonsense."

"I don't remember how to do it, anyway. Doesn't it say in scripture that 'improper rituals make for divine resentments?'"

"That's a misquote."

"Enough of this," I say, pulling my hand away from her. "You can't just shove me along into a bath and think that I now have to perform your superstitious rites."

Part of me thinks that she'll recoil in shock from the remark, but she simply turns and keeps that calm gaze on me.

"You're not doing it for me, dear. Let me inform you of something. I've kept vigil in this Study for thirty years. Throughout that time, I've become very good at knowing when someone is crying for help. It doesn't matter what race I come across. When someone is in enough pain, it becomes plain on their face, and no amount of pride can mask it. Your mask is well and truly shattered."

The cheeks on my face flush red with heat. This scolding from some stranger in a robe is too much for me. I turn and start to make way for the other building to escape. I get to the door into the library.

"Arthur, if you leave now, your pain will eat you alive."

I grip the doorknob, fist clenched as tightly as I can muster. Why can't I turn it? What part of me is stopping it, wanting me to stay here with this self-inserted grandmother? I can feel her gaze on my back, with her disgusting loving spirit. Giving out emotional nurturing for anyone with a pulse. But something far worse is being realized. The more I hate it, the more I realize I want it.

I finally let go of the knob and turn back around.

"Fine! Fine, have it your way, woman. Let's do the blasted Observance."

"That's the spirit," she smiles.

The abbess comes up to open the door next to me and leads me into the sept, between a row of pews into one of the saga-keeping rooms. Inside is a room cut in half by a wooden-mesh screen and a door. On one side lies a table with a chair, and partially visible through the mesh is a stack of papers, a quill, a brass about as wide as the papers, and an unlit pair of candles, one red and one white.

As soon as we enter the room, the abbess's motions become quieter and more careful, as if there's someone fast asleep in here.

The abbess motions for me to have a seat at the table and gently opens the door for herself to pass through. As soon as we both sit down, she starts to pray.

"Keeper above, ever watching, ever writing," she begins, "another soul comes to record his saga, and yours. May he gain insight and wisdom from your teachings. Please state your name, scrivener."

"Arthur."

"Your full name, please."

"Arthur Fey."

"How long has your saga been unwritten, Arthur Fey?"

"Wouldn't the Keeper know all this already?"

"We're not saying it for his sake."

Of course. How could I have not known that?

"Abbess, it's been… about six years since my last Observance."

"The Legacian has much to teach you."

She pulls out a matchbox from somewhere in her robe and lights the red candle. She then picks up the candle and slowly overs it above and around the stack of papers. I guess once they're nice and blessed, she sets the candle back down, takes the quill, and quickly writes something on the top stack of paper before picking it up and holding it over the candle. When the paper catches fire and is about halfway burning, she sets it into the tray and lets it burn itself out. She then takes the quill back up and gets it ready to write.

"What are the greatest parts of your tale?"

Mother and the hospital machines. Your funeral casket. The hatred and satisfaction of both. Keeper above, don't go into that. That feeling of familiarity pops up again with those flashes of memory, as well.

"Uhh, getting into Oxlen and attending courses there."

"What insight was given to you during this time?"

"I learned much of this world, the World Before, and how both function."

She writes down something. I'm unable to read it through the mesh. She then picks the paper up and burns it in the same fashion as the first.

"Continue."

"I left Oxlen a few years after that, on amicable terms."

"What insight was given to you during this time?"

"I don't know."

"Search yourself."

Oh, of course, it's that simple. Just take a peek behind a mental cupboard. There's insight right there for yo—

The feeling of familiarity slams back into my mental focus, perfectly clear. You and mother are here, in this church.

I shoot up from the chair, trying to untangle the repressed memory.

"Please sit back down, scrivener."

"Hold on a moment. Where do you keep the dead here?"

"That is for after the observance."

"No, no, no, it's not. It's for right now. It's somewhere on the upper floors, right?"

"Please, focus on the observance, scrivener."

"Enough, woman," I shout. "Answer me, or I swear I'll tear down this screen and set the church ablaze with that blasted candle. *Where* are the dead *buried?*"

She sighs and returns the quill to the inkpot.

"They're above the sept. On the door to the right when you leave this room."

I rip open the door and rush out in a frenzy, rushing upstairs with some strange desire to see your and her urns, both of your scribesheets. The stairway to the mausoleum is narrow and made of stone, winding as I run up them. Yet another heavy wooden door sits atop the stairs in this temple of heavy wooden doors, and I have to shove it a little to get inside.

The mausoleum is tall and cold, a library of the dead. Shelves and shelves of urns stretch across the length of the Study, with stepladders on tracks alongside each row. I race to the "F" category and go down the line until I see my surname. Eventually I find them, a pair of urns on the second row. The scribesheet is still fluttering from my dash to find it, runes glittering in the dim light. At the top of scribesheets states the day.

Here lies Caddock and Leanna Fey.
Passed on the 6th of Uninox, 676 P.E.

The runes of the Keeper's Script march down the scribesheet in two columns, outlining the lifelong story for you and mother. They speak of your time in the military, mother's taking-on of the mantle as matriarch of the family, after the passing of grandmother. It's idyllic and like a fairytale. Completely divorced from reality.

As my eyes follow along the curvature of the lines and breaks in the writing, memories of a childhood forcefully forgotten come back, in bits and pieces. You were a forceful teacher, and some would call that abuse, sure. But there were other memories, too. Prettier ones. Summer days of blooming flowers and mandolin strings, played by our family steward Wilhelm. The pride on your face when I finally landed a blow on you during fencing. Painting a basket of citrus with mother by a roaring hearth in winter mornings. A childhood so picturesque, beautiful even. Times before we moved to this accursed country.

Once you accepted the "New-Colonian, Old-Blood" grant and uprooted us to this city, then I was forced to wake up. Wake up and see the misery of the city. Beggars coming alongside our carriage whenever we left Founder's Square, pleading for hope. Your friends jokingly talking of the accidents at their steel mills, and how if "those people were put in the mayor's seat, they'd run the country into the ground in a day." As if the city wasn't already scraping against concrete.

Keeper above, that's when it started. The resentment against you and her. Even as a boy I felt like I didn't deserve such grand things. What did I do to get silver cufflinks and daily banquets? What child even needs silver cufflinks? So idiotic. When your investments… What am I saying, it was gambling the whole time, wasn't it? When your gambling cost us our grand estate, I remember being terrified, but also a little happy. I wasn't forced to be a hypocrite anymore. But once we started living somewhere more "middle-class," I yearned for those better days.

What a miserable person I am. What I've always been.

I want to blame you and mother for all this. I really do. And maybe in some way, you're both responsible. But your control over my fate ended years ago. It was over once you both fell from the sky. I've done nothing to turn it around ever since.

"Well, Caddock, Leanna," I say to the scribesheet, "I hope you're proud of your little boy. The proud scion of a noble line, moping and drinking his days away as he's hunted by a criminal elfblood. The final branch, the last of an entire era of ancestors! It's so pathetic, isn't it?"

It's like I'm trapped in a self-devised maze. My history makes me pitiful of myself, and then anger aims at that pity. And it *never* blasting stops.

Anger builds and builds, seething from my pores. Void below, I don't know what to do with myself! I grab the shelf and shake it as hard as I can, screaming. Ceramic urns rattle and shake along the shelf. I let go of the shelf and start to kick at it instead, and then I trip up even doing that. The impotence. The spotless impotence of myself.

"I'm sorry. I'm so, so sorry."

Tears fall from my face, and shudders and sobs shortly follow. The more I feed these thoughts, these circular thoughts, a gap widens between me and the rest of the world. And I don't know if I can stop it.

Then I feel the press of a tin flask in my coat pocket, and reassurance fades in through the misery. Of course, the one friend that never leaves. How foolish I am to forget.

I wipe my eyes and nose on my sleeve, pull out the flask and take deep draughts from it. At the other end of the mausoleum, the door from the stairs opens and closes. Someone to kick me out, no doubt.

My last few moments with you are spent in a fantasy. One where you live and hold me in your embrace.

What a wonderful thing to imagine.

CHAPTER 37

A graybeak is perched somewhere above me, cawing incessantly. The blasted thing and its racket are forcing me to open my eyes and finally wake up. Wake up back to my lovely alleyway palace, with newspapers to keep me warm from the morning chill. That abbess thought she could resign me to a pitiful cot among other castoffs as if that wouldn't drive me insane.

The sun sends bright beams out over the buildings, sharp yellow reflections from metallic fire escapes going right into my eyes. Daily life is already beginning. The same old rhythm of humans, dwarves, and elfbloods going to work, or home, or wherever. In the span of a few months, I went from giddily watching the worker bees march along from my apartment window to homeless and patchy. Worker bees are much larger from the ground. It'd be quaint if it wasn't so suffocating and boring.

I look over to see that my hand is holding something, an empty bottle, and throw it against the wall to watch the splash of glass. The sudden noise makes a few passing suits jump, but then they continue on their way. "Just another loony vagrant," they must think. It must not be anything new. I couldn't bear the result of counting my silvums, but I must be near the last of it by now. A few more bottles and diner lunches before I'm completely bereft.

I get up and rub my temples. One would think that after enough drinking, the hangovers would get less and less severe. But such hopes are that of fantasy. At least it's something to cloud the pain of yesterday. I don't even want to consider those memories again. Those inner insights and bitter history, they hurt too much every time. As I rub my temples, I also struggle to remember fragments of the dreams from last night. The actions and scenes have faded, but the faces still remain. The faces of people that have been left behind, living and dead. While the dead depress me, I miss the living. Every single one of them. Every co-student and professor, childhood instructor, and manor maid. I miss all of them. I even miss Wolfrind, that sorry bastard that used me to party. More than anything, I miss Elizabeth, but I can't see her now. Not like this. There's no need to do that to her.

But I need to talk to *someone*. Even if it's just to talk about the blasted weather. The period of me enjoying solitude is long past. Something needs to change.

That leaves me with at least one person I can pester.

"Very well," I sigh. "Let's give Wolfrind a ring. See if he can be my savior."

While stretching the soreness out of my lower back, I move out of the alleyway and into the busy sidewalk traffic. A little space is made for me in the crowd, to account for the social leprosy, and I'm able to walk along until I see a telephone booth. Looking around again, I discover that this must be in the poorer area of the Acre. Displays both neon and not are showing signs of disrepair on most building edifices. Letters are missing, and tubes are worn or popped. A metal sign of a café with a winking dwarf's head is missing the open eye. A burn mark is all that's left behind of it. Bricks are crumbling and leaving pieces on the sidewalk. The smell of garbage and moldy food is carried on the wind from the overflowing dumpsters in the alleyways. These businesses are dangling by a thread. One bad day or harsh thunderstorm from bankruptcy.

On the side of an intersection resides a telephone booth, with a few missing window panes and flaking red paint revealing the steel underneath. The door whines when I peel it open and close it back shut again. I take out some of the paltry coins I have left still and insert them into the telephone box. After a short while of chirping, the operator chimes in and asks for the number.

"Yes, get me Ophidia 48-216-80, please."

She complies, and the line clicks further. Is this even Wolfrind's number still? He tends to move around frequently.

The more I think about it, the more I hope he doesn't answer. To come to a person like him in such a hopeless state as this. So vulgar. A juvenile sense of embarrassment washes over me. I need help, I know I do, but to get that from a person like him. It's a fool's dream.

Then a lance of worry shoots through. That's right, Astraea! She's still hunting me, isn't she? Fey, you are such an idiot. To drag him into all this, simply to ask for silvum or a shoulder to cry on.

I start to hang the receiver back up before the clicking stopped.

"Hello?" comes Wolfrind's voice from the receiver.

Void, void, void. To hang up? To not? What should I do? Some more sweat dampens my armpits.

"Hello?" he says once more, dragging out the last syllable out of annoyance.

I wince to myself and bring the receiver back to my ear.

"Hey there, Wolfrind. It's me."

"Me who?"

"Oh, sorry. It's Arthur. Arthur Fey."

"Ah. I see. Hey there, chum. It's been quite some time, hasn't it? How have you been?"

His tone is fake. He's pretending to be happy that I called. This is a mistake. I knew it.

"I'm sorry to have called you. It sounds like I interrupted something. Have a good day."

"Oh, come now, I have a few moments to spare. Tell me, how have you been? What have you been up to?"

"You know me," I awkwardly chuckle. "Always working and striving."

"Really? That's good to hear. Are you still doing that 'business acquisition' thing?"

"No, no, not anymore. I quit all that."

"That's a shame. To bigger and better things, right? How about Gren? He's still working there?"

You bastard, Wolfrind. You wretched bastard.

"I'm afraid not," I say, barely suppressing tears. "He's quit too. We aren't talking too much these days."

"That's too bad. Hey, are you crying?"

"I don't think so. You're probably just hearing some interference on the line or something."

"I see," he slowly says. "Well, it's been good catching up with you, Fey. But I have to—"

"Wait, wait. Listen, Wolfrind. I, uh, I need a favor. Or a few favors, depending on how you quantify these things."

"Quantify what?"

"I'm, uh, I'm hiding from some not-so-nice people. And I could use a place to stay for a short spell until I'm on my feet and all that, you know?"

"I see," he says flatly.

"And, and I hate to impose! I really do, you know that. But I don't really have anyone else around that I could turn to. So, I'm hoping that you could... You know..."

"Fey. Are you on the run? Are you wanted?"

"W-what?" I chuckle again, like a fool. "Nothing like that. It's just debt and all that sort of nonsense, you know how it goes."

"Uh huh. Well, I would, Fey. But uh, I'm in the middle of moving again. The lease was finished here, so I decided to move on and, well, there's just no room in my place right now. It's all full of moving crates and the like. You know how it is."

"Yes. I sure know how that can be."

"But uh, hey, you can always try going to a Study, right? They have missions all over Ophidia. I'm sure they'd love to have you!"

I knew this would be a waste of time. Selfish bastard only wants me around when convenient. What a useless human being.

"Yeah, I'm sure they would. Great advice, there, friend. You've been as helpful as you've always been."

He lets out a polite chuckle.

"No problem, chum. I'm always here if you need anything."

I was stupid enough to risk getting him involved, and he can't even make it worth the trouble. Worthless.

"I appreciate that. Ah, actually, one last thing before I let you go. I am, in fact, on the run. These people who are after me, they might be looking for my friends and acquaintances. Nothing serious, probably, hopefully. They're likely wanting to see if anybody will know where I am. So, keep an eye out, will you? If an elfblood or anyone mentioning an elfblood comes around, just steer clear. Do you think you can do that at least, Wolfrind? Can you, at the *bare* minimum, save your own sorry hide, friend?"

"W-what? What are you talking about?"

"It's no big deal. It'll all blow over soon. I hope so for your sake, at least. Do your best to keep an eye out in the meantime, okay?"

"Fey, what in the Void did you wrap me into!"

"It's nothing, Wolfrind, have a cool head, will you? You're in the middle of moving anyway. Now that's a great idea. If you were lying to weasel out of helping somebody, that is."

Nothing but a dull hum comes from the receiver. He's in disbelief.

"I imagine this is the last time we'll be speaking. Have a great life, you miserable *leech*. Keep sucking off of the underbelly of the wealthy in my memory."

"You son of a whore, Fey! You better not have sicked any gangers or orcs on me! If you did, I swear when I find yo—."

And a dull click comes from the telephone box as I return the receiver. At least this waste of time ended with a morsel of catharsis. Good riddance.

Somewhere deep inside, thick guilt starts to settle in. But something else tells me that it won't matter. Astraea knows better than to go after him over nothing. I'm just another nothing. It doesn't matter.

I melt back into the sidewalk traffic and head back the way I came. To return to my newspaper-laden palace.

It's definitely a terrible idea, but I could go see her today. I should see her today. Ever since the day at the park, it's been curt phone calls and delayed dates. And now she's probably the last living person I can ask for help from. How embarrassing.

Keeper above, I hope Gren is okay.

Should I even risk getting her involved? She'd definitely be at risk during all this. Another weakness that could be used to torture me. But I can't handle this anymore. The loneliness and suffering. I've never been stoic enough to fight back against crippling isolation. I've always had people to bemoan to and be around. Now that's all gone, and it's killing me.

My back alights in pain as I stand up, the result of hours smushed against the brickwork. Some more empty bottles fall from my lap. A pounding headache also awakens now that I'm forced to move around.

Bile rushes upward, and I keel over and vomit a little. Where does Elizabeth work again? The *Gazette*, was it?

I look back up at the moving crowd outside the alleyway.

"Excuse me, sir," I call to the first person I parse out from the crowd, an old dwarf. He doesn't respond.

Three passengers later, someone acknowledges that I exist.

"Yes?" an elfblood woman stops and responds.

"Could you tell me where the *Gazette* office is?"

"Uhh… Oh. You head down the street that way"—she points to the left of us—"and take a right once you hit the spinning dwarf advertisement."

"Thank you, ma'am."

She nods and continues on her path. A small kindness. I'm alive, after all.

The pilgrimage to the *Gazette* begins slowly, as achy muscles cramp and protest. But, eventually, it becomes a haze. A mirage of electric signs, both turned on and off, passing suits, and sunray gleams off of metal vehicles. It almost becomes a trance until motion above me catches my eye. A large wooden advertising sign affixed to the side of a building across the street. Words and colors splash across the sign, and on the right side is a crude painting of a dwarf, attached to a spinning wooden plate that's separate from the sign itself. Turning to the right and carrying on, I eventually reach the rotating glass doors of the *Ophidian Gazette* offices.

Then the realization settles in, and my headache pulses quickly with my racing pulse. I'm about to see Elizabeth, aren't I? She will walk in and have no choice but to see me, a shattered wreck of a man, reeking of alcohol and covered in stains. She's going to reject me. She'd be insane if she didn't. Void below, how ludicrous is this situation? Me begging for a savior from a woman who has no want for it. Stupid, so stupid.

No other options, though, right?

"Blast," I mutter. "Blast it all."

I quickly take a deep breath, wince from the pain of quick movement, and push the revolving door on its axis.

The reception area is somewhat cramped, with the walls behind me and to my right being floor-to-ceiling windows and the other two consisting of white brick. Popular editions of the newspaper are framed and equally spaced from one another along the walls, and a woman sits at a desk by the set of double doors, typing away at a typewriter.

"Yes," she chirps. "How can I help you?"

Once she looks up and at the mess of a creature that is I, her expression changes from politeness to concern.

"Is Elizabeth Drummen in?" I say. "I'm family."

"Is she expecting you, sir?" she asks, not convinced.

"Hopefully," I say. "Tell her Arthur is here to see her."

"Right away. Would you have a seat, please?"

I sink into a leather armchair a few steps away from the revolving door. She opens one of the doors near her desk and ventures past it. Yesterday's edition sits on a coffee table in front of the chairs. Having a look wouldn't be a bad idea.

FOREIGN SPIES AND TERRORIST MOVEMENTS? GOVERNESS ADDRESSES RIOT CONCERNS

Ophidian Governess Faea Adalbun hosted a press event to address the public's concern about the Business-Market Trade Proposal, a Statehouse legislative bill that has garnered a great amount of public controversy since its inception. Grassroots political movements such as the New Colonian Liberation Party have gained a great amount of traction by way of protesting the enactment of this proposal.

"The fear-mongering over this humble bill," Governess Faea stated, "is difficult to understate. What is essentially a method for working people to buy portions of businesses, so that they have long-term investments and financial mobility, has been smeared as a way for entrepreneurs and the wealthy elite to make off with more ill-gotten gains. This flawed public perception has led to an excess in civilian injuries and arrests, both here in Ophidia and in other major cities like Traitor's Pass and Wintercrest. Decisive action needs to be taken before protests turn into riots. I even have trusted sources telling me that our former ruler nation, the Huanshun Republic, is using the unrest to reassert political pressure to revert our nation to the centuries of servitude we've only barely escaped from. For the noble pursuit of public welfare, I am branding the NCLP and movements like it as terror organizations and enabling police forces to take necessary measures to prevent any more innocent blood from being spilled."

"Fey," Elizabeth says, with a tone dripping in shock.

The newspaper falls from my hands when I see her. She's as beautiful as the day I first saw her. Curly hair tied back into a loose bun. Eyebrows upturned in worry. Hazel eyes to match her lovely skin.

"Oh," I say.

I should have prepared something. Anything at all would've done for this.

"Hey there, Elizabeth."

"What are you doing here?"

"I— I was thinking— I don't know."

"Why are you such a mess? Is everything okay?"

Come now, something light to alleviate things. Anything. Anything.

"No," I say quietly, tears starting to form. "As much as I'd love to say, nothing is okay."

"Aww," she coos.

Yes, I know I'm pathetic.

"I was hoping… Well, I just— I just have nowhere to go, and my house burned down, I'm sure you've heard, and—"

"Wait. That fire on Starfall Road? That was your building?"

After a moment, I nod.

"Fey, are you in trouble?"

After an even longer moment, I nod again.

I can't look at her, but the feeling of confusion is palpable. Here I am, vomiting my situation onto her, hoping for some sort of answer. So selfish.

"Well, Arthur, this is a bit sudden if I'm being honest."

"I understand. Sorry to have bothered you."

"No, no. I can't turn you away when you're in so much pain."

She gets a little too close and takes my hand. She's wearing a rose-scented perfume. The thought of her smelling me fills me with disgust.

"I'll go tell my editor that I'm going to have lunch, and then I'll bring you home. Okay?"

"That sounds wonderful," I whisper. "Thank you. I mean it."

"Just sit tight for a moment, alright?"

She hurries back through to the offices, and I fall back into the chair. The receptionist is staring as intently at her typewriter as she can. This encounter must be a goldmine of gossip.

Elizabeth returns with her purse over her shoulder, and she takes me by the hand and leads us through the revolving doors. She hails a cab carriage, and we start to ride back to her apartment.

As soon as silence fills the carriage with us, my face is flush with that hot feeling of shame. I can't believe I'm so desperate as to rope in this innocent woman into it all. She doesn't deserve it. Not one bit. I can even feel her eyes on me. She wants me to spill it all out first. As if that's not a terrible idea.

"You can talk to me, you know. I won't judge."

Outside, a newsboy on a corner stand gets shoved over by another boy.

"This is all off-the-record, after all," Elizabeth says, chuckling at her little joke.

The newsboy chases after the other kid, newspapers fluttering along the crowded sidewalk.

"Arthur! Talk to me. Please?"

I look over to her and yet again have no clue what to say. I lean forward out of my seat and close the window to the driver, cutting off the sound of clopping horses and city noises.

"Well, those people I worked for. It turns out that they aren't the nicest people."

"What do you mean, 'not the nicest people?' Are they criminals?"

I let out a deep breath that I didn't know I was holding.

"Something of the sort."

"Arthur," Elizabeth's tone is low and tense, "Are you wanted? Is there a bounty out for you?"

"What? No, no, nothing like that. Security Affairs and the police have no idea. Just my previous employer. She wants me dead, probably."

"Probably? What do you mean, probably?"

"I mean probably," I raise my voice a little. "You can't just send in a letter of resignation and have a firm handshake about this sort of thing. I just left."

"Look at me, Arthur. Right now, look at me."

I comply.

"What did you do for these people? And don't lie to me."

All sorts of lies race past too quickly for me to choose. So, I choose the dumbest thing to say.

"Extortion, mainly. I got money for them from people who didn't want to give it up."

Her eyes go wide, and she backs herself a little into the corner of the carriage.

"They had blackmail on me, Elizabeth," I say, shaking my hands. "They were going to lock me up for 30 years or more if I didn't go along with them. I had no choice!"

"Every criminal says they didn't have a choice."

"Oh, don't give me that. Like you understand what happened, what I went through."

"Did you kill anybody?"

The red-hot wash of shame over my face again.

"What?"

"You heard me. Did you kill anybody?"

"No! Of course not."

"You have a gun on you right now, don't you?"

The press of the revolver in my backseat reassures me.

"Elizabeth, I was the negotiator. That's it."

"Then open your coat, right now. Show me."

I sit a little forward in the carriage seat and hold open my ratty long coat. She puts her hands into the pockets and pulls out my empty flask, setting it down.

"Alright, show me your backside now."

To the void with this woman.

"What do you mean?"

"Don't play dumb, Arthur. Show me there isn't a gun tucked into the back of your pants."

No getting out of this, then.

"Fine, fine. You want to see it? Here it is."

I draw the revolver and hold it upside down in front of me.

"You've done it. You've figured me out."

Elizabeth's eyes widen again, and her face is stuck in one of shock. The reaction is oddly grounding. Normal people are afraid of this sort of thing. The hot wash of shame comes once again.

"Elizabeth," I begin, setting the gun down on the row of seats in front of us, "I'm not going to hurt you, you know that. I have done some terrible things, but I'm no evil mastermind, killing for amusement. I've never even killed anyone."

Internal shock hits from the last sentence, then an obvious realization. Bjorni, that's right.

Elizabeth's expression softens a little, but she still doesn't speak. She has no idea how to respond.

"I'm—" I stutter. "I'm— I'm done, alright? I'm done running and hiding and lying. So, here, I'll tell you all of it. Is that alright with you? Do you wish to hear it?"

Her eyes soften more, returning to normal.

"If you want, I could get out of the carriage right now, and you'd never see me again. I can figure something else out. You shouldn't have to help me like this."

"No. No, don't do that. I was just. I wasn't prepared for this to be my day at all. But I don't want you to leave. Please, tell me what happened. But don't lie to me."

"Of course, I won't."

I struggle to remember it all. The bits and pieces fly past in blurs that are hard to recognize.

"So, this all started earlier this year, near the beginning during the warmer season. I was a dropout of Oxlen, with no family to fall back on and barely any silvum to speak of. So, I went to the only true friend I had, a half-orc named Gren. He's from the Yard, so you can imagine the past he's had."

The carriage lurches to a stop suddenly. A car abruptly cuts in front of it, into this street lane. The carriage driver shouts and waves his fist at the car driver.

"Gren had a plan for us. So we'd have some money to keep ourselves alive while we figured out what to do long-term. It involved robbing a secured place in the docks. And I know what you're thinking. No, I didn't harm anybody. I held up this revolver and convinced the guards to let us through. We stole what we were after, but it angered some powerful people. These people rounded Gren and I up and said we either work for them or get sent to prison for stealing an arcane artifact."

"Hold on a moment, did you aim the revolver at them? Was it loaded?"

The haze of cabaret parties and other jobs fog up the details.

"I can't say for sure, but I think so. But if I did, my finger was off the trigger. It always was. If I ever killed an innocent person, I'd do myself next."

Elizabeth looks outside the window near her and takes in a breath.

"I probably shouldn't, but I believe you. Continue."

"So, the work for these people was some sort of extortion or racketeering. We'd go to businesses that already fund other criminal organizations and trick them into paying us instead. I only had to draw my gun once, and it was because the man we were after tried to kill me. Our leader also used my bloodline during public dinners with the upper crust to gather sway for whatever it was that she was doing. She never told me what. And as evil as it is to admit, I was fine with it all. Instead of slaving away in some office, I got to work a few times a week and get a load of silvum for it. But then we started working for that political movement, the NCLP. Once all that started, the evil became too much to bear. They were trying to embroil me in interrogation and the murder of innocents. The day I saw them kill a Statehouse legislator was the day I ran."

"Keeper above," Elizabeth says, exasperated, "and all this while we were seeing each other?"

"Yes. Terrible, isn't it? Maybe I deserve all this."

"And you haven't killed anyone during all this?"

She doesn't let up, does she?

"Yes, I have. One person. A dwarf. He led us on behalf of our leader. I shot him after he shot and killed Gren."

Elizabeth clucks her tongue, emitting an "aww" before stopping herself.

"Keeper above, Arthur."

"Yeah, I know."

"Such cruel fate to one man."

Visions of that elf and his branding irons come back to me. Is it fate, or is it my choices?

"It's sickening."

The carriage comes to a stop. The driver turns in his seat and opens the little window. I lunge and grab the revolver before he has a chance to see it.

"Chunneling Road. We've arrived, sir," he says. "Miss."

"Thank you, driver," Elizabeth says, handing silvum bills through the window.

We exit the carriage, and I'm allowed a moment of chivalry by helping Elizabeth down. Her apartment building is a grand brick affair sitting squarely on the corner of Chunneling Road and whatever other street. I then open the door to her apartment building for her, and we enter the cramped elevator together, alone.

"206 is our stop," she says.

"No penthouse for you. What a shame."

She snickers a bit. Being so close to her, I can smell the rose perfume again. Keeper above, I hope I don't offend her nose too much.

"You know," Elizabeth says, "It's strange. The things you've done would be enough to make anybody run in fear from you. We always read about the terrible criminals and their deeds. But... There's something about the way you carry them. Your troubles. I don't see you as a criminal, Arthur."

"How pitiful is it to say that I think you should?"

She looks at me with her saddened eyes and hugs me, tenderly wrapping her arms around my chest. I'm stunned for a moment but then do the same. Feelings of attraction amplify until they're unbearable. This woman is too much. I'm going to kiss her.

"Hey Elizabeth," I whisper.

"Yes?" she whispers back, looking up at me. Her eyes say it all.

I go in for the kiss, lips pressed tightly against hers, hands on the small of her back. She returns in kind instantly, arms moved up to behind my neck, and my worries of overstepping boundaries evaporate. We stay like that for a few moments, relent, and then go in again. Some sort of spell comes over me; the feeling of affection is stronger than I'd imagined. Too strong.

We finally back off a little and gaze into each other's eyes. She takes her right hand and gently holds my face. Electric attraction shoots down my back. Keeper, I could have her right now.

But do I deserve it?

I wasn't honest with her. I can't remember where I lied, but I had to somewhere in the story. From the first time we've met, I've tricked her. Through it all, I've gained a love built on deception. It's disgusting what a part of me thinks I can get away with. Nothing this good just happens to someone, drops into their lap clear as day. I've stolen it from somewhere, somewhere in the past, I've lied or hurt someone to get this sort of result. And what actual story ends with a love like this? It's too good to be true. No, I don't deserve this.

"I'm sorry," I whisper to her, with tears bulging out of my eyes. "I'm so sorry, Elizabeth. I shouldn't have done this. I shouldn't have come here."

"Done what, Arthur?" she croons, wiping the tear from my face. "It's alright; you're here now. You're safe."

"No, I can't do this to you. Bring my woes into your life like this. It's not right."

I break away from her and have to press my palms into my eyes to keep the sobs from coming.

"Arthur," she whispers.

Her worrying tone, how low and sweet and lovely it is, makes my heart want to leap from my chest. The tenderness is burying me alive.

"Arthur, you're panicking. Take a few deep breaths. Come back to me."

"You'll be a casualty. You can't have that. You need a man who makes sense. Not me. I've already endangered you too much. Void, I'm such an idiot!"

The elevator door opens, and I surge out, repressing the tears as hard as I can. The stairs are a few steps away, and I run toward them.

"Arthur! Come now, you don't have to do this. We can figure it all out. Please!"

She screams my name one more time as I shove open the stair doors and run down the stairs. More damage, how much more is necessary?

In a few moments or a few hours, I'm outside the building, running in some direction. I run as far as my lungs will let me. Then when I pant too much and have to stop, the realization of what I've destroyed, what I've tricked myself into believing, settles in. I really did think I could just walk away with a woman like Elizabeth, didn't I? While still being hunted by Astraea and Keeper knows who else? Stupid, stupid, stupid! The ground I'm standing on starts to feel so far away. Everything is so far away. The gap is filled with complete, angry, depressing pain.

When I return to my senses, I find my hands blooded a bit, stinging from hitting the brick wall in yet another alleyway. I lean up against the other building, sinking to the floor until I'm lying against gravel and old newspapers. I could go for a smoke right about now. But when I open the pack of pipes in my coat pocket, they're empty. I could stare into this empty pack forever. It's too perfect of a symbol.

"Arthur Fey," an ancient, croaking man says. "Scion of Vizegard the Wise?"

I can feel the presence near me, but I don't care to look.

"Go away."

"We reach you regarding the pact."

"Didn't you hear me? Leave!"

I turn around and see an old man in a tan long coat, with slacks and loafers to match. I throw the empty pack at him.

"Leave me!"

"I cannot, Arthur Fey. The pact has been fulfilled, and you are summoned."

"What blasting pact?"

"The pact of Rivenfell. Do you wish to see your kinsman, the half-orc known as Gren?"

"Gren?"

I get up from my stupor.

"What did you freaks do to him?"

"We brought him into our care. He awaits you."

CHAPTER 38

Gren is strapped to a gurney in a treatment room in the middle of an abandoned mental asylum. I guess the arcane freaks found it fitting. One wide windowpane sits above Gren's bed, showing that of an old brick facade. The window has been shattered long ago, most of the shards littering the floor. The man who summoned me is beyond old. Wrinkles and creases cover his cheeks and forehead. A thin gray mustache rests above his upper lip, and wispy gray locks fall from the top of his head. He's wearing a long tan overcoat and matching fedora, made of fabric that looks about as tired and worn as his skin.

"The half-orc's recovery was most troubling. His conscious brain functions ceased for a short time before he was successfully resuscitated."

"Wait a minute, Gren died?"

"In a manner of speaking, yes. The damage to his body was substantial. Many organs were failing when we brought him into our care."

"How did you save him? What did you do to him?"

"We did what was necessary, ancestor of Vizegard. It would be wise of you to show gratitude for the lengths we've gone to."

"Right," I say, looking to the floor. "Sorry. It's just. It's been a rough few days, is all. Stressing, you see."

"Yes, you are taking the news of being wanted rather poorly. But no matter, you will meet your fate all the same."

These sorcerer types and their fetish with destiny, I swear.

"A word of warning, regarding the half-orc's new state. His body has healed, but his mind has regressed as a result of the necessary treatments."

"What? What do you mean regressed?"

"As far as the half-orc is aware, he is but a young babe, not yet in adolescence."

"What in the Void are you talking about?"

I can't help but clench my fists.

"When his mind momentarily ceased to function," he says, going back to Gren's sleeping form, "Portions of it were damaged. Those portions, too, were healed. But the healing could not replace the memories and cognitive patterns that were lost. In a sense, he has experienced a rebirth. He is made young again."

A profound regret tumbles onto me. These sorcerers have crippled Gren, and it's all my fault.

"What in the Keeper's name did you do to Gren?" I shout, reaching to grab the old man by his lapel.

As soon as I make contact, an unseen force pulses from him and knocks me to the ground.

"We did what was necessary," the old man says, brushing his coat lapel. "Decisive measures were needed to fulfill the pact and keep him alive."

As much as I want to get back up and throttle this vile old man, his protection would make the effort wasted. So here I continue to lay. Bits of glass have embedded into my hands as well, stinging them.

"When will he be back to normal, sorcerer?"

"Your contempt is plain, not that it makes any difference. It is unknown whether his memories and personality will return to normal or not. These changes will likely be permanent."

"So, Gren will have the mentality of a child for the rest of his life?"

"It is likely."

"In what reality does that make any sense?"

"It makes perfect sense if you knew the ways of the arcano-sphere, as your ancestors did, scion of Vizegard."

I heft back up onto my feet, trying to wipe the bits of glass from my hands. Small cuts pour droplets of blood from the resultant holes.

"May I see your left arm, scion?"

"No, I don't think you may."

"I'll refrain from performing anything to the presence that's on your arm. I simply wish to observe it."

Once I get most of the glass out, I roll up my sleeve with my bloodied hand.

"Fine, but Keeper help me if you even start to mutter some sort of spell."

He takes a step closer to me and leans forward to get a closer look at the tattoo. He brings his right hand up to hold his chin, studying the design on my arm intently. I can almost feel his eyes run up and down the serpent, reading each of the harsh dwarven letters alongside it.

"Interesting. To see a guardian brand take so well to a human. Your lineage does you much justice, Arthur Fey."

"What are you talking about?"

"This thing is not some mere invasion of ink upon the skin. It's lived through many generations. Protected centuries of dwarven ancestors. And now it's been handed off to you. A very peculiar development. Did the dwarf who gave this to you die?"

"Yes."

"Did you kill him?"

"That's none of your business," I say through clenched teeth.

"Ah. I see. The ceremony of 'Cle Vhaela' is one infrequently conducted. Those must have been dire circumstances. You must count yourself very fortunate indeed, descendant of Vizegard."

"Can you *please* stop bringing him up?"

"Why do you wish that? Is the comparison between his legacy and yours too uncomfortable for you?"

Anger explodes from inside me, and the impulse to reach for my revolver ignites in my mind.

"My apologies if I offended you."

"Your apology is spat on, wizard," I say through gritted teeth. "Leave Gren and I be. Now."

"As you wish."

The mage produces something from his pocket and smears it on his hands, before snapping his fingers. In the span of a breath, the room is preternaturally dark.

Speak the words "pig iron," and he will reawaken.

More voices in my head. The trickery never ends.

The room returns to its normal brightness, and the old man is gone. A wind blows between the buildings, shifting Gren's blanket slightly. He slumbers so peacefully. Who am I to disturb him?

When I do disturb him, when he does finally wake, he won't be the same. As soon as I wake him up, I'm letting go of the older Gren. The one that always has little impulsive schemes and so many inane but endearing stories. The one that can party and drink as I do. The one that protected me as one would a little brother. The one that I need now more than ever. He might as well be dead and gone.

"Remember that last big party that we had, Gren? The one at Monarch? You were so out-of-place with all of Wolfrind's friends. Then again, when aren't you out-of-place?"

I turn to the wooden half-shelf that sits across from the bed and sit on top of it. All that comes from Gren is the passing of air from his nostrils. No shifting or even snoring. He's always had a snore.

"Such a journey the two of us have had. We two idiots. And we're both still here. Hunted and penniless, but we're still here. I should be thankful, you know. You're alive and kicking, and we have so much more trouble to get in. So, why does it feel like you're still dead?"

The chasm between me and everybody else deepens. If Gren's mind has regressed enough, he might not even know who I am. Once he gets up, I bet I can count the number of people in this city who care about me on one hand.

I pull out my flask and finish the rest of it. There's nothing to be done. Just survive. That's all there is now.

"Alright, enough sulking. Pig iron."

His breathing briefly stops, and his eyes open. He looks around the room, and his face goes to worry when he sees me.

"Mister, where am I?"

He doesn't say Arthur or Fey, just mister. Such an innocent title and it wounds my heart.

"You're in the remains of an asylum, Gren."

"How do you know my name?"

He straightens himself up onto his elbows. His eyes have a youthful naivete in them. It's so uncanny.

"Have you seen my mom? Her name's Bregna. She might be looking for me."

I refrain from telling him his mother died ten years ago.

"She's away on vacation. She left me in charge of you. My name's Arthur, but you can call me Fey."

"Whatever you say, mister."

"Fey. Call me Fey. Please."

"Okay, Fey."

Keeper above, even the way he says my name. His voice is still deep and booming, but something about the rhythm of his speaking, like the cadence of a frightened boy.

"Why am I here?"

"You were sick. But you're better now, and we can leave."

"Shouldn't there be doctors here? And why's the window broken?"

"Budget cuts. The hospital has been getting poorer for a while now, but it's alright. We can go, come on."

331

I hop down from the half-shelf and go to Gren's bedside.

"It's alright, I'll take care of you, Gren."

"Why's your coat so roughed up? Are you one of the streetside men my mom always talks about?"

"No, I'm not. Listen, all your questions will get answered eventually, but we need to go, so get up. I'll take you out for frosted treats. You like those, don't you?"

"Ooooh, I sure do."

As with all children, the mention of sweets motivates Gren to comply with my demands. He springs up from the bed, shoes crunching hard on broken glass.

"Whoa, I don't remember being this tall."

He looks down at his body.

"Or this big."

"Puberty's started for you. That's all. Come now, follow me."

I start to leave the room, and he walks behind me.

"How long will my mom be gone for?"

"She didn't tell me. But I'll bring you straight back to her as soon as we get word from her. And Gren."

I turn back around to make eye contact with him.

"Don't talk to anyone besides me, understand? And if someone looks like they want to hurt you, let me know."

"Okay."

"Promise me."

"I promise."

He offers his pinkie to swear on, and I smile and wrap my pinkie around his big stub.

I start to lead the two of us out of the hospital, but I stop and face him again. I have to try, at least one more time.

"Gren, are you sure you don't remember me, even just a little?"

He ponders the question before shaking his head.

"Take a moment to think about it. *Please.* Look closer if you have to."

I step closer to him and look deeply into his eyes. There has to be a flicker in there somewhere, something, anything.

He eventually looks away, visibly uncomfortable.

"This is weird, mister. Are you sure my mother's not around?"

"Stop calling me mister, I beg you. Either way, it's no matter. She'll be back in due time. Now, let's get some frosted treats."

"Oh, yeah, let's," he cheers. His gruff voice echoes in the asylum halls.

Even as he lives and breathes, the dull ache of loss still remains. It's never going to leave, either, is it? Goodbye, old buddy. I'm going to miss you more than you'll ever know.

CHAPTER 39

A dollop of frosting rests atop one of Gren's tusks, and just like a child, he doesn't know or care about it.

A short walk away from the abandoned hospital is where we found the nearest bakery: a modest establishment run by an old woman. A small display of sweets and treats sat between all the stacked shelves of bread. Gren's childhood has returned in full form. As soon as we entered, he pressed his face to the glass and eagerly drooled at all the baked mini-cakes and stacked frosties. I couldn't get my silvum out fast enough.

He's burning through the mini-cake as if he's been starved. Bits of it are flying from his mouth and falling all over his lap as we sit outside the bakery in the setting sun.

"Slow down, Gren. You're getting it all over your face."

He stops for a moment and remembers to breathe.

"Sorry, Mr—" he cuts himself off. "Sorry, Fey. I'm just so hungry, is all. I don't remember when the last time I ate was."

"That makes sense, but you're meant to savor it, not wolf it all down. The quicker you eat it, the quicker it's gone."

"Oh," he says, with some realization on his face. "You're pretty smart, mister."

He stops eating the treat for a short time while still intensely looking at it. A battle of willpower reads across his creased brow and narrowed gaze.

He doesn't last long. Soon enough, he finishes the rest in a few massive bites. In some ways, his characteristic naivete hasn't changed.

"What exactly do you remember from before you woke up today?"

His tongue works along his lips, looking for any leftover frosting. I point to his tusk, and the remainder there disappears quickly.

He scrunches his eyes to somehow help him remember.

"Umm, I remember being with my mommy, somewhere in the Yard. We lived in a little apartment with a leaky roof. A friend knocked on the door and asked her if I could come play. We... We ran down the street lookin' for somethin' to use as a ball."

"How about anything recent? Anything closer to today?"

"What do you mean? This was last week."

His memories predate his run-in with the Yard's gangs. He's still pre-pubescent, as far as he's concerned.

"Oh," he says, his face lighting up a little. "We ran into an old guy while we were looking. He was very, very old. And he wore..."

He closes his eyes to think harder.

"A yellow coat and hat. But not really yellow. Like a light yellow."

"Keeper above," I mutter.

Those vile sorcerers infect everything they touch. Nothing is sacred, not even memories.

"He came up to us and said somethin' to my friend. And then, next thing I know, I'm in a bed lookin' up at you. I don't think that hospital was really a hospital, either."

"I told you, son, it's just budget cuts, is all. They took good care of you."

Son. I can't believe that slipped out.

"What did they take me in for?"

"Well, your mother was called away to help a friend, and you fell down and hit your head in that little apartment. You must have been reaching for something on a high shelf in the kitchen, I imagine. So, when she found out and took you in to the doctor, she also, uh, called me to keep an eye on you."

"That's all pretty weird. All that happenin' like that. Why didn't she come get me before she left? And what did she leave for again?"

"She didn't have time. I told you that." I lean forward in my chair. "Listen, you need to stop asking so many questions. Worrying about all this is bad for you. She'll be back before you know it. Let's just enjoy ourselves in the meantime, alright?"

He tucks his hands under his legs and tightens his shoulders. I'm sure he'd kick his legs too if he wasn't fully grown.

"Okay," he says flatly. He's probably unconvinced, but little children know better than to keep poking adults. At least adult strangers that their mother has entrusted them with.

The facade is maintained for now, at least. Even though that's what hurts the most. The fact that he may never be able to handle the truth. The necessity of this lie. While he escaped death, a facsimile of life has been resurrected in death's stead. We may as well have never met. Never stolen from my estate the first time he broke into my home. Never played at criminals and taken from my neighbors as some sort of juvenile vengeance. And we never had that last great party before I was sent off to Oxlen, when both of you were still alive, and life was fated to be grand and mundane. What's the point of bonding and suffering together if this unnatural reversal is the result?

As Gren looks up and down the avenue, people-watching and not having a care in the world, I'm wholly swallowed by regret. Every time I look at him, he looks back with this sort of blank glance. Like I'm just another person on the street, except he has to put up with me because his mother is making him. At least in his mind. I can already feel the facade cracking, and it hasn't even been a full day.

I roll up my left sleeve to take another look at Bjorni's "gift." Such a strange turn of events. Bjorni sets this upon my skin without so much as a word to how it could be useful.

"What's that?" Gren asks.

"A tattoo that is, allegedly, alive. A parting gift from a… From someone I used to know."

"What happened to them?"

"They had to leave, too. I'm never going to see them again."

"They must really like you to give you something like that."

"Maybe once they did. But not anymore."

"Why?"

"Gren."

I give my best impression of the stern adult stare.

"Oh yeah, sorry. I still like it, though. Can I touch it?"

I think for a moment before sighing.

"I don't see why not."

His thick finger rubs along my forearm, brushing the length of the serpent.

"Does it need to breathe?"

"What?"

"Since it's alive like you said."

"To be perfectly honest, I have no idea."

Gren's finger stops at the serpent's head. He looks closer at it then pokes it with force.

"Wake up. Come on, wake up."

"That's enough." I pull back my forearm.

"I was just tryin' somethin', is all."

"I understand, and I'm still putting an end to it."

"Okay," he pouts.

His eyes wander the street again. Soon enough, he's looking at the ground, kicking his legs at passing bugs and loose pebbles. It's cute, in an absurd sort of way.

There it goes again. It came along when we first entered the bakery as well. In little flights, I can feel some sort of ease about the two of us. Is this what you felt, Caddock, when I was a young child? The pleasant comfort of an adult watching a child? We watch the way their brains come to terms with existing and learn how to make everything less boring and more funny. The sense of ownership adds to that, too. Every time a child does something miraculously inane, a smile spreads across the parent's face. *That's mine,* they must think. *That's the next chapter of my lineage right there.*

It could be called a gift, me having to take care of him like this. I can almost appreciate it. But then I'm reminded of what was lost to gain this. So much of his life and story are dead. I'm the last one who knows anything about it. If I go, a piece of him dies with me.

I must stop. All that is too much to think about. For now, we have to find a place to sleep. Concrete and beds of newspapers are no place for a child. I feel my pocket of silvum and guess how much I have from ruffling the leftover bills and coins. We can probably manage a stay at some dingy hotel, at least for a night or two.

"Did you enjoy that treat then, Gren?" I ask, rising from my seat.

"Yeah," he smiles. "Are we getting another one?"

"Not right now. It's getting dark out, and the bakery is closing soon. We have to find a place to stay for the night. Have you ever stayed in a hotel before?"

"No. What's that?"

"It's a home away from home. Come on, let's go find one. I hear they have radios in them, so you can listen to music while you lie in bed."

"Whoa, that *does* sound fun. And then tomorrow, my mommy will come around and pick me up, right?"

"Perhaps, son. Perhaps."

I reach up and rub his bald scalp while we walk down the road. He smiles and grabs my head to put it in a playful headlock.

"Easy," I shout. "Easy now."

He just laughs.

A few more days of this should be nice enough, at least.

CHAPTER 40

"Are you enjoying that sandwich?" I ask Gren.

"Yeah, mister," he grins. "Axeboar sure is tasty."

We're sat in another diner, biding our time until something inevitably happens to us. Astraea and the elf have yet to finally put a bag over my head for the last time and drag me off. I'm starting to think that the head-shaving did a lot more for disguising me than I initially thought. Olur must have been onto something after all.

Despite the inevitability of being found, I lack any sort of plan. Unless drinking and feigning being a parent counts as one. I know no one and have nowhere to run to. Maybe I should go back to the Yard, after all, bring those three back their beloved friend.

I look over to Gren, and he's chomping down into his sandwich with wide-open eyes. There's no way I could explain this to them. They'd probably kill me. Maybe it'd be worth it, though. I'd be dead, but at least someone I care about is safe and sound. A release from all this doesn't sound so bad, either.

With a full stomach, I push my plate away from me and motion for the waiter to come over.

"Can I get you anything else, sir?" she asks.

"Just the check, please."

As she walks away, I reach into my pocket for some silvum. Strange, my usual pocket's empty. Then I check the other one, which is empty too. Bizarre. Soon I commit an exercise of fumbling, going through every pocket in a quest to find anything that can be used as tender.

"Everything alright, Fey?" Gren asks.

"Yes, no worries here. I forgot where I put my wallet, is all."

Soon enough, I find some silvum in my breast pocket. Relief washes through as I pull it all out.

Five silvum and some change.

"Here's your check, sir," the waiter says, handing it to me.

The total sum for a few sandwiches and a cup of blackbrew is twenty silvum and six half-pieces.

Keeper above, we're destitute.

"Just, excuse me for a moment, miss, please," I say to the waiter, rising to move to the bathroom.

I rush over and lock the bathroom door as quickly as I can before falling into a pit of despair.

So, this is it, then. The last of my ill-gotten gains, gone. The deepest embarrassment that could happen to someone like me. I may as well have been imprisoned. It was all spent in the span of a few days, too. Some nights at a hotel room missing its lamp and a few cheap dinners. That was as much as I could get. I'm more like you than I care to admit, Caddock. I have a son for a short time, and I'm already close to leaving him with nothing. To be honest, there wasn't even much of an attempt at getting over this chasm of financial and existential ruin.

Scalding hot water pours into the sink and onto my hands. The burning helps take my mind off of it all. I put my hands in for as long as I can bear before instinct rips them out and repeat the process. I keep catching glimpses of myself in the mirror affixed above the sink. Glimpses of my patchy beard and fuzzy scalp. The area below my eyes is a lot darker than before. Strange considering sleeping is all I'm able to do now.

"So many grand things," I say to the sink, "Were in store for Arthur Fey. All those grand expectations from all those *idiots*. Rose,

Caddock, that oaf at Oxlen. What a terrible idea it is to heave things onto children like that. Just makes failing all the easier."

The water burns too much, and I rip my hands out of the sink again. My hands begin to turn a deep shade of crimson, and the burning intensifies. This should hurt far more than it does.

And that's when I finally look into my reflection fully. Bits of dirt and grime are all over my face, clinging bits of beard together. No matter how much I bathe, I can't seem to ever fully clean myself. So wretched and disgusting, all of it.

"Why can't you do it, you fool? Why can't you be happy? What's so *hard* about it?"

"Stop looking at me. Stop it! Enough!"

Mammalian rage takes over, and I try to rip the mirror from the wall, but it holds fast all the same. A man too weak to do anything, equal parts mad and lucid. The cycle of pitifulness and anger is too much.

The revolver beckons once more. I pull it out from a coat pocket and look at it. A look at the aged metal of the barrel is a look into the abyss. A look into an exit from all of this. It would be so easy, so painless. What's to stop me right now, right here? No one left to know or mourn me. No funerals to speak of. Wouldn't be needed anyway. I'd be just another pitiful drunk dead in the city. Maybe that fate is deserved.

"Mr. Fey," Gren's muffled voice calls from the other side of the door, "you okay in there?"

His words bring me back to the present, where I'm pushing the revolver under my chin.

"Yeah, Gren. Just washing my hands is all."

"Are you sure that's all? I heard yelling."

The youthful worry in his voice. The worry of a child too innocent for life and death. Every time he acts like this, I want to cry.

"I just hurt myself for a spell. I'll be out in a bit, alright?"

"If you say so, Mr. Fey."

His lumbering footsteps recede into the diner, and I'm left alone once more. I want to do it. I want to end it so much. But I can't. I can't do that to Gren. Leave him alone and scared in a city that doesn't care about him.

Once he's taken care of, I'll get him to his friends in the Yard. Only then can I consider such things.

I reholster the revolver and unlock the door, exiting back into the café dining room. People are looking toward me but turn away as soon as I close the door, pretending they didn't just hear all that. Gren's standing a few steps away, confused.

"See?" I say. "All done. It wasn't anything serious."

"Why are your hands all red?" Gren asks.

I look down at my hands.

"Ah. The water was far too hot. It burned my hands as soon as I set them in. That's what I was screaming about, remember?"

"Oh."

"Come now. We're going on a field trip. I'm taking you to see some old friends."

"Do I know them?"

"You sure do. You haven't seen them in a while, but they'll remember you. I promise."

"Oh boy. You sayin' we're going for a sleepover?"

"That's exactly it."

"Yay!"

People around the diner are shooting inquisitive looks at us. The same sorts of looks strangers give to invalids. Like if Gren just stopped existing, things would go back to normal.

"It's going to be a great time," I get in real close to whisper to him. "But for now, we're going to get up and leave as quickly as we can, understand?"

"Why? Are we in trouble?" he whispers back.

"No, not yet, and we won't be if we leave right no—"

"Is everything okay over here?" the waitress says, standing right behind me.

"Yes, quite fine, thank you. I must have dropped my wallet somewhere is all. You know how it is."

"Do you remember where you last had it?"

"Well," I ponder, tapping my chin to keep up the act, "It was likely at the till over there."

"I'll go look for you."

As she turns and takes a few steps away, I reach over and grab Gren's monstrous paw.

"Now," I whisper harshly. "Now!"

The two of us rush out of the diner into the cooling autumn afternoon. A breeze washes over us, bringing the smell of baking bread and salted meat. We dip and weave between people until we get a block or two away from the diner. One more place I'll never be able to go to again. Not that it matters.

The lowering sun casts yellow rays onto laughing couples and groups of friends. Denizens enjoying the end of the week. I let go of Gren's hand and keep moving down the sidewalk.

"Follow me, Gren."

"I am, I am. You don't have to say that every time."

I lead Gren from block to block, somewhat guessing and somewhat getting us closer to the Yard. Some people turn around or stiffen a bit when they realize we're behind them. Whispering to one another about the vagrant stalking them. A few cross the street to get away from us.

The more time that passes, the more I sober up as well. Slowly but surely, I lose my grip on the only comfort left. I can't even get angry anymore. All that remains is hollow resignation.

"…And that will be just the beginning," a voice shouts from the next street over. I turn and can make out a large crowd overflowing from the boulevard onto the main street. Cars and carriages are piled up and clumsily trying to maneuver away from the blockage.

"What's going on?" Gren asks.

"Not sure. Let's find out."

I get Gren in front of me, and the two of us cross the street toward the crowd. The closer we get, the more the chill of the evening is immediately dispelled by collective body heat. People are tightly packed and agitated, cheering on the voice at the other end of the road. The smells of the working masses become overpowering.

There's something about the voice that's addressing the crowd, too. It's familiar. Wait, that's who it is. The man I shot and ran away from, Mr. Clarke. Looks like he's healed up nicely, then.

Clanging police bells are already sounding off in the distance, no doubt coming here. We're not going anywhere. I need to see how this plays out. Gren and I get as far into the crowd as we can before there are too many bodies for further progress. I can make out a ramshackle stage nestled between two carriages, upon which stands Mr. Clarke and his NCLP goons. The monster that enables Astraea and her wicked machinations. They're now wearing some sort of green armband on their left arms. The sight of that vile man breeds a cold animosity in me.

"We have been warned," he shouts, "by economists and guild masters the world over, about what would happen should that trade proposal come to pass. About the stipulations that corporations would have over the money of the working masses should they be tricked into investing. For the love of the Keeper, you've heard it all already, haven't you?"

A resounding yes comes from the crowd.

"And if you've all heard it," Clarke continues, "then our political leaders have, as well. And what did they decide to do today? Ratify it into law! Today is a historic day. Today you and I have been surrendered. Our liberties and financial freedom have finally died at the feed of our Statehouse's greedy benefactors. Railroad and silver tycoons all throughout the country laugh and jeer at us! They laugh and jeer as we work and starve. Look to the right and left of you.

Houses on this very street are abandoned and dormant, long deserted by families now too poor to afford them. Now, tell me, my dear New Colonians, is this the legacy our ancestors conquered the New World for?"

Men and women of every race scream no, driven near-mad with class resentment.

Something stiff presses against my back. The unmistakable press of a gun barrel.

"Time for your suffering to come to an end, Fey," a female voice whispers in my ear. "The Betrayer sends her regards."

I try to turn and look at the gunman, but the gun just presses more into my back.

"Ah, ah, ah," she whispers. "Can't have that, can we?"

I quickly become equal parts relieved and terrified. The end I'm entitled to has come too soon. Gren needs to be safe.

"Not yet," I shout behind me. "Just wait for the speech, at least, okay?"

"No time for that, Fey," she says. "Bye-bye now."

"Are you satisfied with today's trials?" Mr. Clarke screams. "Have you been rendered pacified by your long working hours? Or are you ready to act, here and now?"

The crowd moves and screams in response, knocking apart the gunman and me. Gren is visibly scared, clinging close to me in response to the noise.

"Gren, push forward," I shout. "Now!"

"Why?"

"Just do it, move!"

He turns around and starts shoving people out of the way, carving room for us. I tightly grip the shirt on his back and follow. A quick glance backward shows the gunwoman getting the pistol knocked out of her hand by unwitting agitators.

"Then we march to the Statehouse," Mr. Clarke triumphantly screams. "We tear down the steel gates, we take history into our own hands, and we tell those corrupt politicians this: We will *never* lay down again!"

Mr. Clarke and his cronies hop down from the stage to lead the crowd eastward, toward the Statehouse building. The screaming of the crowd is unbearable. Clarke's words have driven these denizens feral. They shatter windows and smash cars as we all march along toward the street. Police with blow horns behind us try to cow the madness, but it's dramatically futile. Officers form a line behind the crowd but are too sane to try and fight back against the teeming horde.

Gren and I are in the middle of the tidal wave of bodies. I'm gripping the back of his shirt as tightly as I can as people shove us back and forth, and we're barely staying on our feet against the momentum. Even in the vibration of it all, I can feel my hands shaking in adrenal fear. My ears ache from the wall of noise. Screams and shouts are penned in between the buildings, echoing off of brick until they're incomprehensible. Some people ripped out a nearby fire hydrant, and a pillar of water shoots into the sky and drenches all of us. Faces are contorted into hateful masks as humans, orcs, and elfbloods let loose their frustrations onto the city itself. In the space of an evening, civilized man reverts to feral animal, letting loose a deafening cry of collective chanting and screeching.

The street starts to widen into a square, and the outline of the Statehouse building breaks the horizon up ahead. It's above us, with the road going up a slight incline. A police line is forming in front of it, with a few pointing rifles at the crowd. Another officer with a blow horn is shouting at us all to stop. A scant line of twenty officers stands against untold hundreds. Bottles, rocks, and bricks fly out from the crowd at the officers. They hold their arms up to protect their faces from the debris. The sergeant continues to shout something in his blow horn, but he may as well be screaming too. It's unintelligible. The rest of the police line threatens with their rifles in vain. How can these people not be worried about getting shot? How can they be so raging mad?

Someone in the crowd throws a wine bottle with pin-perfect precision, and it shatters square on the forehead of one of the officers. It knocks his cap free from his head, and his face starts bleeding profusely. His compatriot to the left of him looks over and shouts something in anguish. He then turns back to the crowd and fires in a moment of enraged weakness. The wall of bodies is stunned for a brief second, the collective rage having never taken this into account. Then a few more people scream in outrage, and vengeance must now be taken. Terror envelops the rest of the policemen's faces as they realize what their coworker's done.

Then the crowd screams even louder and charges the officers, overpowering them immediately. They disappear below the heaving mass, and I can hear the cries of trampled men somewhere beneath the unified noise.

Gren and I get forced against a telephone booth, and people struggle to get around it and us.

"Gren!" I shout at the top of my lungs. "Get on top of this!"

He doesn't reply and scrambles atop the telephone booth. Once up there, he reaches down with both hands and scoops me up as well.

The telephone booth heaves over a bit from the sheer force of bodies, and some people attempt to rip it from the ground. But the solid steel of the walls luckily holds, and the effort dissipates quickly. The two of us are granted a sliver of solace amidst the flood.

The crowd reaches the tall wrought-iron gates in front of the government building and rattles them with their hands. The guards on the other side of the fence hold up their batons in intimidation but are just as terrified as the now-trampled policemen. Slowly but surely, the gates start to buckle under the immense weight.

Something flutters on a nearby rooftop, and I turn to see a figure with a thick robe fluttering in the breeze. Its hood falls away to reveal a middle-aged human man. He raises his hands above his head and moves his mouth in some sort of rhythmic chant. A shape rises in the air behind him, and a green glow emanates from it. The shape is small but distinct. It's, without a doubt, the box we recovered from the frontier. I see visions of Bjorni's face screaming at me to take the box, back in the temple.

Keeper above, what has my forgetfulness enabled?

The smell of ozone and burning sulfur fills the air. Nullification powder from the street gathers in clusters and spins upward from spaces in the crowd and the box trembles. Winding pillars of nullification powder aim and combine into a nexus just above the gate. The maddened crowd, in waves, feels the change in the air and starts to fall silent.

The man on the rooftop ages years with every passing second, hair graying and creases in his skin multiplying. Suddenly the box flings open, and a luminous ichor flows out from it toward the gate. The ichor stretches out the further it goes, and images of ancient stone buildings and shifting bodies can be seen inside of it. That nightmare I had back out on the frontier comes back to me, with that message scrawled along the wall:

The World Before has followed us.

When the ichor meets the spinning powder above the gate, tendrils of the ichor shoot out and lance tens of members in the crowd. Everyone the tendrils touch become corpses, their skin desiccating instantly. More and more people die to the vile magic before a shockwave blows out, crumpling the gate down and nearly knocking Gren and me off of the telephone booth. When I reorient, I look back up at the rooftop to see the caster's body falling onto the street.

Silence falls over the square. Half of the crowd is dead, and the rest slowly realize what happened. People scream as they find out their friends, brothers, sisters, and lovers are dead. A woman shakes the lifeless body of her husband.

Or he was lifeless before his eyes open.

He grabs her throat and rips it out, viscera spraying outward. The corpses reanimate and rise from their resting place. Then they turn upon their friends and family and become machines of murder. As much as I need to, I can't look away. Eyeballs punctured in their sockets. Stop looking. Bones sticking from desiccated and dried flesh. Stop Looking. Veins in legs and arms ripped open and shooting little volleys of arterial spray. Faces twisted into masks of unbridled terror. Stop. Looking.

Gren cries and screams next to me, and I break away from the scene to hug him.

"It's alright, Gren," I shout. "I'll get us somewhere safe."

To my left is a large tenement window within jumping distance.

"Follow me!" I shout.

I draw my revolver and shoot the window twice in the frame. Chunks of it shatter, but it doesn't completely. I take a step backward and then leap from the telephone booth. Bursts of glass cut all over my skin. I tumble forward into a living room, banging my shoulder against a couch. I heave myself back onto my feet and look back out the window at Gren, immobilized by fear.

"It's alright, Gren," I scream. "It's safe in here. Just jump, buddy. Jump to me."

"I can't," he shouts back.

"You'll be safe in here, I promise."

"The monsters will just find us in there. I know it."

"I'll keep you safe in here, Gren. I'll make sure you see your mother after all this. Just trust me. Please."

He looks at me, around the street one more time. Some of the corpses are shuffling down the street in our direction. He covers his ears and closes his eyes, screaming and jumping in through the window. I have to dive out of the way to clear in time.

When I look toward the front door, I see a family in the middle of barricading the door. My coat sleeves are shredded and growing damp with blood, and I've wet myself. I'm about to pass out.

"Sorry about all—, all tha—."

CHAPTER 41

Adrift somewhere warm and static, all that can be heard is a multitude of whispers. A few voices are older than the rest.

"Is he gonna be okay?"

"...No arteries were nicked. It's mostly superficial..."

"...Is that a gun?"

On and on it goes. I keep getting pulled back there, that place that's cold and hard.

The visits there are brief before I return to this realm of shifting forms and concepts. It looks like somewhere I've been before. But it was more concrete, then. Somewhere more livable. It hurts to try to remember. It was a place of abandonment. Dilapidated streets with patches of green sprouting from the concrete. Something etched on a wall. There's a sense of fulfillment from the memory, too. Like it has reached fruition, and I saw it coming the whole time.

It's too much effort to bring forth from memory. A waste of effort. It's far better to exist and nothing more.

The whispers come back and forth again. They whisper about how bad it is outside, and how much one of them misses me. I should be doing something, but it's impossible to remember what.

Then I appear on a hilltop at noon. The cloudless blue sky gives bright light to the longgrass, flowers, and nearby oak tree. In the distance is a chateau that I haven't seen since I was a boy. Or was it only yesterday?

"Hello there, my dear boy," an old voice behind me says.

I turn to see an old man. He's dressed in a petticoat and smoking jacket. He moves with a limp, and whenever he moves a little quicker, some unseen tin bell rings on his person. He must be going to a ball soon.

"Mr. William Sigesar," he continues, curtseying. "Great-great-grandson of *the* Sigesar, at your service. I hope I'm not interrupting anything."

I look over the saturated green longgrass of the hilltop and fluttering leaves from a nearby oak tree. I get the pressured feeling of being late for an appointment. Some dinner reservation or some such that I'll be missing.

"I'm running late for something," I say.

"I think you have more time than you realize, Arthur. Right now and later on."

"How would you know that, Mr. Sigesar?"

"Ah," he guffaws, "Sigesar was my father and the few before him. Please, call me Will."

The shadows of the longgrass and flowers start moving further to the left. The sun is setting, with small clouds starting to form in the sky.

"It's a queer thing," Will says, brushing dead leaves from his petticoat, "how ancestry goes, isn't it?"

"What do you mean?"

"Well, take a look at mine. The Grand Sigesar, a man so grand that his first name became the family surname. He rises to power, conquers the known lands, and dies to an elfblood assassin. His family stays in power for a few generations until I, the only living heir, come along. A man so melancholic and medically insane that I found marriage to be a dwarven scheme and women to be spiteful shrews. Due to these discoveries, children fully fled from the equation. I squandered the royal treasury and didn't care about the anti-loyalist insurrections. Suddenly, one fateful misty day, poof, my carriage explodes from gunpowder charges."

"Yes, I think I remember reading all of that in junior school."

"Did you?"

I look up from the longgrass at him.

"Did I what?"

"Read it in junior school? That portion of human history is awful dark for children."

"Probably. What was that time called? The 'Sigesar Splintering?'"

"That's right. When one empire became twelve nations. As they often do. As divinely ordained as he was, no amount of austerity can prevent such things, can it? We always fall victim to our choices."

A distant part of me gets incensed by this. Too many recent voices have given me such powerless, defeatist rhetoric. Is falling into deterministic pessimism always the ending path for the old and "wise?"

"It's always fate and destiny with your types."

"No other way to make sense of it, I'm afraid."

I scoff before I can stop myself.

"That can't always be the case. It can't be."

"Well, sure. I was medically mad. Nothing to be done about it."

"Enough. Enough of this."

"Of what?"

"This line of thinking, this sort of apathy is pathetic. Your kind needs to stop wallowing in the excuse that is fate."

Will brings up his hands in a passive gesture, with a smile on his face.

"I beg your pardon if I've offended you. I'm just an doddering man trying to help a young boy who's astray."

He's goading me. The batty codger is taunting me. I try to walk away, but my legs don't want to work. I'm trapped in this wide-open field.

"Oh, what's this?" he says.

I turn around to see him holding up a mirror, reflecting right at my face.

"Stop that."

"What's the matter? Don't like what you see?"

"Enough!"

He walks over to me, delicately holding the mirror at head level.

"There it is, Arthur," he whispers. "There's the summation of your fate. All the grand things others wanted for you, and here you are. Pretty sorry state, isn't it? Almost as sorry as a mad old man like me."

I get a glimpse of a view of me in some dingy café restroom. I hate it.

As soon as it's within reach, I slap the mirror from his hands, and it falls silently to the ground.

"Oh, butterfingers, me. Sorry about that."

He circles around behind me.

"Maybe it's a curse on us aristocrats. Maybe one day, all noble lines eventually destroy themselves. Could be a natural thing. Just an eventuality."

"No. I'm still here. I can still change things."

"That right? You can still be a hero, Arthur, and save the day?"

"To the void with being a hero. I can still do what's right."

"Yes, *yes* Arthur," he jumps a little into the air, bells tinkling once more. "Change, atonement! Such exciting things, such comforting notions, perfect for a hero like *you.*"

He circles back around behind me.

"However, there's still a scary choice to be made in the kind of heroism one will seek, what variant of exaltation one can achieve."

"What in the void are you talking about, you loony old bat?"

"Heroism can oft have a certain finality to it, can't it? The warming valiance of the grand sacrifice, lying down everything for some grand goal, or to protect some cherished loved ones... But what about the other choice?"

He circles back around in front of me.

"What about the meeker option? Of struggling and suffering, and getting ever closer to that ideal self? What about bearing the whips and tortures of life, dragging one's mistakes uphill day-by-day, for the sake of hurting others less and hurting yourself less? Could that be the heroism you've been seeking all this time?"

I look into his vacant, sunken eyes and am at a loss for words.

"I... I don't know."

"Barely anyone does until it's time to choose."

Will comes closer to me and puts his arm around my shoulder.

"Do you promise to try for this dream of yours? Do you swear?"

"Of course. I need to."

"Say it aloud. Say, 'I, Arthur Fey, swear to set things right, at any cost.'"

"I, Arthur Fey, swear to set things right, at any cost."

"Ahh, very good. Very good indeed."

He brings himself right in front of me, and I can smell his rotting teeth.

"Well, Arthur," he says, grabbing my lapel, "it's time for you to figure it out."

He shoves me to the ground, and I fall at an incredible velocity.

My eyes snap open, and the vision of a dingy living room unfolds in front of me. The waking world returns, where things make sense again. I sit up and feel sore all over my arms. I'm on some mattress sitting in a corner of the room, opposite the hallway and near a fireplace. An old armoire is pushed up against the window, covering most of the shattered panes. This house has been abandoned for some time before I and whoever else came here. The wallpaper is tattered in several places, with small holes in the wooden planks. A man, clean-shaven and stocky, sits on a nearby sofa, reading a book. He looks at me when I shift around.

"Easy, friend," he whispers, putting the book down and coming toward me. "Your wounds are still closing up. If you flex your muscles too much, they'll open back up again."

I'm wearing only pants and a stained undershirt, with bandages all along my forearms and some on my left leg.

"What day is it?" I ask.

He brings a finger up to his lips, motioning for silence.

"Two or so after," he whispers, looking toward the armoire blocking the window, "whatever the void that was. You've just been in a deep sleep, and we didn't want to wake you up."

I start to get up from the mattress on the floor, and he gingerly tucks his hands under my arms and helps me. My left leg is still sore, so I walk a little slower than usual to the broken window. A gap exists between the leaned armoire and the opening. Shapes of bodies line the streets. Then comes the smell. An overpowering stink of rotten eggs and body odor. I snap my head away before I take in too much detail.

"Those," the man says, "things didn't stick around for too long. They ravaged the streets for one night before falling apart and becoming dead again."

Just like in the stories of the World Before. The Great Undeath would use the bodies for his attacks, then drop them like toys when no longer needed.

"Where's Gren?"

"Upstairs, with my wife and three kids. It's safer up there."

"If those undead were only here for one night, where is everybody?"

"We're not sure, but… Here, just have a listen."

He walks over to a nearby radio, in much better condition than the home itself, and slowly turns up the radio knob. A flat male voice starts to say:

"Attention. Attention. This is a message from the New Colonian Armed Authority. Martial law is in effect. Stay in your homes until further notice. Anyone found on the streets will be subject to arrest. Anybody openly bearing arms will be subject to lethal force. This serves as your only warning. Plans for citywide evacuation are underway. Stay tuned for further updates. Attention. Attention. This i—"

The man turns the radio back off.

"That's been playing since the morning after the attack. A few breaking news segments talked of bombings at police departments and the like. Since then, the city's become a warzone. Gunshots have been going off around us constantly. There have even been roving looter gangs in the streets a few times too."

That damnable elf must be behind this. Or Astraea. Either way, some lunatic got their way.

I also can't get that old man out of my mind.

"I just had the weirdest dream," I whisper. "Just before I woke up."

"Yeah, we've all been having nightmares since the attack. My wife, Elaine, says it's just from trauma, but I know better. Whatever magic went on out there screwed things up."

"What makes you so sure?"

"I was a combat medic at one of the frontier forts. Whenever shamans were in the area, every one of us had nightmares for weeks."

"Keeper above."

"I know. But hey, dreams are just nonsense anyway. I wouldn't think too much about it."

A dream that precise, being only nonsense?

"I'm Jim, by the way," he whispers, putting his hand out to shake. "You're Arthur, right?"

"Oh," I whisper, clasping his hand. "That I am. Gren tell you that?"

"It's all he talked about, how you were watching him for his mom or something. That and wanting to play games with my kids. Is he... alright?"

"Not really, no. He had a complication during a surgery, and now his brain will always be like that."

"Oh. Wow. I'm so sorry to hear that."

"Me too."

"You want me to get your friend for you?"

"Yes. Please."

He comes over and takes a peek through the window. When he doesn't see anything, he starts for the hallway.

"Oh, uh," he whispers, stopping in the doorway, "your revolver's on the table over there. I just borrowed it while you were asleep. Hope you don't mind."

I nod and smile. He continues up the creaking stairs, and I pick up the revolver from the table, clicking open the cylinder. Four unspent rounds are still in it.

Setting the gun back down, I look up at the water-stained ceiling and wonder. Am I to just sit and hide in here, in this den of strangers? Something about the notion feels compellingly wrong. Something I'm forgetting, or someone.

Elizabeth!

"You're sure he's awake?" Gren's voice booms down the stairs. "Jenny played a trick on me twice over it, and I don't wanna get sad again."

"I'm sure, buddy," Jim whispers. "And for the fifth time, keep your voice down."

"Oh," Gren says, dropping his volume. "Right, sorry. Bad guys."

As soon as he gets to the last step, he sees me, and a wide grin spreads across his face.

"Mr. Fey!"

He runs up and sweeps me into a choking hug. Pain alights along my arms.

"Gren. My wounds!"

"Oh, right," he says, putting me back down. "I just didn't know I'd miss you so much, is all."

He looks back at Jim, who's shushing him like a librarian.

"Mr. Fey," Gren whispers, getting really close to my right ear, "do you think you can take me home to my mom, now? I don't really like it that much here."

"I'm working on it, sport. Say, Jim. Have any gangs or looters been around here today?"

"Not really. But it's only noontime. Day's still young."

"Good, because my friend and I here have to go."

His face alights in shock as if I told him we're about to get bombed.

"You sure? Besides those miscreants, Armed Authority soldiers are sweeping through the streets, too. It's dangerous out there, Arthur."

"Dangerous or not," I say, walking to pick up the revolver, "I have someone waiting for me. And I hope she's still alive."

Jim nods and gets out of my way. I pick up the gun but stop myself from holstering it.

Do I really need this over Jim and his family? Should I really disarm them like this? Gun or not, I still have a ten-head high mountain of muscle as a defense mechanism. With the right words, Gren can still fight. The stories of the tussles he got into over his mother's honor, even when he was just a few years old.

No, no, we'll be safe. I can't say the same for Jim.

"You know what, Jim? You keep this. My friend and I will be fine."

"Oh, Keeper, I— I don't know what to say. Thank you, Arthur, truly."

"Well, it wouldn't be fair for me to get treatment and not pay, would it?"

I flip the gun in the air and grab it by its barrel. He smiles and nods, taking the gun.

"The hammer tends to stick, so make sure it's not stopped by rust or something before you fire."

A deep pang of regret rings through me.

"Had such a thing happen to me."

"I've been cleaning it, but thank you, Fey."

"Good. Shall we, Gren?"

"Watch out meanies. Here we come."

Jim pulls back the hammer on the revolver and tiptoes over to the front door. A few pieces of furniture are stacked against it, but the three of us set them aside enough for the door to open. Jim cracks the door open and peeks down both sides of the street. Next to the mattress is the remains of my longcoat, shirt, and shoes. I slip them on, taking time to avoid reopening wounds.

Where did Elizabeth live again? Channeling Street, or something like that?

I get back up and rejoin Jim and Gren at the door.

"Say, Jim, do you know where Channeling Street is? Or Charnelling Road? Something like that?"

"Chunneling Road, you mean?" he says, eyes still affixed out on the street.

"Probably, yes."

"Four blocks or so east of us. Fastest path is wading through the wave of bodies and taking a left."

"And the not-fastest path?"

"Going back the other way down the street and crossing another two blocks."

"That sounds more pleasant."

"We heard more gunshots that way, so be careful."

"Wonderful."

"Alright," Jim says, opening the door all the way. "It's clear. Go, quick."

"Keeper watch you, Jim," I say, pushing Gren out the door.

"You boys, too."

Jim slams the door shut as soon as we both exit. The sound of scraping furniture comes through the door as soon as the locks click.

The hairs on the back of my neck stand up once we're out in the stinking open air. The rotting smell of corpses is almost too much.

"Mr. Fey, I think I'm going to be sick."

"Cover your mouth with your jacket, Gren. And take my hand. Whatever you do, don't let go."

His massive fist wraps around my hand and squeezes a little too tightly.

I lead the two of us down the stairs. Some corpses line the sidewalk past the stoop. I try to step over a few but then snap the arm off of a fourth. We then scurry past the stoop as quickly as we can, heading in the opposite direction of the Statehouse. Soon enough, we're away from the pile and heading down the street.

Two rifle shots echo from somewhere south and, hopefully, far away from us.

Abandoned cars and carriages clog the street completely, with only a few of the carriages having dead horses attached to them. There's a score of bodies here and there, but most of the corpses are that of automobiles after a certain point from the Statehouse.

The more of utter death and destruction I see, the more I can feel my mind wanting to regress into childhood and cry. And after those urges comes an almost-automaton-like rationality. A distance is being set between me and the bodies at my feet. This will be the urge I act upon.

Gren and I get to an intersection, and I lean against a building edifice and take a look to my right, eastward. More abandoned cars and carriages, with bodies near some of them. But further along the street, some bodies are alive, and they're beating each other.

Three men with black armbands are beating a man in an olive-drab uniform. Revolutionaries versus the state, a scene perfect for a painting. Their shapes are a little far off, and their shouts are indistinct. All I can hear are echoes reverberating off of the tall buildings. Once the soldier is on the ground and holding his hands up to beg for mercy, one of the armband men draws a pistol and executes him. The shot rings off of the brickwork.

"What's going on?" Gren mutters.

"Bad men. Very bad men doing very bad things."

A second armbanded man picks up a rifle near the soldier's corpse, and the three of them turn our way and walk toward us. Void.

"Run, Gren. Now."

I spin us back the way we came and sprint away from the intersection.

"We're going back to the pile of people."

"Yes, because we need to. Cover your nose with your jacket, and don't look at the sleeping people, alright?"

It doesn't take long until we pass the house we were just staying at, and the bodies make running difficult. I'm forced to look down and pick my steps carefully. Bodies sunken and bloated sit on top of one another, with viscera in every possible combination covering them. Necks, arms, legs, eyes, hands. All severed or splayed open in violent and unnatural ways. I have to focus and fight down the urge to vomit.

"Can I look down now? I keep stepping on top of people."

"No! We'll be through it soon, just trust me."

Then we reach the square in front of the Statehouse. Near the central fountain, the bodies are all desiccated and stacked almost up to the top of it, like the undead went to a central point and just fell apart. Flies fill the air around the piles; a cacophony of buzzes sounding all around us. A vile sucking sound comes from below Gren.

"Eww, my foot fell into something."

"Keep your eyes up, buddy," I say, looking back.

His foot sank into a dead woman's chest.

"It's just a pumpkin. Pull your foot out, and don't look down!"

Gren does what he's told, and the two of us start to turn left down the intersection. That's when I hear a shout back the way we came. I steal a quick glance behind us and see the armbanded men heading our way.

"Gren, keep your eyes closed and follow my voice."

The two of us sprint through the swamp of death. We trip and stumble almost every step, but Gren's hand never leaves mine, and he doesn't go into shock despite the fetid smell, so I can only assume he's doing as he's told.

"Why do the sleeping people smell so bad?" Gren asks, with a voice that's in the middle of deciding whether to be scared or not. "Are they—"

"No! No, they're not. Don't think too much about it. We'll be away from them soon."

After a few minutes, the swamp starts to clear, with the street reaching a state of relative normalcy. We round the intersection, and a bullet hits somewhere behind us as the men try to get a shot off before we get out of sight. Gren yelps at the sound.

We're not going to make the four blocks before they can get a sightline on us. We'd be dead before we made two of them.

A large carriage is lodged on top of an automobile in the middle of the street. That will have to do.

I clamber up to the door and find it unlocked. The carriage itself is empty, and curtains are drawn over all of the windows.

"Gren, get in here. We're going to play some hide-and-seek."

"Uh, is now the best time for that?"

"Just do what I say, please."

Gren climbs on top of the car and gets inside the carriage, and I almost join him.

Wait, this spot is too obvious.

"Gren, come back out, please. This spot is too obvious."

Gren groans and comes back outside, and I close the door, leaving it slightly ajar.

To the left of the carriage is a house with a door off of one of its hinges. I rush us up the concrete stairs and try to force it open, but something is wedged on the other side.

"Gren, could you plea—"

Gren rams the door open in one thrust of his body, with something wooden splintering and breaking on the other side.

"Good lad."

A thin hallway is directly inside, with some chairs and tables stacked near the door. An opening is directly to the right, with more further down the hallway, mostly obscured in darkness. The door is somewhat broken, but from the outside, it looks fine. I wedge a chair against the door and pull us into the living room, where a curtain is drawn over a window, obscuring most of the room in darkness.

"Perfect," I mutter.

Gren vomits back in the hallway, and I feel the urge to do the same, now that my focus turns back to that fetid stench.

"Sorry, I don't know what that smell is, but it's too icky."

"That's alright. Can you do me a favor and come here with me? We're going to sit and wait for a spell and see if the bad men are still following us."

"Okay."

He comes in from the hallway and sits down on the floor, and I nestle up near the window, drawing the curtain back as minimally as possible.

"You sure I stepped in a pumpkin? It stinks. Bad."

"Shh, sport, just be quiet for a moment. Take your shoe off if you have to."

The clouds above the sky have thickened, giving a uniform diffuse light over the piles of mechanical wreckage in the street. The neat rows of buildings across the street are desecrated with smashed windows and doors. Some windows are barricaded, but most have been left shattered and open. A loud thumping is coming somewhere nearby. Turns out it's my heartbeat.

My heart drops into my stomach as the men pop into view. Their weapons are still drawn and swinging around as they poke into cars and around corners. Once they get closer, their talking becomes intelligible.

"Keeper, that pile back there," the blond-haired one says, shrill syllables bouncing off of the street. "The stink's still in my clothes, I swear."

"Stop talking about it," the one with the hat and rifle responds. "I'm already close to losing my mornmeal."

"Boys," the third, a dark-skinned middle-aged man, shouts. "Focus. Human and half-orc male. Both bald, just like she said. If we lose them, we're dead."

My heart sinks again, further than I thought possible. So, that elfblood witch hasn't forgotten about me.

The dark-skinned man points at the carriage with his revolver.

"Check it," he says.

The other two stalk up to the carriage and the unarmed one swings open the door while his rifled friend points into the inside. They stay outside, barely peeking into the carriage. The rifled one holds his aim, and the two don't move for a few moments, listening more than anything else.

"It's empty, Sinclair," the hat man says.

"You don't know that, you coward. Check inside. Now."

The rifle is pointed at the only unarmed one.

"You heard him, Conty. Check it," the rifleman says.

"He said it to you, you moron."

"Horun," Sinclair shouts, pointing his revolver, "check in the carriage *now*."

"Okay, fine," Horun yells back, swinging his rifle down in anger.

The two finally peek their dullard heads into the carriage, Horun first, then slowly comes Conty. Sinclair's gaze scans the nearby wreckages before looking up at the buildings across the street. No, no, no, don't look up here, you bastard.

"Like I said, boss," Horun says, "nobody."

"They're hiding somewhere. No one could clear this block that fast on foot."

Sinclair's eyes stop on a shattered window. A few moments pass, then he pulls up the revolver and shoots at it.

Gren winces and emits a shallow cry.

"Shh," I hiss at Gren.

"Void," Sinclair spits. "Thought I saw somethin'."

"Now what?" Conty says.

Sinclair's gaze turns to our side of the street, scanning the windows. I drop away from ours as soon as I see what he's doing. The curtain flits back and forth from my rapid motion. Please don't tell me they saw that.

"Conty," Sinclair says. "You go back and look into the bodies. Horun and I need to check somethin'."

"Aww, why do I gotta do it?" Conty says.

"Boy," Sinclair shouts, with the mechanical click of the revolver to enunciate.

"Fine, fine," Conty says. "Always gotta pull out the gun to make a point."

"Horun," Sinclair says, dropping his volume. "Check that house with me. The curtain moved. I know it."

Of course.

A thin ray of sunlight barely lights up the room. All I can make out of the living room is a long sofa near a dead fireplace, with a small parlor sofa sitting opposite it. Staying low, I scurry to the fireplace and pick up a poker lying on the ground beside it.

"Are they coming?" Gren whimpers.

"Yes."

In the space of a few creaking footsteps, I lie in ambush in the corner between the doorway and the window.

"You hide behind that chair, alright?" I whisper, pointing at the parlor chair.

"I don't think I can fit, but I'll try."

Footsteps tap against the concrete of our house's stoop. One of them tries to open the door, but the chair wedged under the handle holds.

"It's locked," Horun's muffled voice leaks through the door.

"Is your brain working," Sinclair asks, "at any time of the day? It's wedged, not locked."

I look back over to Gren. He isn't hidden at all.

"If someone comes in here," I whisper, "tackle them. As hard as you can."

His frightened gaze looks from me to the doorway. The two men heave against the door once. Twice. Thrice. And it finally crashes open, the hinges snapping off of the door, letting it and whoever was shoving it fall onto the floor. Two bodies scramble up from the ground and get back outside, just past the outer doorway.

"We know you're in there," Sinclair shouts. "Just come on out. Make this easier for everyone."

Wind passes along the street and whistles through the opening.

"If you ain't who we're lookin' for, we'll let you go. Keeper's honest truth."

Only the wind responds.

"Horun, get in there. Check that room first."

A moment passes, and a footstep clacks against the door, followed slowly by another. The rifle barrel is the first to pass through the doorway into our room. What a fool. Then it starts to aim further inward, toward Gren. After the rifle comes his right shoulder and part of his head. That's when I bring the fire poker down on his dullard skull, and a thick cracking sound comes out of it.

"Unnh," Horun slurs, collapsing to the floor.

Gren's yelling fills the apartment. My hands are on the rifle before it even hits the ground.

I pull back the bolt to check if it's loaded. It is. Fortune favors me.

Sinclair's revolver booms one time, shredding the wallpaper in front of me. I dive to the floor as another bullet passes through where my torso was. I fire back, and his footsteps stomp back down the stairwell. Reflexes pull the bolt of my rifle back and get me back on my feet, leaning beside the window. I have only a few heartbeats before he can get an angle on it. Using the rifle's barrel, I whip the curtain aside and gain a full view of him halfway down the steps, eyes wide in fear and revolver breech open. The fool's reloading.

That's unfortunate.

With one deep exhale and squeezed trigger, a high-caliber round bursts open the window and punctures his chest. His body tumbles down the stairs.

My hands start to shake, but the work isn't over. A third is running out in the street. I step over Horun, dead or not, and peek out the open doorway. Conty is coming toward us, half a block away. But as soon as I come fully outside and aim the rifle at him, he stumbles and turns to run away. The shot is tricky. He's falling over himself and moving erratically, weaving between cars and corpses. Breathe in. Take aim. The rifle's front is heavy, and my shaking hands aren't helping anything. The front sight sits on his chest. Squeeze the trigger. The rifle kicks and roars, but I miss and leave a hole in the car in front of him.

"Please," Conty screams. "Don't kill me!"

I pull the bolt back and take aim again. Breathe in. Aim. Squeeze. And the gun clicks.

Of course.

Dropping the rifle, I rush down the steps and pick up the gun from Sinclair's body. A revolver about half the size of my previous one, with a cylinder for five shots. It'll do. He loaded one bullet. I snap the breech closed and aim the revolver, but Conty is nowhere to be seen. Void. To the void with it all.

"Stop hiding in the corpses, you coward! I won! Against the three of you blithering fools, I won! Come out of that filth and *die*! You deserve death, and you know it!"

Time passes. He doesn't pop back up from his hole. Now the wind is the only response for me.

"Fine! Fine, you coward. Run back to your master. Tell Astraea that I'll kill her on my way out of Ophidia!"

A surge of adrenaline follows those words, along with some sense of power. Who's a driveling sob now?

Oh, wait, Gren!

I rush back up the steps and into the house. Gren's still hiding behind the parlor chair, weeping to himself. He's sniveling and crying harder than I've ever thought possible. Snot and tears run down his face. Never have I thought I'd see such an imposing man reduced to a state like this. It's so unfairly pathetic.

"Hey," I say, low and relaxed. "It's alright, Gren. We're safe. We're safe now."

"What did you do to those men?" Gren says, voice thick with phlegm.

"I stopped them from hurting us. It had to be done."

"Is he—, is he gonna be okay?"

His finger meekly points to Horun. Or since he isn't breathing, Horun's body.

"Sure he is. Listen, they had to be stopped. They would've done bad things to us, buddy. And you did such a good job. Just like I told you. Not all men, or boys, I mean, would've done that."

I reach out my hand to rub his back and try to reassure him, but he recoils from the contact.

"Did, did you kill those men?"

His timid eyes lock with mine. Lying now is impossible.

"I did what had to be done, sport. To keep you safe."

"I—. I— I just wanna go home."

He sobs and cries louder than before, filling the room with his weeping song.

"There, there," I say, trying to pat his back again. He lets it happen this time. "We're going there next, okay? We're going to find my friend, and then we'll get you straight home. How does that sound?"

After a few moments, his sobbing starts to settle down.

"O-o-okay," he mutters.

"Good lad. You're stronger than you think, Gren. You can stop hiding now."

Gren gets up from behind the chair in stages, still unsure if he's safe or not. As he looks at the floor again, I get between him and the body as much as I can.

"That's a good lad. Now, can you close your eyes for me again and take my hand?"

He does as he's told, and his grip is tighter and more painful than before.

"A little less tight, there."

With baby steps, I lead him over Horun's body, out of the house and down the steps, past Sinclair's body, and next to an overturned car nearby.

"Good job. Now, hold tight here for a tick. I think I forgot my watch back there."

He stays standing with his eyes closed, and I sprint back to Sinclair's body to search for some bullets. Between his vest, shirt pocket, and pants, four more rounds were found. Enough to fully load the small revolver.

"It's better than nothing."

Once the gun's loaded, I go back to Horun and see if he has any spare rounds, but none are found. What a useless man. I return to Gren and take his hand, keeping the revolver drawn in my main hand.

"You ready?"

"Mhm," he nods.

"Good. Let's go find Elizabeth."

CHAPTER 42

Wherever the fight is, it isn't in Gusilp Cross. Once we reach Chunneling Road, I look about once more before crossing the street, and the entire area is as silent as a tomb. No souls, hostile or not, are seen all along the streets and boulevards. Just more urban wreckage and decay.

The glass-and-brass doors that comprise the entrance to Elizabeth's apartment building are shattered and almost off of their hinges. A mirage of shoeprints covers the floor from the entrance to the stairwell. I press the metallic button to call the elevator, and it still works.

Hold a moment. Getting into a metal box isn't the best idea, is it?

Gren and I enter the stairwell and climb the narrow flights up to the second floor. Gren has been silent ever since we left that home. Whenever I look back at him, he always avoids eye contact, and the impression of resentment is palpable. I suppose children redirect stress to the nearest adult. That or he's before the violent stages of his life. A pure form of Gren, in a place that'll eat him alive. Keeper above.

I creak open the door leading into the second floor slowly, sweeping my revolver along with my gaze. Compared to downstairs, the hallway is pristine. There are some scratches on the walls, but that's about it. A lush carpet lines the floor between the rows of doors and cushions our footsteps as we creep along. Elizabeth's room is either 204 or 206. After a few beats of no movement, no ambushing men with armbands, I lower my gun.

"Good," I whisper. "Seems safe enough."

As we approach her home more and more, something that I've been feeling the whole day magnifies. Some intermingling of dread and expectation. More than anything, I hope that she is alive and here. She has to be. She just *has* to be.

When we reach 204, I get close to the door and tap my revolver against it to knock.

"Elizabeth? Elizabeth, are you in there?"

No response.

"Elizabeth. It's me, Arthur."

No response again.

Please be here. I don't think I have the power to be hopeless.

"Elizabeth," I shout, crossing over to the other door and slamming my fist against it. "Are you in here? It's me, Arthur!"

I hear footsteps and get back a little, keeping the revolver aimed at leg-level. A few locks unlatch, and the door cracks open enough for an eye to peek out.

Elizabeth's beautiful, anxious eye.

"Oh," I say, taken aback. "Hello there."

Her eye scrunches up and looks like it's about to cry before she flings the door open and rushes out to hug me. Gren jumps a little from the flurry of movement.

"What do you think you're doing here, you big stupid *fool?*" Elizabeth says into my shirt.

A few of her tears dampen the spot below my collarbone.

"I was swept away in a riot and jumped through a window," I say, hugging her back. "Made me reconsider a few things."

She laughs and holds the hug for a few moments, looking up at me with a big smile.

"Inside. Hurry."

The three of us get into her apartment, and she locks the two deadbolts and lodges a chair underneath the handle. A modest kitchen and living room adjoin in a singular room, with a platform to the left having sofas and a radio. Behind those is a balcony glass door, covered in thick false-wood shutters. The cyclical drone of the man declaring martial law plays quietly from the radio.

"So," Elizabeth says, coming up behind Gren and me, "who's your friend?"

"Hi, lady," Gren says. "I'm Gren. My mom said that Mr. Fey could take care of me while she's away."

"Oh," Elizabeth says. "That's, that's good to hear, Gren."

"Hey, Gren," I say. "Why don't you see if there's anything else playing on the radio?"

"I sure hope so."

Once he kneels to fidget with the dials, I lean in close to Elizabeth's ear.

"He's my best friend, just with the mind of a child," I whisper. "Surgery gone bad."

"Oh, no," Elizabeth mutters.

I pull away from her ear, and our eyes meet. None of the chemistry has faded. We don't hold out long before we embrace again, lips locking for a few moments. I pull her in as close as I can before my arms cry out in pain.

"Ooh," I wince. "Forgot about that."

"What's that?" she whispers.

I look over her back at my forearm bandages. Some wounds have reopened.

"Nothing major," I say. "Just need to change some bandages, that's all."

She looks behind herself and sees my arm as well.

"I'll go fetch some from the restroom," she says. "Were you outside when it happened? The attacks?"

"Yes," I say. "And the both of us saw far too much. Wait, attacks? As in more than one?"

"That's what we were led to believe. Reports were frantic before the Armed Authority took over the airwaves." She starts to head to the right door, behind the sofa. "At least three major bombings, at the Statehouse, Mountain Guild Bank, and somewhere deep in Plimred Yard. They said at least a hundred pounds of explosive was used collectively."

She says it so matter-of-factly. The most violent event in recent memory, and she can't help but be a journalist about it.

"Here," Elizabeth says, returning to me. "Do you want me to change them?"

"Yes, more than anything."

We sit beside each other on the sofa, near a playful Gren whose imagination transforms the radio into something he's communicating to.

"Breaker, breaker," he says. "We lost you, Captain."

"Nothing on there, Gren?" I ask.

"No," he says, pouting and turning away from his game. "It's just the same guy sounding bored over and over."

Elizabeth takes in my right arm and starts to undo the bandage. Dead skin and scabs peel off with it and leave behind sharp stings. When she pours a bit of alcohol on them, they sting even more. The pain isn't that bothersome, though.

"So, were there undead," I ask, "at the other bombings too?"

She stops and looks at me. "What?"

"Gren and I. We were at the Statehouse, when it all happened. Some sorcerer was on a nearby rooftop and opened a portal to some blighted nightmare. It turned a lot of people into the undead, just like in the World Before."

Elizabeth's eyes are as wide as I've ever seen them, eyebrows cocked to match. It must be impossible to imagine such a thing if you didn't see it.

"No," she says, starting to collect herself. "No, the other bombings were just nitron-laced explosives, as far as the news told us. I didn't see anything. I was home. Once the looting started, I stayed inside and locked my door." She pauses for a moment, still in shock. "And you saw them? The undead?"

Last night replays itself. Rotted teeth tearing plump flesh and arteries. Husbands gorging upon wives. Murder and consumption for its own sake, noxious and senseless.

Death consuming life.

"Yes, I did."

Elizabeth stops wrapping and takes me into a tight hug. Every time she touches me, I feel so secure.

"I'm so sorry, Arthur. I'm so sorry things happened like this."

"Why are you sorry? Did you do all this?"

"No. It's just… You know what I mean."

"It's not so bad, either way. After all, if things shook out differently, I might have never met you."

"Oh, stop," she says, chuckling a little.

After a few moments, she pulls away and gives me a kiss on the cheek, returning to changing the bandages.

"They're coming over the hill, Captain," Gren says, with his best impression of a military officer. "Watch out."

"I really missed you," I say to Elizabeth. "You know that?"

"Me too. If only you didn't run away from me like a fool."

"Indeed, I must confess: That was probably the stupidest thing I've ever done. I was… I just… It was too perfect. You were too perfect. I didn't want to destroy it like I've done everything else."

"But by running away, you did destroy it. Just prematurely, without the good parts that come before the end."

Keeper above, this woman.

"You're right. I hope I didn't do any permanent damage."

Elizabeth smiles. "Not anything you can't fix, eventually."

She taps my bandaged arm.

"But I'm still mad at you."

"That's deserved, and ow."

"Are you bleeding anywhere else?"

"My left leg."

"A— Atten—" the radio man's voice cuts through the static. "…update on…"

"Gren," I say. "Stop on a station for a moment."

He moans in frustration and lets go of the knob.

"The Armed Authority has established an evacuee camp in the Upper West Grove, in front of Klemen's Gate. This camp is available only to residents north of the Grengara River. If you are found by Armed Authority forces, comply with any of their demands, for your safety and theirs. Attention. Attention."

"Thank the Keeper," Elizabeth says.

"Time to move," I say.

"Can I keep the radio," Gren says, "to play with?"

"No, it'll be too cumbersome."

"I got something for you, Gren," Elizabeth says, rising from her seat.

I pull the revolver from my coat pocket and check the hammer and cylinder. No rust, as far as I can tell.

Elizabeth goes into her bedroom for a moment.

"Should I pack some spare clothes, do you think?" she calls out.

"No," I shout. "The less we carry, the easier it'll be to travel."

"Of course, of course."

She returns to the main room with a wooden toy soldier in her hand.

"Here," she says, handing it to Gren. "A false sergeant, dwarven-made. My father used to collect them, and you can have this one."

A bright smile beams from Gren's face.

"Thanks, Elizabeth."

Elizabeth tousles his bald head.

"Don't mention it."

I stalk over to the front door and undo the locks. Opening the door and peeking through the crack. No movement at all in the dusty hallway.

"Where is everyone?"

"Hiding, like us," Elizabeth says.

"Hmm,"

"Is it safe?"

I look back from the crack and see Gren holding her hand. My paternal nature has lost out, it seems.

"Safe enough. Come on."

I'm the first through the door, revolver drawn, and the two close behind me. We cross quickly down the hall. Our footsteps against the carpet are the only sound during our trip down the hall and the flights of stairs. Once we reach the broken glass of the building's front doors, crispy cold air brushing my face, I realize that my internal compass is in disarray.

"Which way is Klemen's Gate?"

"Northward," Elizabeth says, pointing her finger to our right. "That way, I think."

I skulk just past the entrance and lean against the wall, peering down the wide avenue of Chunneling Road. Gray skies and diffuse light cover the street and its destroyed inhabitants. A chute of water sprays into the air half a block down, the result of an uptorn fire hydrant. More rifle shots somewhere behind us, but not a living body on the streets. But who knows how many lie in wait in the dozens and dozens of windows, all along the block? Any second, we could get shot down in transit. A clothing store across the street is dim and smashed open. Bobbing and weaving between hiding spots it is.

"Are you two ready to run?" I ask.

"Why? Is someone out there?" Elizabeth asks.

"Maybe," I say. "Too many potential shooting positions to tell for sure. Get behind me."

Once I hear their footsteps stop just behind me, I tense my entire body, prepared to act.

"On three," I say, "stick as close to me as we can. We're going for Letterman's across the street. One. Two. Three."

Muscles all along my calves and thighs erupt in motion, running as fast as I've ever had to in my life. As soon as we step off of the sidewalk onto the first lane of traffic, my lungs already begin to burn. Somewhere behind me, Elizabeth and Gren are panting. We cross the second and third lanes, the concrete divider, the three lanes on the other side, and stop once we cross the threshold into the darkened clothing store. My entire body aches from the effort, and I can feel the cuts on my leg reopening.

"Alright," I gasp. "We didn't get shot at. That's good."

"Do you want me to carry you, Elizabeth?" Gren asks, perfectly composed.

"Yes," she pants and smiles. "Please."

Gren's massive arms scoop her up in one deft motion, and he holds her without a struggle.

"How chivalrous," I say.

"What's that word mean?" Gren asks.

"Nothing. You're a good kid, Gren."

Starting in the distance and closing steadily is something blaring from a speaker and a car engine. The three of us press against a wall beside the door and wait.

"Attention. Attention," the same male voice ricochets along the street, getting louder as it gets closer. "An update on the evacuation of Ophidia. The Armed Authority has established an evacuee camp in the Upper West Grove, in front of Klemen's Gate. This camp is available only to residents north of the Grengara River. If you are found by Armed Authority forces, comply with any of their demands, for your safety and theirs. Attention. Attention."

I get close to the door and peek outside, seeing a large open-air truck with a long truck bed instead of rear seating and some sort of treading instead of back tires. Six olive-drabbed soldiers fill it, rifles and pistols in hand, along with a large pair of speakers emitting the radio broadcast.

"And so begins the exodus," I say.

"Should we go out to them?" Elizabeth asks.

"No," I say. "I'm not trusting anyone until we see Klemen's Gate."

They continue down the main street, broadcast fading with the distance, when a bottle crashes against the front of the truck and explodes in flames, setting the driver alight. Six orcs and four humans with wrenches, cleavers, and other crude weapons surge out of a nearby building and charge the soldiers. Five of the looters are shot dead before they make it to the truck, and the rest mob the truck and attempt to club the soldiers. I've seen enough.

Moving away from the entrance and further into the shop, a door behind the counter leads to a dim stocking room, where knocked-over mannequins wearing dresses, petticoats, and smoking jackets are piled hastily all along the floor and near a metal door on the other side.

"There's an alleyway back here," I say. "Come on."

When I look toward the two, I see a fine black longcoat on the floor, left alone in the chaos. The one on me is covered in mud, holes, and a bit of dried blood. The decision makes itself.

We come out of the clothing store into a narrow alley, almost made into a hallway from the fire escapes and close-proximity buildings. We traverse through it slowly, with me in front sweeping the revolver past dumpsters and up at the occasional window. People rush past the mouth of the alley on the other side, and we duck behind some trash cans to hide. But moments before they disappear, they appear unarmed and with children. More scared-witless folks, just like us.

"Hurry," I say, getting up to run to join the sparse crowds.

I stop just at the alleyway opening, and once Gren and Elizabeth reach me, I grab onto the end of Elizabeth's dress, now chest-level with me.

All along the street, families appear at doorways, stealing glances of the outside world before they rush north. A glimpse of comfort emerges when I see kindred spirits like this. They still avoid each other, and me when they see the gun. We spill out onto the road and go between cars and raised stairways as we make our way north. Gentle murmurs of parents urging children and stomping shoes on concrete fill the air. Parents try as hard as they can to keep their young ones quiet, as we all scurry from cover to cover. Whispering any and all assurances so that whoever is doing the killing doesn't find us.

Whenever a gunshot rings, we all stop and wait a couple of moments. When no further shots or cries of pain follow, the herd reawakens and continues along.

We sometimes see movements in windows, too. But it's always scared civilians catching a glimpse of us before slamming their shutters closed. The violence is strangely always just off in the distance. Gunshots never get too close, and the bodies we come across are never fresh. It's as if a tidal wave of death washed throughout the city overnight, and the decaying fish and seaweed are left behind in its wake.

Even though the air is cold, sweat pours down my chest and back. The tension of expected violence makes my hands shake like nothing else, like it's always the second before a job went bad.

"Are we there yet, daddy?" a girl asks her dad behind us.

"A few more blocks, sweetheart, promise," her father says.

Soon enough, the military presence reveals itself. Sandbag barricades and abandoned Armed Authority jalopies crop up here and there on the street. Checkpoints made in hubris when the state thought they had control of Ophidia. Left behind when the forces of terror became too much to bear. There's evidence of conflict, too. Scorched out windows, blown apart carriages, and dried pools of blood. There are also one or two military bodies. An officer's body lies against his vehicle, torn in half. Not too far from him is a body half-burned. Its legs and chest are completely charred. Its face is untouched, eyes sunken and gray. I can't say why, but that thing has to be a shaman. Keeper knows what horror they're unleashing in the poorer districts, where nullification powder is barely spread at all.

Up ahead past a few families is a quick scuffle of movement and gasps of alarm.

"Are you civilians?" a crisp male voice barks. "Hands, let me see your hands!"

We all immediately comply. The family in front of us ducks down and reveals an Armed Authority officer leaning up against a set of sandbags holding his bloodstained leg. His other trembling hand holds an automatic pistol, aimed at the lot of us.

"All of you, single file," he commands. "March past me, no quick movements. The checkpoint is four more blocks north of here. If you have any weapons, dispose of them before you reach the checkpoint, or else. Understood?"

Quiet and defeated murmurs of assent come from the families. They start to form a line, with us in the back.

"Void," I whisper. "This is going to take forever."

A shot rings out, hitting somewhere behind me, and all sense of civility shatters. People scream and dart for the closest cover, most rushing under vehicles or behind stairwells. Elizabeth grips my hand and pulls Gren and me aside behind a nearby carriage.

"Remain calm," the officer yells. "Maintain composure, please!"

Another shot almost hits him, and he dives behind the sandbags he was leaning on.

Children are screaming and crying, their parents powerless to soothe them. From a certain angle, this must look like the street itself is in hysterics.

"Everybody, stay down," another voice calls down the street, back the way we came. "We don't want to harm any of you. We just want that officer, the one cowering behind the sandbags."

"The only thing you'll be getting is a bullet, reprobate," the officer yells.

"We have explosives, officer. Comply *now*, or else we start blowing apart children!"

Families scream and plead for mercy.

"I have to do something," I say.

"No, Fey," Elizabeth whispers. "Just stay down. We don't know how many there are."

I lean out for a moment to get a glimpse of where they are. About ten men are back the way we came, crouched behind cover with rifles aimed our way. Far too many to take care of. I could kill one or two, maybe, but then I'd be shot dead.

"Enough, enough," the officer screams. "I surrender! I'm coming out!"

His hands spring up above the sandbags, one still holding his pistol. Leaning against the barricade, he slowly and painfully stands back up.

"Throw out your handgun," the criminal yells.

The officer does as commanded, the pistol skitters along the street.

The criminals rush toward us, boots stomping on the street. In a few seconds, they have the officer surrounded. Two or three watch behind them, rifles aimed at the rest of us. Each of the gunmen wears a red armband on their left arms. How many different factions are tearing Ophidia apart?

Their leader is a middle-aged man with pale skin and balding blond hair. Like his friends, a bandana is pulled up over his nose. He ambles over to the officer and tucks a pistol under the officer's chin.

"Good to see you again, Lieutenant," he says. "Thought you could get away after all those raids this season? Thought you and your dwarven-backed cronies would get away with letting this country *rot*?"

The officer spits at his face, dampening the bandana.

The gunman laughs and pistol-whips the officer. The crowd shrieks in response.

"Please," one of the nearby women pleads. "Just let us go!"

The gunmen start to get antsy around all of the crying civilians. Their rifles sweep over men, women, and children erratically. No way in the void will this end well.

"All of you get out from your hidey holes," the leader screams. "I will not ask again!"

People shriek and plead again. We can all feel what's about to happen next. They never planned on letting anyone go. Too many witnesses to tell the military where to find them.

"That means you three, too," a shrill voice says behind us.

I turn around to find one of the riflemen with his rifle aimed at us. As soon as our eyes meet, his widen in recognition.

"Keeper above, am I lucky today?" he says. "She'll pay me in gold when I bring you in."

"Wait, please," I beg. "You don't have to do this."

"Do what? Make a fortune and get away clean? And who are these two?"

Elizabeth whimpers, and Gren hides behind her.

"Got yourself a little family, do you?" he says. "What's your name, miss?"

"Get away from me," Elizabeth says.

Their leader is shouting something again, and more people cry in response. But I don't care.

Our captor gets a little closer to Elizabeth.

"Come now, miss. I won't bite," he grins.

"You touch her," I say, "and you will die *choking.*"

"Really? Little old Arthur Fey, the one who can't stop sniveling and drinking, is going to grow a spine and fight me? No way in the void will you put up a fight, even if I do this."

He slides his rifle over his shoulder and snatches Elizabeth. She knows better than to scream at this moment, so she covers her mouth to suppress herself.

In a blur of movement, I reach back to draw my revolver. Pain alights along my left arm, and the muscles tense on their own. My left hand makes a fist and swings itself, dragging the rest of me along with it. It lands squarely on his jaw, sending the both of us off of our feet and into a stairwell. He grunts in pain and slams down the stairs, with me right above him. A few of his teeth scatter past his head. I try to move my left arm, but it's possessed, not listening to me in the slightest.

"Stop," the man says. "I'm sorry, plea—"

My left hand grips around his throat, tightening like a steel cord. The bump in his throat moves frantically, going up and down with his breath. His throat is as rigid as it hopes to be, and my hand keeps tightening. I never imagined a throat to have so little to give.

"Don't," he chokes out. "You don't have to do this."

A gunshot rings out near the officer and his captor. More screams follow it.

I try to pull back, to relent. It doesn't listen to me. My palm pushes into his throat. It forces the air and muscles out. His limbs wriggle helplessly in protest. His limp hand brushes my face, another plea for mercy.

"I'm sorry," I say.

More gunshots echo out, more screaming.

Finally, his tunnel collapses. The cartilage or muscle or whatever blasted thing I caved in causes him to wheeze. His eyes bulge open in panic. Both of his hands grip mine, trying to pull it off.

It's too late. He can't breathe.

The burning pain in my arm subsides. I regain control of it. I fall onto my back, getting a few steps up and away from him. His eyes look at mine again, wide open, and he tries to mouth something, but all that comes out are the wheezes of a dying man.

A few seconds later, his body goes limp in stages. First his legs, then his arms, and finally his head goes slack. All muscles release the burden of life and drool dribbles out from his mouth.

Elizabeth is standing at the stairwell in absolute shock, both eyes tearing up.

"What happened?" Gren asks.

I go up past her and stop Gren from looking.

"Come with me, Gren," I say. "We have to go. You too, Elizabeth, come on."

I grab her hand and pull her away. Her body complies even though she doesn't want to.

Peeking back around the carriage, the officer and lead gunman are dead. Several civilians are too. Someone must have grabbed the officer's gun and set off the powder keg. The rest of the families are being chased and shot at down the street by the surviving gunmen.

"Elizabeth, Gren," I turn back to them, "take each other's hands, don't let go. We're getting to that checkpoint."

Elizabeth reaches out and grabs my hand as tightly as she can. Gren holds hers in turn. I draw my pistol and lead the way.

Darting off to the right, we enter a small alleyway, dodging detritus and corpses that dangle from fire escapes. The streets are much the same. Although this time, more waiting is spent to see if any of those armed lunatics find us or are waiting to shoot anyone who passes. As soon as no one shoots me in the back or the front, we rush from cover to cover, the same dance as before now done in a frenzy. Gunshots continue to ring out in the direction of that band of murderers. The chaos and evil never stop.

After some time, we hit a major intersection, a miniature square that's surrounded by theaters. The signs are blown out, and glass litters the streets. More carriages, bodies, and vehicles, all left behind in death. How is Gren handling all this?

Looking back at him, his face is blank and distant. His eyes have the stare of inattention. He's retreated far, far within himself, and who knows when he'll come back out. At least Elizabeth seems to be a comfort to him. She'll be a better parent than I ever could.

We reach a turn in the street, and once we cross it, soldiers with large emplaced rifles behind sandbags are stopping a mass of civilians who've gotten here first. I lead the three of us into the gathering as much as I can before families start to push back on us. Soon enough, we're all so close together, we may as well be one great blob of fabric and flesh. Relief cuts away the tension, and I pocket the gun back into my coat. We made it. We're safe.

"Maintain civility at all times," a sergeant atop a military truck shouts. "You'll all be processed and safe in due time. Those with weapons will be summarily punished. No traitors will be allowed to leave the city limits!"

Void, that's right. What the officer said earlier, I need to get rid of this thing.

"I'll be right back," I whisper to Elizabeth.

I turn around to leave, and at the edges of the crowd are more of them. A few more of those armbanded bastards, undoubtedly looking for me. I aim my face downward enough to hide it and still keep an eye on them. They fan out and pick through the crowd, turning around people that look vaguely like me, men who are slim enough or who have a bald enough head. By the time they'll get to us, we'll be past the checkpoint, surely. Safe passage assured to wherever the state decides to herd us.

But it won't end simply like that, will it?

Astraea's a capable and vindictive person. As long as she's alive, the hunt may never stop. As long as we're somewhere populated enough, one of her snakes will probably lie in wait. A lifetime on the run, do Elizabeth and Gren really deserve that? Looking back, it's something I've been doomed to since the first day, isn't it? As soon as I agreed to live a life like this, a peaceful end stopped being a possibility.

Still, the three of us, once we get somewhere remote enough, could have that idyllic life, perhaps. A small wooden cabin, harvesting Old-World plants on a small plot somewhere closer to the southern border, where the beastkin tribes don't lurk as much. A life like the folk out in Fallund. A simpler life, free from the void-cursed control of the city. Could that be what I've wanted? Maybe my paranoia bars me from considering that path forward.

That strange man from my dreams comes back to me, as well. What was his name? I fail to remember. For some reason, against all reasonable logic, I consider his words as well. As if my leading myself to Astraea would even constitute as some grand sacrifice. Bringing myself to her like a lamb to slaughter. Quite the heroic notion, isn't it?

One of the armbanded men triggers a fight with a father who's had enough and gets a punch to the face in return. Several nearby families look back in mild panic.

No, no, I can't do this. I can't simply run away. Every day would be a day of dread, wondering if they'll finally find us. I must handle this first. Astraea must be dealt with.

Only then will the three of us be able to live, truly live, and perhaps I can drag myself toward being a better person.

I weave back through the crowd to get to Elizabeth and Gren before I get the chance to second-guess myself.

"Elizabeth."

She looks at me, scared and comforted.

"Yes?"

"I... There's... T-there's something I need to handle. I need to do it alone before I can safely say we're going to be alright."

Tears form at the corners of her eyes.

"Arthur, no," she whimpers.

"I'm sorry, Elizabeth, but this is the way it is. She'll never stop hunting us if I don't."

"Who? Who won't stop hunting us?"

"I'm going to handle it and come back, understand? I'll find both of you, I promise. I promise upon my life."

The tears fall down her cheeks, cutting a sheen through dirt and grime.

"You can't do this to me. Not again. *Please.*"

"I wish I couldn't, but I have to. Take care of Gren in the meantime, will you? For me?"

She tries to blink the tears away, but they flow down even faster.

"You bastard. You're just the worst, aren't you?"

"Yes. Yes, I am."

I grab her hand and kiss it before brushing her cheek.

"You're the best thing that's ever happened to me. I lo—"

"*Don't,*" she stops me. "Don't even think of saying that. Not yet."

She brushes the side of my face, as well, and leans in for a kiss. It's the most electric one yet.

"Now go, before I change my mind."

I nod and go to Gren.

"I'll be back, Gren. Keep her safe until I do, alright?"

He turns his head, and once our eyes meet, he's still looking past me.

"Okay, mister."

"Good. Good lad."

I pat him on the shoulder. He doesn't react.

"I love you, Gren. You were the best friend I've ever had."

For a second, he doesn't respond. Then, a flicker of recognizance. Maybe it's my desperation for it to be so, but in that brief instant, his eyes lit up.

I pat him on the shoulder again and leave, weaving between people fast to get away from them. In a way, this is death, too. Consigning myself to this. A necessary one, but pitiful all the same.

The chasm between me and everyone else may never be crossable.

The first armbanded cretin to spot me is a wiry woman, almost half my size. She shoves her friend and points at me, and within seconds they surround me.

"Just take me to her," I grimace.

"With pleasure, Mr. Fey," the woman says.

One of them grips the back of my coat and pushes me. No one in the crowd dares to interfere. They're all too miserable and terrified to be noble.

I steal one glance back. A blink of an eye's worth at those two. Gren's hugging Elizabeth, her face buried in his chest.

So close. We were so blasted close.

CHAPTER 43

They announced that all civilians that have yet to evacuate just hunker down so armed forces can reestablish order. We passed a few trucks with large speakers announcing as much on the way here. The soldiers driving the trucks looked me dead in the eye and just kept driving, pretending not to see the three armed people escorting me rather forcefully. I guess everyone's just doing the bare minimum and nothing else during times like these.

The trek from the checkpoint to wherever we are now, near Oxlen University, was desolate and depressing. One of the bandits felt the need to continually jab me with his rifle. They frisked me as soon as they got a few blocks away from the military's prying eyes, finding my revolver immediately. Panic bites at the back of my mind. No semblance of a plan of action. The tattoo is continually burning, seeping further and further into my arm, almost reaching my chest. It periodically twitches, and I have to grab it with my other arm and try to keep it still. Now's not the time. Not yet. Perhaps it'll be my saving grace.

Gunfire echoes from several directions. Once or twice, we had to duck down when it sounded like it was close. Panicking civilians watched from windows and did their best to hide from us once they saw us. No outside intervention to save me this time.

"Where are we going," I ask.

"Somewhere familiar, aristocrat scum," the woman bandit sneers at me.

We cross Hignen Boulevard and enter Serenity Park. World Before trees and bushes line aged sidewalks. The desolation of the city has freed this little square. Halfway through the walk, I see Oxlen's archway, now half destroyed, and my stomach drops.

"No," I say.

"Oh, yes. The students fled the first night, and we took it over," the woman says. "Looks like your curriculum is getting longer."

"How do you know so much about me?"

"She completely filled us in. In case you tried to hide out nearby. Guess what else?"

"What?"

"Once you're handled. Elizabeth and Gren are next. No loose ends."

I stop walking and turn to stare her down. My tattoo burns. It's as if I stuck my arm in a boiling pot.

"You touch a hair on their heads, and I swear."

"What? Swear what? You're a pathetic, young *nothing*. The game is over, Fey. You're done."

A barrage of automatic fire erupts from somewhere inside the Oxlen campus. All three of the bandits unsling their rifles and crouch down.

"Was she expecting anybody," one of them asks.

"'Course not, you dolt. Walter, stay here with him. You, with me."

They set off, crouched and rifles aimed at the ground. The last bandit aims his rifle at me and shoves me onto a nearby bench.

"Don't get cute now, you hear?"

"Shame you don't have handcuffs, isn't it?"

He grimaces and jabs me in the stomach with the butt of his rifle.

"No speaking, louse."

He stands a few steps away, awkwardly aiming his rifle at me while looking at Oxlen.

A sharp pain jabs into my right arm and pierces into my torso. I grunt in pain and double over.

"What's your problem?"

"Nothing, it's nothing."

Visions of somewhere a long time ago flash before my eyes. I look to my left and right and see rows upon rows of dwarven soldiers, each driven berserk by a bright tattoo that grows along their body. A dwarf in a robe is chanting something in front of a glowing runic table.

What in the Keeper's name did Bjorni bestow upon me?

I shake my head and look at the bandit. His right eyebrow is quirked up and he looks as if he's trying to see if asking something will garner anything worthwhile.

Just then, more automatic gunfire erupts from Oxlen. The bandit drops to a crouch and aims his rifle that way.

My arm lurches forward, tattoo glowing through the shirt fabric. Guess now's the time.

My arm jabs the bandit across the jaw, knocking him off his feet and his eyes momentarily roll into the back of his head. I then regain my balance and punch him again, and again. He fires his rifle in the air, near my head. I grip the rifle and try to yank it free from his hands. His eyes return to normal and his face is one of abject terror.

"Don't! Please don't!"

"Too late for that!"

I jab him in the jaw with its butt. He folds over and crumples to the ground.

I spin the rifle and aim it at him, waiting to see if he'll get up. Some more gunfire reports come out of Oxlen.

After he doesn't get up, I crouch down and run his pockets, looking for spare rounds. I find one more stripper clip with about six rounds on it. I pocket them and run towards Oxlen.

Just then, some more visions. A dwarf on a rock is yelling and pointing his axe at a beastkin village, somewhere deep in the shifting forest. I'm shorter and filled with rage. I'm eager to kill the denizens of the shifting forests. I know the dwarf on the rock. He's Lodrun Voidwater, a lieutenant of the Grimaxe clan, whose main purpose was to protect dwarven mining expeditions. This is somewhere northwest of New Colonia, about 250 years ago.

I shake my head again, and my vision returns to normal.

There's no way in the void I'd know all that. I roll up my sleeve and look at the tattoo. It's burning a bright deep blue, and runes are starting to appear in my skin. The serpent's getting longer, and growing along my arm.

"Whatever in the void it is you're doing," I say to it, "Can it wait until we get to Astraea?"

It just pulses in intensity. No words or anything enter my mind. Just the subtle impregnation of memories that aren't mine.

I rub my eyes and groan. "Right. Let's do this, then."

Before entering, I look up and down the road to see if I'm safe, hiding behind an abandoned carriage. Nothing on either end. Just shuttered windows and the wind blowing the inept powder up off the street.

I pass under the broken archway and onto the corpse of Oxlen. Windows on several buildings are shattered, and discarded books and bags line the paths. I walk past Gregory Guillihon's Hall of Rhetoric and see tossed suitcases and backpacks all over the ground, books and notebooks tattered and strewn all over the stairs. I feel the urge to call out for Timothy, or Kedriff. I wonder whose corpses I'd come across if I entered these halls.

Just past Anna Hnona's Hall of Sciences I see the first few bodies. Armbanded men and women like the ones that chased me filled with bullet wounds and the rifles beside them hurriedly disarmed. I fight back a primal terror as I get close to them and check their pockets for spare rounds. Nothing.

A few more steps forward and I see a stranger, a trooper of the opposing force. An elfblood man in a dark red three-piece suit. A hat that matches the suit is thrown a few steps away. He has no gun to speak of, but there's a lot of small pistol cartridges piled beside him. He had something automatic, which means his comrades probably do, too.

A barrage of rounds explodes the ground beside me, and I fall backwards, scramble to my feet, and take cover behind a nearby pillar. Some more rounds pound into the concrete, sending flakes flying in every direction. I unsling the rifle and check the chamber. It's loaded. I slowly scan the rows of windows across the campus until I see him. A man in a dark suit aiming a machine gun at me. I duck back behind the pillar.

"I'm not one of them, you know," I shout.

"All the same to me," he shouts back.

Another intense exchange of rounds comes from deeper in the campus. I look out and see the origin. The Hall of Administration. Bodies are in disarray all along the stairwell, and the front doors have been exploded open; a gaping maw leading into the building.

The man pounds some more rounds into my pillar. He's trying to freeze me. Keep me in one spot so reinforcements can come and finish me off.

Something I don't have time for.

I raise the rifle and lean it against the pillar. This gets more rounds sent my way. I wait for a pause. When there's no gunfire, an eerie silence comes over the entire campus. Silent enough for me to hear him reloading.

I rotate until I see the window he's in. Breathe in. Relax. Finger on the trigger.

As soon as he pops up, I fire.

Dead on target. A pink spray goes up behind him and he drops.

I rack the bolt and look amongst the sea of windows. Some shattered, most of it not. Especially on the upper floors. Another barrage of automatic fire spills out of the Administration building.

I sprint to the blown-out entrance and stop at the doors, or rather where the doors used to be. I peek my head in for a moment and dive back, in case anyone's watching. All I caught was bodies and bloodshed. Dozens, at least. I peek once more, and when no gunfire spills out at me, I enter.

Bodies of every race are found here. Humans, half-orcs, elf-bloods, dwarves. Too many dead to count. The direction of the corpses shows where Astraea's crew did their last stand. Amidst all the blood and viscera, I take a peek at a few of Astraea's men, and see what I assume to be sword wounds. Some of the elf's men are not far ahead, with bullet holes all over them.

Keeper above, I'm in over my head. My body starts to shake and I can't stop it. I look down at my rifle. I blink and it becomes a greataxe. I look up to see my kinsmen charging through the shifting forests, cutting down beastkin shamans that shoot ivy branches out of the ground.

"Dammit, enough of this," I hiss under my breath. I slap myself in the face and return to reality. The burning sensation in my arm is almost too much.

Keeping my head on a swivel, I enter the hall, swinging my rifle frantically at every possible opening. Part of me knows it's futile. If someone was going to ambush me, they'd be able to do it.

I step over the first collective of bodies, bandits shot in the back as they went for the stairs. Another one is dead on the first landing of the stairs, behind a machine gun emplacement. A few men in suits next to him, with a pair of opposing bodies on top of one another, blades buried deep in their stomachs. It's all so barbaric.

A sharp burning pain shoots directly from my forearm to my mind. I shout in pain and drop the rifle. A flash flood of hundreds of memories assaults me. Battles, rituals, funeral ceremonies. This thing has been with dwarfkind since the Exodus. I'm the first human it's been attached to. Warnings from a dwarf runecrafter echo in my mind. "The humans can never get ahold of this," she says, "They'd be unstoppable if they got their hands on it."

I drop to my knees and clutch my head, unable to stop the torrent. The pain overwhelms me and I land on top of an armband half orc.

***

I'm unsure of how long I've been like this. Seconds, minutes, hours. It doesn't even matter. I know the entire history of the Grimaxe clan. I've seen their battered history. So much bloodshed and carnage, for some shiny stones in the ground. I'll never understand this race. With each memory, something continues to take shape, just outside my periphery. It has a name, I think, and it's trying to show me something.

Eventually, the memories slow down, the closer to the present time they get. Tattoos are given more and more sparingly, most are laid to rest. One day, a few decades ago possibly, the dwarf most recently given to it sets out of home, driven to exile for killing his clan leader over what to do with some human refugees. He has a bundle on his back, and sees Ophidia in the distance. Years go by, as a mercenary here, a bodyguard there, until he meets Astraea. She smiles at him and promises a job worth more to the free world than anything he's ever done. He's killed dozens of gang members and secret operatives in her name. The more bodies he piles up, and the more silvum he acquires, a certain morose ennui starts to envelop him. He struggles more and more to find a point to waking up, a reason to get out of bed, but he does so. He's a good soldier, as he was trained to be. That is, until he starts to work with a man with spectacles. Mr. Clarke! Clarke sends him on mission after mission, fighting alongside striking workers and even breaking into homes to kill police commissioners, politicians. Wetwork for political gain, something he promised himself he'd never do.

Finally, the sequence slows to a crawl, the dwarf takes a shot of whiskey and looks in the mirror. Sure enough, it's Bjorni.

"Klenahn, *vigne.*"

The tattoo simmers at a low brightness on his head.

"Fey, if you get this and don't die, use it to stop her. She's failed. Whatever that elf has planned is going to happen. Astraea knows this, and she's got something far worse in mind. She's turned bitter, she wants the whole city, even the country, to burn."

He rubs his eyes and turns from the mirror.

"Don't let her survive the chaos, and if you fail, don't let her get to Volhansk first."

He opens a bottle of whiskey and sighs.

"*Vigne.*"

***

I gasp awake, covered in sweat. I look outside to see how much time has passed. The sun is still high in the sky. Some more gunfire comes from upstairs. It only must've been a few minutes. To say I'm disoriented would be an understatement. How far ahead of me did Bjorni plan for? And what would drive a man like him to suicide? Not even to mention Volhansk. What does someone like Astraea have to do with a nation that's still recovering from a civil war?

I need answers. Now.

The burning in my arm subsides. I roll up my sleeve to see the tattoo's design still progressing up my arm.

"Help me end her, and you can have me."

The tattoo pulses twice in brightness.

"That'll do."

I rise from the pile, pushing up from a body that breathes its last gasp, and go up the stairs.

I go from each floor and wait for gunfire to dictate whether to go up it or not. The second floor was another bloodbath, with bodies of both sides lining the hallway. The third floor was blocked off with piles of desks, utterly impassable. Halfway up to the fourth floor, a hand grabs my pant leg.

I swing the rifle down and see one of the bandits who took me in, the woman. A sword has her implanted against the ground, and a puddle of blood is below her.

"The elf's men... Got here first... Go and die to them... you *coward*."

I shake my leg free and the light fades from her eyes fast. Never in my life did I think I'd be able to move through so much death with ease. Maybe the incident at the Statehouse numbed me more than I thought.

A wide set of double doors await me on the fourth floor. Gunshots echo through it, so I guess this is my stop. I press my ear to the door.

"Void, she's putting up a fight," a masculine voice says.

"She's down to knives, she won't last much longer," another, deeper voice says.

I brace myself and ready the rifle. I see the tattoo running down both of my hands. Such exponential growth.

"Keep me alive, get me to her," I whisper.

I kick the door open and two men with pistols look at me, bewildered. I shoot one in the stomach and the other draws. No time to pull the bolt.

I throw the rifle at him, and it cracks as it strikes across his head. He drops to one knee and loses grip of the pistol. While he's struggling to stand back up, I pick up the pistol and shoot him twice.

I take out the magazine and count the bullets. Three shots left. As I attempt to loot his pockets, a man in a suit backs out of the administration main office, firing into the door. A knife flashes out of the room and lands in his neck. He staggers, shooting until his gun runs dry, then falls over.

She idly walks out from the room, pulling the dagger free from his body.

"Astraea," I shout, "Here I am!"

She looks up, confused, then a vicious snarl creeps across her face.

"Oh look," she says, "A nice ending to my evening. Killing the measly human who *betrayed me*!"

My upper body ignites in heat and I draw the pistol. She throws a knife and knicks my ear and I fire twice. One catches her in the leg and she dives back into the office on the second shot.

"Now, how in the void did I betray you," I ask.

"Come now, Fey, don't be coy. You killed my lieutenant, the finest dwarf I had, you met with Faustus and were allowed to leave alive. How do you expect me to not put the pieces together?"

"Faustus? You mean the elf?"

"Don't play dumb, Fey."

I take a few steps forward and aim into a room. The entire left half of this floor is interconnected.

"I'm not," I say, "I still have no clue what all this is about. That strange creature, whom I assume you used to work for, gave some grand speech about his plan to overtake this country, and then thanked me for the box. That's it."

An echo of laughter fills the halls.

"Oh Fey, you're either far more crafty or far more daft than I expected. How'd a sniveling little aristocrat like you find himself in the center of all this?"

"I have you to thank for that. What did you do to Bjorni?"

Silence fills the halls.

"He couldn't keep killing. He was at the end of his rope for years. Now that he's seen what I have to do to undue all this, he decided it was too much."

"And what is that, exactly?"

"You know what happened in front of the Statehouse?"

I sweep the next room, and continue slowly down the hall.

"What about it?"

"Imagine that, but multiplied. Faustus's nation will be that of corpses."

"Is that what you have planned in Volhansk?"

"No more questions!"

I pass the next room and aim my pistol in it. More abandoned school bags, briefcase.

She dives out of a door behind me. I spin and fire once. The round goes far to the right.

She's on top of me, with a strength that far outweighs her slim frame. My right hand is stopping hers, dagger in fist. A sharp coldness floods the back of my head. I could die, right here, right now.

A flooding warmth overwhelms me, and I shove her off. She cracks into the plaster wall and grunts. She's winded, has to be.

"You're really going to make me do this, aren't you," I ask.

She smiles and throws her dagger. It cuts through and pounds into my stomach. White-hot pain makes it hard to breathe. She draws another dagger and leaps again.

She's halfway across the hallway when a deep pulse starts at my heart and reverberates throughout my body. She moves more slowly now. A bright blue line glows through my clothes. I don't know what to do, so I yell, as loud and as coarse as I can.

I duck down and spear her, taking her through the wall. Something sharp scrapes up my back, but stops once she crashes through the wooden boards.

We land and sprawl across the ground. I leap up and try to swing at her, but she's already on her feet. Her hands are empty, so she grabs my arm. I can already tell she's going to break it at the elbow joint, so I pull back as hard as I can. She tries to dig her heels in, but my arm gets free. I pull in my limbs and dive into her stomach with my shoulder. She crashes into a metal desk, the orator's desk, and her frame gets dented into it. The shock of the rigid steel threatens to dislocate my shoulder, but somehow it doesn't. I'm struggling to inhale, but am able to get up regardless. She drives her elbows down into my back and I'm forcefully winded. I wrap my arms around her torso, and am able to lift her with no effort. Just the pulsing burning of the tattoo.

Visions of dwarves killing and dying fill my vision. The battle of Newearth Hill, 140 years ago. I'm part of the Grimaxe battalion sent to kill off the beastkin tribes inhabiting what would become a glittersilver mine. I managed to pick up and disarm a shaman, right before it could enact its foul incantations.

"Not now," I scream.

I'm not in a room anymore, so I have to guess where everything is. All I can see is an intense gathering of trees slowly shifting back down into rose bushes.

We're at the orator's desk, which means the windows must be off to my right.

The shaman is dangling above me, whipping its appendages in every direction. I stand tall on my two feet. My brothers cheer me on and tell me to finish the fight.

The window.

I take two steps to the right and throw it as far as I can. The body cracks against a nearby tree, and the tree topples over. The beastkin coughs up blood. I pick it back up again, take another step over and throw it again. Glass shatters as the shaman flies through the air.

Beating drums, roars of triumph, the final throes of victory in a kill well done.

All this must have occurred in about twenty seconds.

I look down at my stomach dampening with blood and fall to one knee. The knife must've been wrenched out at some point. The pulse emits one final time throughout my torso before leaving my body completely.

CHAPTER 44

I limp down the hallways, and find a suit jacket not all that covered in blood. I wrap it as tightly as I can around my stomach, and press into the wound.

"Void's bells," I grimace.

I have to make sure she's gone. I have to make sure all of this wasn't for naught.

In little under a quarter of an hour, I'm limping out towards the front door. I look at the tattoo and find it totally inert. I don't even know what to say about it.

I pass through the main entrance, and go down the steps, a heavily wounded elfblood is limping across the campus. Her.

I look at my feet for a gun, and sure enough, there's a pistol. I groan in pain as I have to crouch down to grab it, and struggle down the steps.

"Wait," I try to yell. It comes out as a hoarse whisper.

She doesn't hear me. I fire once to get her attention.

She stops and turns around. One of her legs is struggling to work with her.

"How in the Legacian itself are you still alive," she asks.

"Could ask you... The same thing."

I get to where I'm about ten paces from her, and aim the pistol.

"Well," she says, throwing up her hands then grimacing at the movement, "You've done it. All my men are dead. I'm dying. You're dying. Was it worth it, Arthur Fey?"

"Not… sure."

"Keeper's sake, I'm the good guy! I was the one *trying* to stop all this! And you and your weak little sympathies had to get in the way. I had to believe you were working for him. None of this would make sense if you weren't! You couldn't be just some tired aristocrat's son with the most impeccable luck in the world, right?"

I push in my wound to try and stem the bleeding.

"Right," she asks, "Right?"

"You'll never get to know, Astraea."

"It's Fe'lona. My name… It's Fe'lona."

I nod, aim the pistol, and shoot once. She drops dead.

I let go of the pistol and meagerly limp my way to the entrance of the college. My strength fails me then and there and I drop to my knees.

So this is it. The entirety of my efforts in Ophidia. So much silvum made. So much blood spilt. And for what? So that a minor crime kingpin would fall victim to the grander machinations of a larger crime kingpin, and take the rest of the city screaming with them. I shudder to think what all this means for the future. Luckily, I'm in too much pain to.

"Void," I grunt, looking down at myself. A slick stain goes onto my trousers, forming a dark red river down both legs.

I sigh and fall back to the ground. The clouds are so pretty. The setting sun on the grand city is something to behold, truly. I try to turn the tattoo back on, but no luck. Guess it's tired, too. Everything becomes more tiresome, and quieter. It's getting harder and harder to keep my eyes open. The battered bark and thick branches of a nearby oak tree speak to me. It's so large and uncaring. The city burns and dies, and it stays there, in the same state it will always be. Our little squabbles don't really matter anymore, do they? The more I lie here, the more I keep wondering, wondering about everything. What was I even so worried about? Leaving now doesn't seem so bad. It's so calm. Everything is so calm.

Wouldn't you agree, Caddock? Did I do alright, in the end?

"This isn't the end, Arthur."

What? There's no way that could be right, right? It can't be. That's not possible. Your voice has that same low timber to it, the one I'd always hear coming down the hall to wake me first thing in the morning.

"Is that you, Caddock?"

You come over and get on one knee beside me. You're wearing the same brown plaid suit you always wore on our weekends out when we'd play by the beach.

"What're you doing here, father?"

"I wanted to check in on you. It's been a spell since we last talked."

"That's because you died, remember? On the zeppelin."

"That so? Maybe I wasn't. Maybe I was sleeping all that time. You know I need my beauty sleep."

You wink at me.

"You know, we're right outside of Oxlen Park. I used to take your mother there all the time. Go ahead and get up, look at the beauty of it."

I grunt and heave and with some considerable effort, lean on one arm and look into the grand park. The walkways, the shrubs, the trees. All as beautiful as the first time I saw them.

"I miss her sometimes," I say.

"I do too, son. I do too."

"We never should have left Veneria."

"You might be right, son."

"So did I do alright? In the grand scheme of it all?"

"What do you mean?"

"Ever since you and mom left, did I do alright?"

You smile and go behind me, to push me further into a seated position. I gasp at the pain.

"Arthur, you did just as well as I ever could've hoped for. You were and are the best son a father can have."

403

Before I can stop myself, tears roll down my face. Then comes the mucus.

"That's all I've ever tried for," I choke out between sobs, "A pathetic goal maybe, but one I've wanted to achieve."

I feel your presence, your warmth, as the tears flow out of me. Minutes pass as I cry and cry, unable to stop. Keeper above, I've never been so pathetic.

Eventually, I'm able to calm back down.

"You know," I say, "I met someone earlier, in my dreams. I don't remember his name, but he talked about us, about our kind. He also said a few things that spoke to me. About the choices people like me need to make; the grand ones or the meek ones. My whole life, I thought I was a meek person. But maybe I was just the wrong kind of meek. Perhaps pain and suffering warped me toward being the wrong kind of meek. It led me to be the scared, hating sort instead of the stoic, patient one. Perhaps meek is the wrong word. I don't know, words are malleable, but I just see what was wrong this whole time now. It came through in glimpses toward the end, but at least they came at all. There's a way out past this. There's a way to tear myself free from this path of woe. At least that, that grain of insight was gained, and by the Keeper above, I hope that is redeeming. Besides, there's still hope. At least I didn't have to make that grand sacrifice, right? I can still see Elizabeth, still guide Gren. I made the right choice. I know I did. I did what had to be done. I know I did. Didn't I?""

Nothing in response. All of a sudden, I can hear truck engines and marching boots. My head drifts to the left and I see military trucks and troops rolling down the street. A man in a white helmet is running towards me.

I smile and fall back flat. I look around and you've left. That's okay. Thanks for the little visit.

Your son's got some things to do on this continent yet.